AT TABLE

Barolo

Matthew Gavin Frank

UNIVERSITY OF NEBRASKA PRESS
LINCOLN AND LONDON

Library of Congress Cataloging-in-
Publication Data
Frank, Matthew Gavin.
Barolo / Matthew Gavin Frank.
p. cm.
ISBN 978-0-8032-2674-6 (cloth : alk.
paper)
1. Wine and wine making—Italy—
Barolo. 2. Cookery—Italy—Barolo.
3. Frank, Matthew Gavin—Travel—
Italy—Barolo. 4. Barolo (Italy)—
Description and travel.
I. Title.
TP559.I8F72 2010
641.0945'13—dc22
2009031586

Set in Bulmer by Kim Essman.
Designed by Nathan Putens.

For L.L., Marilyn and Noel

(my mother and father),

and Jeff, Jodi, and Keiter

Contents

Acknowledgments

Grateful acknowledgment is made to the Illinois Arts Council for its 2008 fellowship.

Portions of this book were originally published in slightly different form in the following publications:

"Raw Meat and Barry White" and "The Unfinished" originally appeared as "Raw Meat, Barry White, and the Brothers," *The Best Travel Writing 2009* (Palo Alto CA: Solas House, Inc., Travelers' Tales imprint, 2009), 103–20.

"I Cannubi," *Gastronomica* 9, no. 1 (Winter 2009): 83–87.

"Global Flavors: Savoring Salumi," *Plate Magazine*, the Bacon issue, November–December 2008, 52–60.

"Breadstick Hydra," *The Best Travel Writing 2008* (Palo Alto CA: Solas House, Inc., Travelers' Tales imprint, 2008), 235–44.

"Italian Butcher Shop Blues," *Gastronomica* 6, no. 1 (Winter 2006): 21–24.

"Italian Butcher Shop Blues," *Best Food Writing 2006*, ed. Holly Hughes (Avalon Publishing Group, 2007), 63–68.

"Dessert," *Brevity* 18 (Summer 2005), online at http://www.creativenonfiction.org/brevity/brev18/frank_dessert.htm.

"Dessert," reprinted in *Creative Nonfiction*, "The Best of *Brevity*," no. 27 (2005): 91–92.

BAROLO

1

The Fewest Idiots

My heart jumps like a toad in a potato sack when the arriving passengers pour into the gate. My neck rockets backward, and the airport ceiling shadows fly like Raffaella's hair. The loudspeaker crackles — Italian first, then English — to placate the delayed. The crew will clean the plane, and then we will board. I watch the yawning arrivals shuffle past my chair, decide which are Italian and which are American by the way they hold their mouths. Some mouths simply look as if they've been exposed to better tastes than others.

I throw my arm around my backpack, resist the temptation to whisper sweet nothings to its zippers, and lean forward. In my lean, between my shoes, I see Barolo, Italy, and Il Gioco dell'Oca, Raffaella's farmhouse bed-and-breakfast. I see Pongo the Great Pyrenees sprinting over Il Gioco's driveway stones; Michele, Raffaella's father, pointing at me, roaring, "Chicago! Chicago!"; Adriana, her mother, shaking tomato-wet hands over her head at the outdoor grill; Raffaella touching my shoulders; her son, Niccolo, throwing a rock at the dog.

My chest swells right here in O'Hare as I remember Raffaella's words when, during my first trip to Barolo, I departed the region via a Satti bus after a mere four days. Though I certainly didn't earn the designation, I felt like a member of the family, and, kicking my backpack against the bus stop sign, Raffaella had said to me, "If you ever want to come back and work the wine harvest, I will talk to some people for you."

These words stained my brain like iodine. I went back to Chicago, then moved to Alaska. Three years passed like a hiccup while I scrambled eggs and fried sausages at Juneau's Channel Bowl Café. It was when Al, a seventy-seven-year-old ex-goldpanner, after a yolkful of over-mediums, espoused his philosophy — *In a world full of idiots, you have to go to the place with the fewest idiots* — that Raffaella's offer rang itself over my frontal lobe. Then Al looked up, took a sip of his coffee, ran a hand down the length of his gray beard, scowled, and spit his drink back into his "Alaska Ship Chandlers" mug.

"Terrible!" he bellowed. "No taste!"

That night, from a pay phone on the wharf, I called Raffaella. When she picked up with her classic "Pronto," I nearly lost my lines: my pleading (but not too pleading) speech about staying with her indefinitely — maybe the entire six months spanning Barolo's fall and winter, more reverently known as truffle season and the grape harvest. I'm hesitant to admit it, but I think I even said something about cleansing the soul.

When I was growing up, food was the thing that emerged from the microwave, steaming and soggy. A rubbery omelet. A desiccated matzo ball in watery broth. A steak going green. A corpse of broccoli. But my mother treated our crap with ceremony. It was with bad food that we dealt with tragedy or comedy or mediocrity. For my birthday, microwaved hamburgers with iceberg lettuce; for my father's, microwaved lamb shanks. It was always something that once had a bone or an entire skeleton. We loved meat. In my family, to die young and full was expected. We gracefully upheld the pillars of heart disease and diabetes. Saturated fat and clogged arteries kept us warm through the winter. In my family, enjoying food meant overeating. I became a fat teenager.

The winter of 1986 I tried so hard to be cool. This was my first year in high school, Bon Jovi's *Slippery when Wet* had just come out, and the December temperatures in suburban Chicago were way above average. You could see the sidewalks through the ice. Girls would come to class in shorts or skirts, and teachers would scold them for their weatherly indiscretion. I tried so hard, but Bon Jovi was this foreign thing — this upsweep of mislabeled heavy metal, rooted in Aqua Net hair spray.

My father had brought me up on classic rock — Chicago's 105.9 WCKG and the rough sexy DJ voices of Patty Hays and Kitty Lowie. The way they talked about Led Zeppelin and Jethro Tull, their voices gruff and throaty, carrying the mysteries of age and cigarette, was enough to make a male high school freshman dismiss Bon Jovi and, in turn, his coolness as sonically trivial.

When driving together, my father and I would pick up McDonald's (he would remove the buns from his two Big Macs and press the four patties into his mouth, one hand twisting the steering wheel) and listen to Simon and Garfunkel and the Eagles. We dissected "I Am a Rock" for its metaphor and contexts and "Witchy Woman," tying the allure of the invisible Patty and Kitty to the windblown black of Stevie Nicks.

But this wasn't cool. Not in 1986. I knew damned well that if I couldn't quote Bon Jovi with some study-hall regularity, I'd never make it to the upper echelon of Adlai E. Stevenson High. The song that year was "You Give Love a Bad Name" — *Shot through the heart!* — and I soon would be, by a rosemary sprig. But I hadn't yet found food, my hopeful catalyst into coolness, and at the time I had to rest with Zeppelin, my thirteen-year-old feelings uncontrived and implacable, hidden in the folds of those short winter skirts.

Given his Big Mac habits, my father was an Adkins advocate before Adkins was Adkins — before it was good for you, then bad for you, then really bad for you. My mother catered to this. Our dinners were spent at the table, the kitchen television always on, politely watching my father struggle through troughs of chicken wings, rib tips. He drank his water from a plastic bottle, one of those with an extended strawlike appendage. (In the refrigerator he distinguished his water bottle from my mother's by putting a rubber band around its middle.) He would stuff his mouth full of meat, swallow, put his hands flat on the tabletop, and regain his breath. *Whooo-whooo-whooo.* Then he would bow his head to the water bottle's straw, not exerting the effort to lift it to his lips, sip a few, then return to the troughs. *Whooo-whooo-whooo*. This, I thought, was eating. As a child I equated fullness with discomfort. If I wasn't uncomfortable, I wasn't full.

As I grew older and my own breathing shortened with each Friday football game in the neighborhood park and my grandfather died at sixty-six, I began to wonder: what was the matter with fruits and vegetables? Somehow I didn't anymore want to be part of a familial food culture that made of the tomato the devil's candy. If I couldn't get into Bon Jovi, perhaps I could get into the four food groups and a little exercise.

I began running, slowly, around the block twice a week. Though barely five feet tall and quite round, I had my eye on a slot on my high school's high-jump team. That over-the-bar descent onto that giant sponge of a mat just looked like too much fun.

I read cookbooks and food magazines, revising my approach to edibles and their role in my survival. In the bathroom I would thumb through the back of *Chicago* magazine's dining guide, circling the interesting places in red pen — the ethnic haunts, the then-nebulous four-star establishments granted the clandestine designation of *fine dining*. I began to check them off.

When the Food Network was launched, I watched it voraciously, taking notes. When I left for college, I left my most expensive graduation gift behind — the microwave. I began cooking — fucking up, almost succeeding, fucking up. I got serious, reading Chef Thomas Keller's treatise on trussing a chicken, Charlie Trotter's manifesto on the potato.

After moving to Alaska, I waited for Ferran Adrià's *elBulli* cookbook to drop below a hundred bucks on amazon.com. When it never did, I read all the free articles about it.

My friends got into cooking. My male friends grew their hair long, my female friends shaved their heads. We told ourselves we were these rebel chefs, self-important culinary militants who were mediocre line cooks at best. At worst, we were overseasoners. A handful of salt. A liter of cumin. We made up jailhouse stories for each other, though none of us had seen the interior of a cell. We drew prison tattoos on each other's forearms with Paper Mate pens.

We called ourselves a catering company and got a few gigs — small Alaskan New Year's parties, aunts' birthdays. We tried to make our own stocks, prepped feverishly. We discussed for thirty minutes how the onion was supposed to be chopped, how each piece was to be a uniform arc. We read articles on the importance of proper seasoning, then seasoned our food improperly. So meticulously, we served our flawed food, received our polite compliments.

I took restaurant jobs — dishwasher, prep cook, server, garde-manger, grill, stock boy for the wine. Watching the other chefs work the line, I realized my militancy was an illusion. These people were for real. In the restaurant kitchen the hierarchy trumped the collegial. I was tired of being yelled at. I would never really be a chef — didn't have the calloused tear ducts for it — and began to wonder: could tasting be a talent?

So I tasted. A lot. Eventually, I shed my excess fat, uncovered the elusive concept of moderation. A concept that was about to be deconstructed, rearranged, and rebuilt by Italy.

As the airport loudspeaker crackles, the entire gate stands as one, all of us travelers on the same ark, ready for an ocean of wine and for boarding. The indefinite status of my stay prohibits me from taking a room at Il Gioco (financially speaking, of course), and I look at my backpack and envision the olive green tent coiled tightly inside. Per Raffaella's suggestion, I am to set up my lodging in her garden, just around the corner from the luscious animal-fat aromatics of Adriana's hallowed outdoor grill. She is allowing me to camp on her property for free.

I watch as the elderly and the children-riddled families approach, then disappear into the Jetway. I think of steel beasts and their bellies and of Jonah and Pinocchio. He was Italian, wasn't he? When they call my row, I stand even before the English translation. I don't need it anymore. I am dumping the crutches. I am starting to heal. My chest opens like a Pentecostal hymnal, a bottle of wine. Against the gray sky the plane shines like a bullet. It is September.

2

Dialing for Raffaella

When I land in Milano, exhausted, it is *septembre*. When I arrive in Alba, Italy, having taken a train from Milano to Asti, then a diesel train to Alba, it is September still. Struggling with the urge to call Il Gioco and tell Raffaella where and how I am, I also struggle with piecing together a vision of her.

I close my eyes, reddened from the all-night flight, Alba's late-morning winds carrying smells never to be found in America: a mesh of rotten grape, mushroom, olive, and stone. Eyes shut tight, an image of Raffaella comes like a Picasso. I can see portions of her overlapped in threes: her blonde hair, her skin, her eyes fanned like abstract postcards. I can't quite make her gel.

My eyes open to a contained assault of people on foot, on bikes, in cars, cascading over orange-roofed shopfronts, pastel facades, white shutters. A medieval dream. Alba rests in the Langhe territory, in the Piedmont's southern corner, sandwiched between the beautiful breads of Liguria (the Italian Riviera) and France. When coupled with the neighboring Roero territory, the countryside is dappled with over one hundred tiny villages, all accessible by car or the less reliable bus systems. The throngs of people brush against me as they pass. They smell good. It must be in their blood.

The first settlers came to the area during the Neolithic period, anywhere from the sixth millennium to the third millennium of pre-history. Alba's "freewheeling" lifestyle of the Neolithic gave way to the obvious Roman conquest in AD 173. The Romans originally named the hamlet Alba Pompeia. The "great" (depending on who you ask — the conquerors or the conquered) Roman emperor Publius Elvius Pertinax was born in Alba Pompeia. When the Roman Empire began its famed decline, Alba Pompeia fell victim to numerous barbarian invasions but began to assert its own stable environment in 1100. When the fascist seduction attempted to bed most of Italy during World War II, Alba remained a rebellious and partisan village, seduced instead by the poetic words of its native son, author Beppe Fenoglio.

The neighboring hamlet of Barolo, equally rebellious, is home to a towering orange castle, forever spewing its narrative. Hovering at 301 meters and housing 676 residents, Barolo has been inhabited since prehistory, later serving as residence to Celts, Ligurian tribes, Romans, and the famed Falletti banking family. The name Barolo comes from the Celtic *bas reul*, or "low place," due to its position in the Langhe.

In order to finally defend itself from century-long barbaric raids, Barolo erected its castle in the year 1000. In 1250 the entire town of Barolo was purchased by the Falletti family, who quickly converted the castle, once an imposing defensive fortress, into their country villa.

The castle-turned-villa housed the last direct members of the family, Marchese Carlo Tancredi Falletti and his wife, Juliette Colbert, until 1864. During this time Colbert, taken with the region, devoted herself to studying its fruits and, with the help of French oenologist Louis Oudart, invented the refined techniques to produce Barolo wine.

Today the region is a strange mesh of the rustic and the cosmopolitan. Shops selling fresh pasta, decades-old wines, and wild boar salami are juxtaposed with display windows boasting designer shoes, purses, and sunglasses. Through the window of one such store I watch a woman in black stretch pants check herself out in a mirror, flipping the edges of her blouse collar skyward. Behind me a string of minicars speeds by, inches from my legs.

While my backpack adjusts itself, impatient on my shoulders, moaning to be put down and unpacked, I notice an orange pay phone at the north end of the train station. The sun throws its light from the black receiver. Soon I am dialing for Raffaella. The phone rings only once.

"Pronto?"

Yes, I think, my blood going warm as coffee. "Raffaella, it's me." Even louder than the mosaic of car horns, her throaty, extended cry is the catalyst I need: my body rocks in transubstantiation, my blood loping up the evolutionary ladder from coffee to wine. In that sound, for better or for worse, Italy snaps into focus, jetlag takes a backseat.

She says, "You are in Alba."

"Yes," I say. My hands shake a little, but I continue, "Should I take the Satti bus to you?"

"No. No, I will send a boy to pick you up."

"A boy?" I ask.

"Sì. Yes. His name is Francesco. Look for a blue car. A, uh, a very dark blue."

"Okay," I accept. "I can't wait to see you . . ." I stop. "And everybody."

"Yes," Raffaella says. "It is good you are here. You work for Sandrone tomorrow."

"What?" I say and close my mouth. The jetlag reasserts itself, drones away like a lawnmower.

"Yes," Raffaella continues. "I tell you about it when you are here."

"Okay," I manage. "Ciao."

"Ciao-ciao."

I take the receiver from my ear and stare at it. Luciano Sandrone. Super Sandrone. Tomorrow already. I am going to pick grapes for the man, nay, the master. I wonder what he looks like. *Huge*, I think, *round, planetary. Jupiter with feet. A grounded comet.* I breathe. Alba rushes into my chest. My backpack stares at me from its slumber. I wonder if it knows. I wonder if it dreams of being stuffed with bottles of Sandrone's wine.

Across the street an old man sets up a vegetable table on the sidewalk in front of his shop. Mushrooms. Cardoons. Garlic. No one stops to peruse. In the cafés well-dressed businesspeople take their espressos standing up at the counter. Mopeds subvert the pedestrian walkways, find their way along the orange cobblestones. Beautiful boys walk arm in arm with beautiful girls.

Cracking my knuckles, I watch a navy blue Subaru tear from the street into the train station's parking lot, nearly splitting a brown-suited pedestrian in two. But the brown suit stumbles on with barely a glance. This sort of recklessness is expected here. The Subaru stops at the parking curb nearest me and shuts off like a clatter of dishes. This must be "the boy" Raffaella mentioned.

The car door opens, and a lanky forty-something man pushes his graying hair into Alba's morning. A distant church clock rings its bells for twelve. This man—this "boy"—must be the god of afternoon. His overcoat matches the color of the car, and he is caped, good-looking, and as well treated as a retired racehorse. His eyes find me. He holds a thin hand over his head as if demonstrating his ability to finger the clouds. I nod and return the wave, my hand no higher than my chest.

"Raffaella?" the man calls, his voice light, dusty, strung in the air like crepe paper.

"Uh," I say.

"Raffaella?" he repeats. "Il Gioco dell'Oca?"

"Sì," I say. "Uh . . ." and I tap my chest frantically, trying to remember the phrase for "That's me"— "Uh, esso io."

"Aaaah," he stretches his sigh like a cat, "italiano."

I laugh.

"Tutto bene?" he asks. "Everything good?"

"Sì," I say and launch my backpack over my shoulders.

"I will bring you," he says and reaches to brace the bottom of my pack, helps me slide it from my shoulders into the car's trunk. He is nearly a foot taller than me. I've never felt my five feet seven inches more. I think of my high school career as a fourth-string high jumper.

"Um, do you work for Raffaella?" I ask.

"Sorry?"

"Um, do you, uh, lavoro, uh, work for, for Raffaella?"

"Work for?" he asks. "Oh, no, no. I, uh, work for, uh, the bank. In Torino. Sixty kilometers, uh, far from Alba. I am, uh, the friend of Raffaella . . . Francesco. In English, uh, Francis. Raffaella say you are americano."

"Yes," I say, walking to the passenger side. "From Chicago."

"Aaaah, Chicago," he says triumphantly. He phonetically pronounces the *ch*.

The Subaru leaps to life, and Francesco rockets us into traffic with a seeming disregard for the other cars. My backpack rolls in the trunk, and I fumble with the seatbelt. He turns to me.

"Only, uh, ten kilometres."

"Sounds good, Francesco."

"You are tired?" he asks.

At the mere sound of the word, fatigue trickles into my legs a drop at a time. I become aware of my joints. My head rotates against the headrest.

"A little, I suppose. Un po."

Francesco turns to the windshield, then back to me. A white motorbike shoots in front of him and, without looking forward, he taps the brake. I yawn and Francesco wrestles the stick shift. My eyes roll back. I decide to trust him.

"Aaaah," he says.

3

The Boy Brings Me

My eyes, exhausted, teeter on the brink. I don't know whether . . .

Upward slopes and rounds of green and is that a window? Oh, the car window. I'm moving on a road and I'm looking out the window and roofs are whipping past in orange stripes and doors and there's a man with a rake standing still and now he's *smeared into the roofs and gone and who is that?* It's Francesco at the wheel. His eyes are ahead and does he know I'm still here? Is this a car seat or *a bed pressing my back? What's holding me up? Am I in Chicago? Or Alaska? I think Alaska. I have to be at work soon. Chop onions. I need a blanket. A lamb shank. My hands aren't moving. They don't want to. Oh, well. Leave them alone.* I see grapes. *And darkness. A cave. A cave with too many windows. Green and heavy light.* My eyes are open now, right? Did we hit a bump? A castle to the right. The top of it. Squares of brick with blanks in between. I can see the sky in between the squares of brick. It's red. The brick. *The cave. No brick here. No yellow here. I'm in Italy. In a car . . . not . . . done . . .*

Crunch and crunch and rolling crunch, Francesco spins us onto the white stones of Raffaella's driveway. I sit up straight at the sound, my mouth wet, spine cold, eyes dry but open. I stretch and stare out the window at the black wrought iron gate sandwiched by two orange brick pillars. The stones maze themselves under the gate, spread into a wide courtyard. I touch my head. My hair is a mess.

Pongo, Il Gioco's Great Pyrenees, stands to one side of the iron gate, fur matted, tail sweeping circular, barking.

"Ciao, Pongo! Tutto bene?" Francesco nods to the dog.

"Pongo!" I muster, and the dog's tail backflips.

Francesco is at the trunk, grappling with my backpack, and I haven't yet closed the passenger door. I take the pack from him and watch a persimmon tree test the air with its orange fruit, threatening to drop its bounty onto the dog's back. Somewhere beyond the gate chickens are clucking. The sky is a washed-out, underfed blue.

In an overcoat wave, like a censor's dot rushing to cover the barking dog, Francesco steps to the gate and works it open with one hand. Pongo shoots forward, curls himself over our legs. Francesco and I knock into one another. It is the bicyclist who saves us as Pongo sprints away to the far fence, barking at a white-T-shirted pedaler struggling along the road.

Via Crosia: snaking from Il Gioco into downtown Barolo, it is a street, a name I long to pencil into the return address corners of countless envelopes. We're only four kilometers from Alba, but this is the sticks, any trace of commerce pushed to the unseen side of the vineyard hills. The Italian air rushes overhead like a fistful of prunes. The Gioco dell'Oca farmhouse stretches massive, peach with blue shutters, the vineyards pushing from behind, lit bone green in the moonlight. Persimmon trees. Hazelnut trees. A covered brick portico housing Adriana's giant grill. Raffaella inherited this nineteenth-century farmhouse from her grandparents, and, after traveling the world in the tourism industry, she returned to her birthplace to run it as a bed-and-breakfast (known in rural Italy as an *agriturismo*). Il Gioco dell'Oca translates into English as "The Game of the Goose," an Italian children's game that, like a morbid Game of Life, takes its young players on a journey through financial ups and downs, marriage, family, and, finally, death. The "winner" is declared when she or he replaces the game piece on the precise square upon which it began. Full circle. Raffaella describes her return to Barolo in terms of this game in a voice measured with melancholic calm.

"My life," she is known to utter famously, "it is the Game of the Goose."

Before I can exhale, Il Gioco's front doors swing outward and Raffaella steps — black pants, black blouse — into the sun.

She is even more *Raffaella* than I remembered her. I hold my breath a moment longer until my lungs go sweet and then push my backpack to the stones. The farmhouse stands its ground behind her. Its front doors once graced the entryway to Beppe Fenoglio's former home. Michele, Raffaella's father, never tires of repeating this fact, as if all the dead writer's poetry and partisanship lie in this slab of golden-knobbed wood.

The white stones slide from under Raffaella's feet like a boat wake, and it appears she really can walk on water, from crest to crest, and never know the darkness and depth in between each wave. The flesh of her face and hands is coppered from simplicity and the force of the Italian sun. She is smiling. Small wrinkles come as parentheses to the corners of her mouth, though the fullness of the lips in between is anything but an afterthought. I try to wave and say hello, but it comes out as more of an unnoticeable wrist flick and a "Gak."

"Come va?" she announces, snapping me from my muteness with the thrusting spread of her arms.

"Raffaella," I croak.

We speak in essentials: the flight, Alaska, my family, her family. Food.

"You are tired," she declares.

"Yeah, I know," I say.

"Well, you work for Sandrone tomorrow. I make it for tomorrow. For eight."

"Eight tomorrow morning?" I ask. I am being thrown to the wolves. I was hoping for a bit more sleep. "You don't waste time," I smile.

"Well, you say you want to pick up the grapes," she shrugs.

"I can't wait, Raffaella," I yawn.

Francesco sings his Italian from behind me. I forgot he was there. Raffaella says something back to him and turns to me.

"There is the garden." She points away from the house toward the Via Crosia fence, where Pongo is still sniffing for bicyclists. "You can put your tent there."

We hug; I am wrapped in her wings, her bird heart beating into my chest. I nearly drool onto her shoulder. Francesco follows her inside as I drag my pack to the garden. Find the perfect patch of grass, flat and soft and under an oak tree, fifteen feet from the chicken coop. Nod to the eight hens shuffling breast first in the soil behind a wire mesh enclosure. They roll their throats in approval or warning as I open my pack, pull out my tent.

4

Enough

This morning, a Wednesday, the rocks of Raffaella's driveway genuflect as the tires of a gray pickup roll hooflike toward the front gate. The horn cries and I walk, still half-frozen from a cold night in the tent, toward the sound. Although I had sweat through every synthetic layer of my sleeping bag last night and woken with a crystalline frost over my entire body, my pace is heated and my demeanor, downright blazing. This is my ride to the vineyards, and when I see the 8:00 AM silhouette of a teased and hair-sprayed Afro through the window, I know that Sandrone himself is not going to be my driver. I reach for the passenger-side handle. The door opens as a hatch, and I step into a vinyl-coated, bucket-seated outer space. But this is no black void. It is filled with the placid grinning face of Luciano Sandrone's wife.

"Ciao," she says from the throat like a roosting pigeon.

"Ciao, ciao, come va?" I reply.

"Bene, bene, e tu?"

"Oh, molto bene," I say.

Luciano Sandrone purchased his first vineyard in 1970 and launched his namesake venture in 1977. Sandrone had to work for years as a cellar man on the Marchesi di Barolo estate in order to save enough money to purchase his first vineyard on the famed Cannubi hill. The Cannubi hill, fronting Via Crosia (in between Il Gioco dell'Oca and downtown Barolo), is reputed to produce impeccable grapes due to its position relative to sun and temperature. Sandrone's vineyard is located on the Cannubi Boschis subplot (originally owned by the local Boschis family), an area known as perhaps the greatest vineyard section of the greatest vineyard hill in the region.

Though his wines have earned him international acclaim, Sandrone is still an object of scorn to many of the region's vintners. In an area where most vintners have inherited their trade and property from previous generations, Sandrone, the son of a bus driver, is widely viewed as a newbie and, therefore, easily dismissed. His wife, Mariuccia, frowns as she tells me this, nearly driving the speeding mini into the weeds.

After careening at breakneck speed through the vineyard roads, eleventh-century castles whipping past as if mere mile markers, we arrive at a row of flatbeds lined with empty red crates attached to one-seat tractors. Then I see them: the crew. They are men and women, some old and hunched, kerchiefed and suspendered, some young and shirtless, overalled and jeansed. Most are huddled in groups of three or four, talking to each other and drinking coffee from plastic thermos tops. The cliques are evident — the young, elegant postharvest clubhoppers; the no-nonsense grandparents dispensing wisdom with their eyes; the children alternately running the rows with their friends and clutching at the pant legs of the grandparents; the misshapen black sheep, surely playing a mental game of *D&D* as they fill their crates with grapes.

Most of these crewmembers are friends or relatives or relatives of relatives of Sandrone. Those who aren't on this rural coffee break are wrist-deep in the vines, hands reaching through the jungle of leaves to the tight bunches of Nebbiolo grapes, careful not to rupture the thin skins, spill their juice.

Nebbiolo, the varietal responsible for Barolo wine, derives its name from *nebbia,* the Italian word for "fog." This annual fog tends to penetrate the Langhe come fall; the air temperature drops, and, because of this, these grapes can rest on their vines, maturing. Though the fog today is thin, the air is still cool, but the crew, sweating, work with their sleeves rolled up. An old woman in a white Sinatra bandana looks toward us, flashing the fleck of gold in her front tooth. Her arms are brown, stringy. I watch her tendons flex like piano strings as she closes her spring-loaded clippers over a branch. Next to her in the same row are two girls in their late teens. They must be someone's nieces. They wear matching short yellow shorts. I stare at the sheen of sweat collecting at the backs of their knees. If I was anywhere but rural Italy, I'd feel like a total scumbag. The old woman says something to one of the girls, and she laughs. The other girl, visibly disgusted, spits onto the ground.

I step away from the car and turn to face the downslope. Apple trees wave in the wind like sails, dropping their fruit. Mariuccia is talking to me, but I don't understand what she's saying. She points her finger over my head in clarification. I turn. A gruff voice rises suddenly over the crewmembers' conversations, and I see a faded blue beret bobbing above the vine leaves. The beret moves uphill and spawns a face underneath, then a neck, shoulders, torso, arms, hands, and legs. The old woman sees him and calls to him in Italian, her sentence ending with a vibrant *Luciano!* He laughs and shakes his head.

He stands only five feet six inches, wears small, thin glasses, a dirty white undershirt, navy cotton pants looped over his shoulders with burgundy suspenders. He is thick and squat, hairy and strong, walks with an authoritative certainty, and has a thin cheroot smoking from his sixty-year-old lips. *Sandrone.* Though only about my height, he looks as if he can hurdle me.

"Questo è il americano?" he asks his wife.

"Sì."

Sandrone turns to face the downslope, stares past a wrought iron table anchored precariously into the hillside. A few crewmembers sit around it, playing cards, drinking glasses of wine, eating what appear to be slices of purple salami from paper plates. Parked in the narrow dirt alley dividing the rows are three dormant one-seat tractors, their flatbeds slowly filling with crates of picked grapes. One driver, wearing overalls without an undershirt, huge arms loosely folded over his chest, leans against his tractor. His torso is giant but hairless, some mutant infant with an adult brain. Another driver angrily yanks a crate from the hands of one of the young clubhopper boys. The clubhopper says something in a high-pitched, ridiculing voice, then curls his lip like a wolf and howls. The last driver flexes his bicep for a group of female pickers — young, old, all of them talking at once.

Sandrone takes hold of the leaning tractor driver, leads both him and me into the rows. The space is tight as an escalator, and I brush against a few crewmembers as we go, uttering my feeble "Mi dispiace." The vine leaves range from luminous green to dead. I step over a series of empty red crates, placed at strategic intervals along the row, waiting to be filled. Carrying the smells of basement, stable, human sweat, and broken fruit, the wind washes cool over the vines, the dime-sized grapes lolling like Lolita.

Sandrone stops at the row's end next to a middle-aged woman, sweat ringing the front of her T-shirt like a bib. Chandeliers of sweat hang from Sandrone's armpits. Clipperless, he plucks a voluptuous bunch of Nebbiolo grapes from the vine with his bare hand, stained a velveteen purple-black. With a pair of carpenter's scissors he begins to prune away all desiccated grapes, grapes with splits in their skins, grapes bearing the white fur of mold. Sandrone shrugs at me, wrinkling his forehead, stressing the simplicity of his lesson. He takes hold of his head in both hands and cracks his own neck. He speaks and the tractor driver translates.

"He says to never throw the grapes into a crate. Place them in there gently."

The tractor driver's voice is raspy, erratic, as if he's speaking through the static of a scratched jazz record.

Sandrone drapes the Nebbiolo bunch at the bottom of a red crate. Then he speaks again.

"He says that when he finishes a harvest, he waits awhile, tastes the juice, the wine . . ."

Sandrone exhales a mouthful of cheroot smoke into my face.

". . . and if the taste isn't wonderful, he throws it awayyy," the driver says, extending the last word like a trailing saxophone.

"Capito. Bene, bene," I say, and I wonder if I really do understand.

I thought working a wine harvest would be somewhat luxurious, but this is farmwork, plain and simple, however elegant the end product. I question the endurance of my hands and back, try to recall my prep chef arm strength, the muscles required to chop thirty gallons of tomatoes, to repeat the same monotonous motion for hours. I think of the poor saffron farmers hand-harvesting some fifteen thousand individual crocus stamens to produce one ounce of spice. I bill myself a crybaby.

"Also," the tractor driver says, "even if the taste *is* good, if there isn't something *interesting* about it, he throws it away."

The tractor driver coughs and fingers a thin scar on his shoulder. He must be in his late thirties, his brown hair cut so short I can see the skin of his scalp.

"Bravo," I say, putting my fingertips to my mouth and kissing them.

Sandrone grunts, his breath struggling to turn over like a motorboat in winter, then stares transfixed at the vines. He hands me a pair of spring-loaded clippers and throws the scissors at my feet. He pats the driver on the back and walks to the end of the row, disappearing over the slope. The driver introduces himself as Ivo, snatches my hand in his, an eagle catching its salmon. His grip is painful, something I can't match, and I'm not sure if this is a display of machismo or if he simply doesn't know his own strength.

"You know," he says, "you don't use your hand. You use the clippers."

He tells me to fill a crate with the groomed grapes, carry it to the end of the row to Tractor Alley, where it can be loaded onto the flatbed, then move down the line, filling another, and another, and another, until I hear otherwise. Somewhere in Detroit a car is being similarly built. Here in Barolo we are building the standout of the wine flight, that one memorable pairing with your venison au poivre and kumquat chutney. It takes repetition and mechanics, amoebas of sweat and thick heartbeat.

I nod and look uphill, downhill, side to side. Sandrone is nowhere to be found. I am left alone with the crew, happy to fly under the radar of the boss. The sky is mercifully bare. Last night Raffaella warned me about governmental air raids by helicopter; that, specifically on the larger farms, these helicopters land, and starched men in suits and expensive sunglasses search the property for those crewmembers working illegally.

As one such crewmember I know I represent a potential liability to Sandrone, as the fine for my presence would likely cost him thousands of dollars. It's not easy to find illegal work here, especially in the wine industry. Fontana Fredda, a large local farm, was recently raided. Whispers of the punishment circulate among the local hamlets with snowballing exaggeration. Sandrone's willingness has everything to do with his friendship with Raffaella, her neck, her hair . . .

The crew clip in rhythm, the sound, an arena of typewriters. Conversations arise, escalate, and die. In the silence the Italian birds loose their shit onto blessed soil. The fog swirls above us, but I can still see the distant hilltop towns of La Morra and Castiglione Falletto, pushing their gaunt castles into the air. The wind blows a few loose leaves to the end of the row. Ivo follows them, rejoins his locomotive. About fifty feet to my right the sweaty middle-aged picker shakes her clippers at me, her pale tongue pressed between her teeth.

With the clippers I snip a grape bunch at its green stem, catch it in my hand, and retrieve the scissors from the ground to begin the pruning. I fall into rhythm, forearms thrust into the thick brown branches, clip, catch, cut, repose, another clip of the stem, a cutting away of the lesser grapes, bursting like arteries to the blade, another soft repose into the red crate. Oenological surgery, hazy anesthesia. The music of non-English swirls in the air, a predrinkable concert hall. I fill crate after crate, move from this row to the one above it, Sandrone, our invisible conductor, surely waving his mad wand, buried somewhere in the slope. I follow the sweaty woman at the safe fifty-foot distance.

Nobody talks about the itch. Maybe they're used to it, or maybe I have an allergy that my pediatrician never tested for, but working with grapevines *itches*. It's a pulsing, venomous sort of itch, a bite from an alcoholic mosquito. My hands in the leaves, fruit branches, a slow rash develops along the backs of my fingers, runs from knuckles to wrist. A sticky purple-white paste begins to form, thick between the fingers. When I press them together, then pull them apart, I can see the skin stretching.

Standing on a slope of this grade for hours is evil on the back, one leg extended behind as a brace, the other bent forward in an awkward and perpetual calisthenic. I increase my pace, work my way up the hill, but the hill only seems to get steeper, the huddle of grapevines taller. Soon I can't see above them.

My back is really tweaking now. I want to sit down, but I can't tell if I'm being watched from some covert perch by some jury with folded arms. The sweaty woman moves mechanically, unfazed, the wind lipping her sleeves, her mahogany arms hard as radio antennae. Her shirt is immaculate. Mine is filthy at the belly, stained purple with grape juice and dirt, the colors of old murder. My heart tries to beat for the fact that my sweat is going to be in Sandrone's future bottles, but the rest of my body really wants to stop working. My hands struggle to open all the way, clawed over clippers, cuffed into scissors. I farmer's blow a nickel of snot into the grass and immediately feel disrespectful.

Clip, catch, cut, repose . . . The itch, the smell, the filth. The old women and teenage girls running circles around me, the old men in white undershirts carrying the full crates without a struggle. The vines in a state of thickening. I never knew that wine and cramps were a permissible pairing. With each new squeeze of the clippers my assumptions about the glamour of wine work become progressively more false. When the choice arises — drink wine or make wine — drink wine, every time.

Woozy, hungry, I clip lazily at the vines. I am ready to dismiss them. In the sky I watch for helicopters. A Nebbiolo grape bunch breaks from its stem, falls at my feet. A couple of grapes are crushed, and I stare at them, their cracked skin, the little juice. I feel like a wife-beater, sheepish, slobberingly apologetic. Picking it up, snipping away the broken grapes, I pray the sweaty woman did not see this.

Sandrone emerges, walking uphill in Tractor Alley. He follows a slow-going flatbed, removing large brown thermoses and setting them in the soil at the end of each row. The sweaty woman shouts something in Italian, her voice heavy and intense, a pile driver falling into a bucket of cream. She tosses her trimming tools into the dirt and takes off for the thermos. Most of the crew follow suit.

Body creaking, I pull a Styrofoam cup from the stack and fill it with the steaming coffee. My thumb and middle finger bear indented red rings, the burrow carved out by the scissors. Sandrone makes a second round with water bottles. The crew drink from them, rinse the resinous filth from their hands, splash water over the backs of their necks.

As I begin to unscrew the bottle top Sandrone pushes his glasses into place, waves his hand to me, and roars, "Vieni qua!"

I prepare myself for some kind of vintner's punishment — the removal of a kidney with a corkscrew or something — exacted because of my slowness, because of my dropping that grape bunch. Lowering my head, exposing my ears for the boxing, I drop my water bottle to the soil and totter toward Sandrone, passing the sweaty woman, her shirt swiping me with its wet salts.

When I get to Tractor Alley, Sandrone turns, his suspender-backs heading toward the empty wrought iron table, barely upright on the slope. On the table is a spread of pink salami marbled with fat, gleaming slices of chalk white cheese, a basket of crusty bread, and a bottle of unmarked wine. Sandrone pulls out a chair and motions for me to sit.

"Pranzo," he says, sweeping his hand over this late lunch. I want to jump up and down, root, root, root for the home team. Eat until I burst, break moderation like a twig over my knee. Cut it down to size. I sit, and Mariuccia appears on the horizon, the sun making a nest of her celestial Afro. She approaches the tableside and pours a glass of wine.

"Dolcetto," she says, naming the wine and its grape, and pushes the glass to me.

If Nebbiolo is the dictator, Dolcetto is the leader of the rebellion. Far less powerful but full of verve. The name means "little sweet one," though the wines are usually dry. Best drunk young, Dolcetto is full of fruit and juice, exhibits a deep, supple purple color and a plummy, almondy taste. It goes perfectly with the spicy, almost tannic salami, which has been made with Barolo wine.

The cheese is a local specialty called Toma, Mariuccia assures me, a heavy cheese made of goat's and cow's milk that the locals claim has three main properties: "It satisfies hunger, quenches thirst, and cleans the teeth." I proceed to test the theory numerous times. Gamey. Viscous. Béchamel filtered through a gym sock. And I mean that in the best possible way.

Ivo and one of the yellow-shorted nieces join me at the table, amassing their own portions of meat, bread, and cheese. Trinity on a wrought iron tabletop. Edible isosceles. The niece throws her blonde hair over one of her shoulders and looks around for more interesting company. To her, Ivo and I must be old bored men.

"It's good?" Ivo asks at my inhalation of the cold cut.

I nod, tell him, "Your English is impeccable."

He pulls at his overall straps with both thumbs, baring an extra few inches of his expansive and hairless chest. He looks like something to project a movie onto. The niece switches her gaze between the table and the sky. Ivo and I are the things in the middle to be skipped over on the way to the clouds.

"Yours too," he laughs, a string of salami jetting from the corner of his mouth.

I laugh back, the paste of half-chewed Toma bubbling onto my lower lip.

The niece looks about to chastise us for our bad table manners, her birdwatching face growing wrinkles of disgust.

Swallowing, Ivo says, "I spent four years working in Medford, Oregon . . ."

He leans in, his elbows on the table, his forearm less than an inch from the niece's. She doesn't move a muscle.

He continues conspiratorially, ". . . on my uncle's Rottweiler farm."

"Are you kidding?" I ask.

"It was my uncle from my mother's side. I wasn't related to him by blood or anything. He married my mother's sister. He's a louse, not an Italian. But I worked for him so I could see America."

"That sounds like pretty dangerous work," I say.

Ivo straightens his back, throws his forearm fast and backward over his shoulder, thrusting his elbow in my face. A large scar, the size of a pen cap.

"Look at this. One morning I was chopping wood." He pauses, shakes his head. "Fuckin' Rottweiler—raised him from a pup—runs up from behind and bites. My uncle had to aim tight and chop his tail off to get him to let go. Not easy. Those little, stubby tails."

I don't know whether he's having fun with me or not. All of a sudden I feel jetlagged again.

"We had respect after that," he says.

I think the niece rolls her eyes, but I can't be sure. She says nothing.

"You're not serious," I say.

Ivo would have been perfect for my Alaskan wannabe chef catering crew. He seems a born overseasoner, a maker of jailhouse stories.

"Now look at this," he dismisses.

He pushes what little hair he has from his forehead, revealing a small vertical scar, hanging above his left eyebrow like a grain of rice.

"I was getting some sun, laying on my back, you know. Rottweiler comes over and claws my face."

The niece drains her wineglass, stands from her chair, surprises us both with her "Ciao." Her voice deep and echoic. Spoken from the bottom of a well.

Ivo grunts. I don't know what to say.

"This," he says, pulling his right overall strap to the side. He reveals a long-healed bite mark on his clavicle.

"Know what this is from?"

"Rottweiler?" I say.

"Yes. A Rottweiler."

Soon our spread is eaten, and Ivo and I rejoin the fields. My body is sore after the sitting, and the vineyards stretch like a marathon. I pray for a spectator to hand me oranges and Dixie cups of water at intervals set in the rows. When I slip the scissors over my fingers, I am reminded of that sweet chore of childhood, putting on an already wet bathing suit, sandy and cooled.

Clip, catch, cut . . . A quiet bruise begins to form along my right palm as I move along yet another row. The vines are supported by a fencelike structure. Sandrone has created his trellis by driving old posts into the ground about ten feet apart. The wood, weathered nearly to white, appears to have been unearthed in some archaeological expedition, pulled from the soil along with Neanderthal jawbones. At the tops and bottoms of these posts Sandrone has run thick steel wire, thinner wire strung along the post middles. The Nebbiolo grapes are held aloft by these wires, the bunches heavy and full, the final Caligulan fever dream realized.

Lunch stampedes in my stomach as I reach between these wires, pluck a tune with tired hands. Wayward nailheads jut from the posts, reaching to catch our clothes. At these points the sweaty woman slows her pace, navigates the nails like a stunt driver. A clipper dance. Like Pinot Noir, Nebbiolo is such a delicate grape, unstable, susceptible to weather and human mishandling. Like a gingerbread house, decadent and easily broken.

The sun by now has burned off most of the early fog, lifting the lid on the green mosaic of vineyards. Endless. Thankfully so. The soil continues to boast its loam and chalk, and we pick upon it, exhausted and hallowed.

The sun lowers, leaks its heat. Only Ivo remains of the tractor drivers, the others having descended the hill, disappearing into minicars and farmhouses lit yellow with candlesticks and the light of espresso machines.

The clubhoppers harvest above me, rustling the vines, their lovely curled hair bouncing, impatience in their voices. Beyond us, in Alba or Torino, there are showers to take, clean clothes to be buttoned and snapped, songs to be danced to, boys and girls to be kissed, beds to be used. The nieces must be freezing in their little shorts. The grandparents hold their tongues, their remaining energies reserved for the last grapes of the day. A few children still run among the rows, playing an alternative version of tag—the fleeing must be caught by the shirt, spun to the ground. Other children sleep in the shadows, their silhouettes heaped like laundry.

My brain wanders, anticipates future meals. I see an entire cow's head pulled from a boiling cauldron, carved tableside and dripping. An unseen elderly voice calls dibs on the eyes. Another asks for more broth. My hands struggle to close over the fork and knife, cut into the soft brown meat on my plate. Here the clippers and scissors reassert their roles, dissolve the vision. Cut . . .

When the air temperature drops low enough for me to notice the wetness of my shirtback, Sandrone emerges from Tractor Alley. He strolls along the rows, surveying our work. He kisses the sweaty woman on both cheeks, and she is dismissed from the vineyard, walking straight-backed downhill.

He approaches me and I stand, clippers in one hand, scissors in the other as if for balance.

"Tutto bene?" he asks.

"Sì, Sandrone," I say.

He squints at the grapevines, scrutinizes the half-full crate at my feet.

"Va bene, va bene," he says, swatting some insect from his face.

He cracks his knuckles and I do the same.

Gently, without kissing me, he says, like a teacher or a voice of reason, "Basta."

He turns, leaves the row. I look up. The sun is low and sharp-edged. Easy to look at. I know what this means. *Enough*. Our work is finished for the day, and I stare at my final bunch of grapes, still clinging to the vine, tapered from branch to tip, curved and teasing as a demon Venus. My hand fumbles with the spring-loaded clippers and the purple cluster falls, lazily weighted, into the sugared net of my cramped fingers. I walk in the orange light, carrying my last full crate, downhill to Sandrone.

5

Four Sips

As the sun drips the last of its caramel (*No — too common*) . . . As
the sun drips the last of its porcini risotto (*No — too savory*) . . .
As the sun drips the last of its hazelnut panna cotta with a glass of
Perdaudin Passito 1985 (*Ah, yes — perfectly overwrought, perfectly
Italian*), I find myself sitting on the railing of a forklift, feet resting
on a square pallet of wood, rocketing down a vineyard trail over dirt
and divots and rocks toward Luciano Sandrone's cantina, the man
himself at the wheel.

His hands are so steady, I wonder if he falls victim to the anxiety
that penetrates the region during the harvest. Sandrone preaches
the gospel of harvesting his grapes at peak ripeness, which sometimes means waiting out rainy weather that can destroy the fragile
Nebbiolo. Vintners here are constantly turning their heads upward,
watching the sky, the clouds, the moon. Harvest or wait? An early
morning picking? Late afternoon? Evening?

So many vintages have been ruined by bad weather. Sandrone's
stoicism must be facade. Surely he loses sleep every time he hears
what could be thunder, rolls over in his midnight bed, reaches for his
notebook, revises his harvesting plan by the red digits of the alarm
clock. Surely Mariuccia stirs next to him, communally sleepless,
running her hands over his back, begging for calm, for clear skies.

So many things can go wrong. If it's not rain, it could be a bad
cork. In 2000 a compatriot of Sandrone, Elio Altare, lost nearly all
of his yield due to a supply of tainted corks that destroyed his wine
with hints of mold, a flavor often described as wet cardboard. The

neurotic drama of the winemaker dissipates only with the sipping, then starts up again the next harvest season.

Sandrone must have been wracked with indecision, but today he doesn't show it. My second day of picking Nebbiolo grapes for the man spanned nearly eleven hours, my body anchored diagonally into a hillside between the hamlets of Annunziata and La Morra, my hands drenched in juice and fruit skins. It was good to see the familiar faces this morning—even the clubhoppers, dark circles under their eyes, were generous with their "Ciaos." The nieces had switched to matching red sweatpants and hiking sandals. The sweaty woman was ready to saturate another T-shirt, Ivo was in the same pair of overalls, the same bare chest. Either the slopes today were easier to handle or my body is developing calluses.

At lunch today I learned that, when offered prosciutto cotto or prosciutto crudo, choose crudo. The cotto designation refers to cooked ham, not a million miles away from an American diner breakfast. The crudo, or raw ham, is the real stuff. The stuff we blanketly call prosciutto in the States. As I filled my belly with the meat, sipping another glassful of Dolcetto, I couldn't help but think of my late Jewish grandmother, Grandma Ruth, a staunch hater of the hog, rolling in her grave, meditating on her favorite meal of broiled orange roughy and bread crusts. A product of the Depression and survivalist approach to eating, she passed her somber eating habits onto my father. Habits that I am gratefully dismantling more and more with these vineyard lunches.

As Sandrone forklifts me among the rows, the unpicked grape bunches wave from the cheap seats, hold their wild history beneath their skins. Nebbiolo has been cultivated since the nineteenth century but wasn't shared with the world until the late 1960s, early 1970s. The reasons for this lapse in time and taste reside in mere theory.

A popular version of the Barolo wine's inception is set in the nineteenth-century Piedmontese hamlet of Grinzane (known today as Grinzane Cavour). Count Camillo Cavour (likely handlebar mustachioed) teamed with French wine expert Louis Oudart (likely tortoise shell bespectacled) on a project of the palate. Up until this point the Piedmont harvested the Nebbiolo grape in order to produce sweet red wines. But Cavour and Oudart, upstarts with then-revolutionary wine ideas, began to experiment with the grape to see if it could produce a mouth-friendly dry red. Another version of the story is that it was not Cavour but Juliette Colbert (likely dressed in a blue wedding cake gown), a member of the Falletti family (who owned the town of Barolo at the time), who teamed with Oudart to produce the wine. Certainly, neither Colbert nor Cavour nor Oudart could have predicted the invention of the forklift and the birth of the man who now drives it so recklessly.

I steady myself on the rails, fingernails carrying ounces of dirt. I must have filled twice as many crates today as yesterday, still dozens behind even the slowest of the grandparent pickers, Ivo hauling the yield onto the back of his tractor, biceps bursting from his bare arms, overall suntan lines developing on his torso, his Rottweiler scars going pink with effort.

At lunch he challenged me to an arm-wrestling match, the sweaty woman, gumming her prosciutto, acting as the unofficial referee. Allowed a handicap, I used two arms against Ivo's one.

An audience developed. The nieces stood close to the flanks of the clubhopper boys, the grandparents watching with solemn smiles, smoothing the hair of their grandchildren. The sweaty woman was nothing if not effusive, introducing us in her strained announcer's voice, a raspy Italian Michael Buffer, her moist palms cupped over our fists. Ivo snarled, his beefy elbow digging into the iron surface of the table, imprinting our skin with its diamond holes. A couple of the clubhopper boys started flipping coins onto the table, calling their bets, the nieces laughing, the grandparents hissing, we back-alley vineyard roosters readying our talons and beaks.

After a countdown from *cinque* to *uno*, the sweaty woman released our hands, and I tugged with two fists against Ivo's one. The skin on his chest began vibrating, predicting the fat that will surely plague him in ten years or so. I bit my lip and rose an inch or so from my chair, an illegal maneuver that the clubhopper boys were quick to point out. The moment my ass hit iron Ivo slammed my two fists against the table, raising his hands in the air. A couple of loose hairs hung at his armpits, catching the light of day. One clubhopper boy collected all the coins, the others looking at me disappointed, astounded at my weak American arms. All the prep cheffing in the world could not have granted me the muscle to defeat Ivo and his telephone pole pythons. The nieces clicked their tongues and called me Italian names. The grandparents weren't at all surprised. Somewhere, from his unseen perch, Sandrone surely planned my expedition to his cantina, my lap in defeat.

Back and forearms aching, I wish this rattletrap forklift ride would end already, but I'm sure we're almost there. We have to be. Bouncing along the vineyards as Sandrone's rickety passenger, the sun staining the hemline of Italy's Piedmont an impossible dusty yellow, I try to lose myself in thoughts of my forthcoming dinner with Raffaella and her parents.

This morning, over a quick breakfast of her mother's apple cake and a saucer of plain yogurt, Raffaella invited me to join her family at La Cantinetta, one of the region's more respected restaurants. The cake's density and graininess revolved around my mouth, moist slivers of apple poking through the crumbs like a groundhog testing the weather, and I nearly coughed the entire pasty mouthful onto the rose lapels of Raffaella's blouse as I mustered an exhilarated "Really?!" Her answer, a much more declarative and much less muffled "Really," was the injection of energy I needed to propel me through a full day of picking grapes for Sandrone, my loss to Ivo. Otherwise I would have surely collapsed by noon.

The grapevines stutter past — purple, green — and I see it all as a skipping record, the earth locked into the steady, needled vibration of Sandrone's reckless voyage over this treasured soil. My knees buckle. My hands are torn with wine purple blisters, the widening pain in my lower back fizzing like Alka-Seltzer, and as Sandrone's foot sinks deeper and deeper into the gas pedal shadows, it takes all of my resolve not to whimper like a child. I pitch and tilt with the slope, the voluptuous darkening vineyard greens rocketing as downed clouds, and I have to hold the metal railing at my waist to keep from falling. In my throat the taste of old prosciutto, on my hands the stink of fruit. Here even nausea is delicious, without artificial flavor. I wonder if this region has even heard of the microwave and its soggy evils.

The pallet drags dirt as Sandrone spins to face me, perennial cheroot extending from his swarthy lips. His glasses fall to the bridge of his nose, he belches a balloon of smoke, and we shoot in a magnificent, jaw-rattling bump from the vineyard into a garden at the rear of his cantina. He cuts the engine and steps out. I rise, adrenaline leaping, spine restacking itself in a slow vertical clicking, to follow him.

Sandrone is reduced to a single charcoal color in the waning light, and it doesn't seem as far away as this morning when he turned us loose into the fields, clad in the increasingly familiar colors of his harvesting uniform: faded blue beret, dirty white undershirt, burgundy suspenders, pants the color of exhausted olives, first cold-pressed, to be sure. He walks toward his cantina like dethroned royalty, humble but with a long-practiced grace. His arms hang low to the ground.

The front double doors are magnificent. They must be thirty feet tall, heavy and regal, scrolled, faded wood. Sandrone reaches for the black iron handle, his briar of arm hair infiltrating his hand. The steel button curves like a soft coin beneath his thumb. The door swings inward, heavy, creakless, and a brief hot belch of indoor air swirls between us.

The cantina is palatial, a seamless mesh of tradition and innovation, a ceiling of raw, unfinished cedar beams, giant windows of curved glass, elevators, two-storied, pot-bellied steel tanks for washing the grapes without removing their sugars. The floor is concrete and strewn with old wine stains, a powder that could be sawdust. The smells of subterranean library, chestnut, oak tree, and raisin couple and uncouple with each step forward.

Sandrone has been criticized and praised in equal measure for his revisionist approach to Barolo winemaking. Indeed, the vintners of the Piedmont have drawn a line in the sand — the traditionalists on one side, the modernists on the other. Sandrone places himself somewhere in the middle, but the local traditionalists place him firmly on the other side.

In making a "traditional" Barolo, a vintner will ferment the wine in massive casks of at least fifty hectoliters, often made of oak or chestnut. The wine will ferment and macerate with the grapeskins for nearly two months. During the maceration process the pressed grapeskins are allowed to rest in the juice until they have rendered a level of tannin and color deemed appropriate by the winemaker. This extended contact with the skins lends the wine greater tannin and, traditionally, a greater shelf life. Oftentimes this process was conducted without controlling the temperature. If a fermenting wine is allowed to get too hot, certain flavors and aromas can be lost. These wines were then aged in equally large casks. The product retained a fierce and delicious local identity that was occasionally criticized as too harsh, too elaborate for the global palate.

In order to "soften" Barolo's taste and image a few revolutionary winemakers began experimenting with the traditional process. In the 1960s these vintners began to control the temperature of the product during fermentation, allowing for a wine that retained a greater "balance" and flavor of the original fruit. These "modernists" then began to truncate the maceration period (sometimes as short as four days), softening Barolo's characteristic tannin. Piedmontese producer Angelo Gaja then began aging his wine in smaller, 225 liter barrels made of French oak. These barrels, known as *barriques,* add nuances of smooth wood, which tend to counteract the operatic tannin that was traditionally associated with Barolo and its Nebbiolo grape. The insides of these barriques are typically "toasted," literally burnt, to varying degrees, adding a complexity and color to the wine that traditionalists dub nonindigenous and blasphemous.

Indeed, the word *barrique* is so volatile in the Piedmont that it can't be mentioned to the locals without spawning lengthy debate. Many claim that the flavor of French oak robs the wine of its locally revered identity, that its flavor in any measure cannot be incorporated into a traditionalist's definition of *balance.* (The late Piedmontese vintner Bartolo Mascarello, a politically outspoken and staunch traditionalist, was known to put the phrase NO BARRIQUE directly on his wine labels. The phrase also adorned the walls and archways of his cantina and was emblazoned on T-shirts that he sold or gave away to locals and tourists alike.)

Sandrone and other modernists began to employ rotofermentors, cutting-edge machines that circulate the skins through the juice, further shrinking the maceration time, and allowing fruit to supersede tannin. The traditionalists scoff at such machines, dubbing them unnecessary "cement mixers." They further claim that in careful hands long macerations and aging in the larger, clean casks no longer need to result in unbalanced, overly tannic wines but wines that truly bear the identity of the region, its grapes, its soil, its climate, and its long history of winemaking practices.

Though he is new to winemaking by the region's ancestral standards, Sandrone's passion for the stuff has infected the world market. And it begins here, on these stained and speckled concrete floors, in these tanks that drone with unseen motors. Ivo and his two fellow tractor drivers are busy unloading the flatbeds. They work wordlessly, eliciting only the occasional grunt. They seem not to notice us, shuffling the crates of grapes.

Ivo seems to be their tractor cult's commander, instructing the other two — the one who flexed his biceps for the girls, the one who was ridiculed by the clubhopper boy — to work faster. After loading the grapes into the rinsing tanks and then removing them, the men empty the bunches into a strange destemming machine, a long metallic cylinder. From the front the machine resembles an industrial washer-dryer, housing a rotating sphere, its lining punched with dime-size holes. Destemming the grapes is necessary to avoid an offputting bitterness in the resulting wine. Once the grapes are poured into the cylindrical hopper, an electric agitator pushes them through a series of rollers and screens. The product is then collected in a large, drawerlike bucket. The three tractor drivers work waywardly with this machine, which seems able and willing to swallow their arms.

Sandrone says something to them, and they snap to attention. He calls the biceps-flexer, Beppe, another large man who, in this close proximity, bares a green tattoo of a square-inch tortoise on his left cheek—perhaps an unspoken retort to Ivo's pleas for quickness. Beppe wears his black hair perfectly parted down the middle. He perpetually carries a set of gaming jacks in his coveralls pouch, is known to take unofficial breaks throughout the day to play a few rounds in the vineyards on the backs of the flatbeds before they fill up. Now the pronged metal pieces and red rubber ball poke from beneath the denim. Ivo has told me that Beppe refers to his jacks as "knucklebones."

The other driver, the ridiculed one, is raven haired, if the raven is molting; he is thinner than the other two. He is half Italian, one-quarter Spaniard, and one-quarter Chinese; the other drivers call him Indiano. In spite of his nickname, his skin is so pale you can see the blue network of veins tracing beneath. Eyes bloodshot and coveralls yellow, he assaults this cantina with his primary colors, stark and unblended. Sandrone watches their clunky ballet for a minute, his hands on his hips.

Behind the destemming machine Sandrone gestures with an open palm to his rotofermentors, and indeed they do resemble stainless steel cement mixers, huge vats adorned with complicated dials that seem imported from an airplane's control board. Beyond them, Sandrone's infamous glass elevator, suspended on cables at the mysterious second-floor offices. I can't help but search my pockets for the torn stub of Willy Wonka's Golden Ticket, half expecting to swim laps in a psychedelic pool of Nebbiolo, lick Dolcetto-flavored wallpaper, tango with tractor-driving Oompa-Loompas. Surely, this is some fantasyland dripping with Fizzy Lifting Drinks. In this tricky smell and whir of space-age machinery I can't help but go gluttonous and spoiled, a fat, expectant child who needs to be filled.

Ancient winemaking. Modern techniques. This is all a sepia photograph of the future. And in it Sandrone drags his feet along the cantina floor, collecting the sawdust into a community of molehills.

We come to another man (the cantina is curiously lacking in female energy), bald as the sun, squatting in fluorescent yellow shorts and a T-shirt with surfboards on it. A fantasy of 1970s Hawaii. Bermuda in the basement. He is about fifteen years younger than Sandrone and is busying himself with a pencil and clipboard. His scalp, so red it seems on the verge of bursting, pushes itself between Sandrone and me. Wooden barrels of various size stretch roadwise behind him. He mutters something in breathless, fast-forward Italian, exhaling as if having just finished a marathon.

"Va bene, va bene," Sandrone scolds, then turns to me.

"Mio fratello, Luca," he says and shrugs.

Another Sandrone. Luca, the younger brother. As we pass him, his casual outfit descends into the cantina's shadows, backlit by the barrels in which Barolo is being reared. He goes back to his clipboard.

The farther we step into it, the more this interior space seems circular and square at the same time, and in these walls, humming with taste and motors, Sandrone leads me among another dizzying array of steel tanks. He explains in very deliberate Italian and less deliberate body language about the strict and fixed water temperature of the washing tanks. After the grapes are delicately rinsed, Ivo, Beppe, and Indiano load them into the destemmer. Sandrone explains, in deep, gruff, Bob Hoskins Italian, that the rollers in this machine must be set just so to allow the soft crushing of the grapes, the release of skinny juice, without bruising the skins, avoiding an intrusion of excess tannin.

Behind us Luca shouts something to the tractor drivers. His voice carries a waver, a lilt that says he is asserting his lesser authority as the boss's sibling. Ivo and Beppe laugh him off voraciously, running their thumbs over their cheeks in some kind of derogatory gesture. Beppe fingers his tortoise tattoo and puffs his chest, the jacks threatening to burst through the cloth of his pocket. Luca's authority seems to carry weight only for Indiano, who snaps his eyes downward in a handless salute, his luminous skin outshining even the fluorescence of Luca's clothes.

The more I see and hear of this place, the more it seems like a secret factory churning out children's stories. Here the men behind the curtain wear overalls.

After the grapes are destemmed and crushed, Ivo and company load the product into Sandrone's cement mixer rotofermentors to macerate and begin the fermentation process. In this stage the circulating grapeskins will lend the wine its red color; the natural yeasts in the grapes will react with the sugars, producing carbon dioxide and alcohol. This prepubescent Barolo is now allowed to go through a brief secondary, or malolactic, fermentation. Here the malic acid in the wine (which can cause an astringent taste) is converted into smoother-on-the-palate lactic acid. Sandrone macerates and ferments his grapes for approximately seven days.

Then (and here Sandrone shoots both arms forward, pointing to the highway of barrels) the juice is pressed, separated from the skins in large mechanized strainers calibrated to a specific pressure, and piped into barrels for aging. Certain winemakers are known to add oak chips to the juice in lieu of (the far more expensive process of) barrel aging, though this is unheard-of in the Piedmont. To be legally dubbed "Barolo," the Nebbiolo juice at this stage must age a minimum of two years in barrels. After this long, patient wait, the wine is then filtered into bottles and sealed. (Whereas cork is traditional, many winemakers are opting for synthetic cork or even screw tops to avoid the ordeal suffered by Elio Altare.) Again, according to the legal standard, Barolo must age for an additional year in the bottle before being released onto a fortunate public.

Sandrone drops his hands to his sides, cocks his head, surely listening to the three tractor drivers bitching about Luca's micromanagement. A grin spreads across his face, and he shakes his head. I keep reaching to pat Sandrone on the back but always stop myself. I'm not sure how he'd react to my touching him. He stands harsh and unyielding, a weathered ship's captain explaining his trade to a deckhand. As a lover of wine I can't help admiring his perfectionism, but, as a member of his crew, I am ready to return to Il Gioco dell'Oca, shower, eat a huge meal, and pass out.

As we walk the cantina fills with echoes — our footsteps, the low grumbling of Ivo and Beppe, the sighs of Indiano, the groaning and settling of the machines. And undercutting it all, the sound of liquid becoming wine, a ghostly slosh, trapped behind wood and steel. We listen to the switching of gears and the laughter of the tractor cult, the sounds of Barolo being made.

Sandrone has trouble walking and talking at the same time — at least, talking to me, dumbing down his Italian to accommodate my nonfluency. We stroll beyond a final steel tank, about to pass under the peach stone archway that leads to the gravel parking lot and, likely, the moon, when Sandrone stops and says, "Aspeta."

This word, a vocal refrain for the man, means "Wait." And I do, but not for long. There is a silence that lasts the amount of time needed for me to crack my knuckles and inhale the wet-rock scent of the place. Then Sandrone begins a story, speaking very slowly to ensure that I understand everything.

A family of New Zealanders (who had also stayed at Il Gioco dell'Oca) visited his cantina a week earlier. He shifts phlegm in his throat and explains that they have a vineyard on New Zealand's North Island and had invited Sandrone himself to their harvest that upcoming March. Sandrone pauses, stares at the ceiling as if trying to divine a text on translation. In this silence I hear Indiano yell in a pinched voice. Standing up for himself. The last straw. Shedding his nerdhood for the rest of the day.

"Allora," Sandrone says, flaring his nostrils. I get the feeling that if I wasn't here, he would verbally beat the shit out of these guys. He listens to the air for a second. The argument has ended. Something loud in this last steel tank switches on and, in the sound of propellers, Sandrone continues his story.

This March he is indeed going to New Zealand but not to oversee or consult, not to bestow a kernel or two of expertise, but to *pick the grapes.* He is going to work the fields, do the grunt work. This man who exports his wine all over Europe and the States, Canada, Japan, Russia, Brazil. Australia, South Africa, South Korea, Hong Kong. He will share my back pain and carpal tunnel syndrome. The rash that has made pickled beets of my hands. An odd brew of respect and revenge shoots into my bloodstream. It is as if Ferran Adrià is going to travel across the globe to mop the floors of a Denny's simply because he is enamored of the restaurant atmosphere. I suppose this is true love. The man is going to *work the fields*.

I try to piece together the proper Italian response in my brain, sifting through old equations: the quadratic, the associative, the Pythagorean theorem. I fuck up. It comes out all nasalized English.

"That is true love," I tell him, hoping he understands. I cup my right palm under my heart as if suspending it in my chest.

"Lavoro del cuore," I manage, looking at his face, at his settled contentment.

I think he understands, but he remains smiling and stoic. A swarthy Buddha. He gestures toward a mop leaning against the steel tank. He pronounces the words *la prossima settimana*. I think that, next week, I am mopping his cantina floors. After the New Zealand story, how can I say no?

My stomach growling in protest, he leads me up a flight of metal stairs just before the parking lot archway. We emerge onto a narrow scaffolding at the near-ceiling-high lips of the tanks. Some are closed at the top and some are open, and I peer inside and see it: the full rippling sea of wine so deep that Indiano, Beppe, and Ivo, riding each other's shoulders like Cirque du Soleil clowns, could disappear beneath it.

The depth of color, so dark, thick as cloth. I turn, still leaning over the tank, and I see Sandrone with a goblet in one hand and a glass wine thief in the other. The thief, used to extract tasting samples, is the turkey baster of the wine world, the bastard child of the eyedropper and the Erlenmeyer flask.

"No," I say to him, understanding right away, "no, it's too much."

After a chunky adolescence in Jewish American suburbia, it's tough to shake guilt in the face of decadence. Growing up, it was okay to say yes to microwaved anything, a freezer full of boxed dinners, but to wine? My father would beat himself up for choosing

Coke over Diet Coke. My mother would only let me and my sister chew sugarless gum. Fat, yes! Sugar? That's for the goyim.

And honestly, for all of my kvetching (that's for you, Grandma Ruth) — *my back, my hands* — I'm indebted to Sandrone just for offering me this experience in the face of legal persecution and threat of air raid by helicopter. And now he wants to feed me his wine. I close my eyes and meditate on whatever engine it was that compelled me to become a dwarf high jumper and clumsy caterer. Compelled me to love food. I open them. Sandrone is leaning over the tank, filling the thief a third of the way with the purple liquid. He splendidly bastes the inside of the wineglass.

"Barolo," he says, "Cannubi Boschis," and hands the glass to me.

I hold the glass to the light, and a ball of rose shines in the middle of the darker purple. The sun from thirty ocean feet deep.

"Prego," Sandrone offers, smiling.

I bow my head and sniff the liquid.

"Oh," I moan.

Earth, truffle, history, time travel, Jurassic.

At glassbottom I see the public schools of America heaping spoonfuls of prepackaged creamed chipped beef onto refined Texas toast. Styrofoam trays with compartments for dessert. Radiated apple cobbler. I picture that small percentage of children who will feel a culinary rebellion growing within them. Pick up a cookbook. Watch a cooking show. Start packing their own lunches.

I sip.

And I feel it — a red carpet unfurl along the length of my tongue, billowing to fill my cheeks, throat, esophagus, stomach, turning everything soft, soft and warm. This is it. The key to unlock my muscles is passing over my guts. Hands melt. Back unties. The elementary school cafeterias of America evaporate somewhere over the Atlantic. And I still have four sips left.

The shadow of Luca Sandrone passes in the distance, bent and extended along the far cantina wall like a vampire trick, the shadow of the clipboard tucked under his arm. No sound from Ivo, Beppe, or Indiano.

Sandrone, impatient, rolls his hand. "Prego, prego," he says, appalled at my slow imbibing.

So I succumb. I down the glass and let the wine massage me as it will. I suppose if I'm going to be here for a while, I'll have to learn to savor more quickly. With a bellyful of vino, my hunger is a lot easier to handle, my glass, coated in translucent wine sheen.

Sandrone reaches for the glass and I thank him, try to tell him how much his wine means to me, but at this moment he probably, and correctly, sees me as a delirious American. He smiles. Nods. Walks me to the far edge of the scaffolding. I peer over the side and see another open-topped tank, filled with grape mash — branches, seeds, skins. This is the leftover stuff from the winemaking process, waiting to be distilled to make grappa, the ubiquitous Italian *digestivo,* a pomace brandy with a reputation for bite.

The tank is steaming, and I feel the warmth of it on my face. Sandrone gestures toward the mash with an open palm, bows at the waist. He is encouraging me to lean in, very close to the contents, and take a smell. The mash seems to breathe, this tangle of vegetal viscera, a lowbrow special effect evoking terrible slaughter. Somewhere the tractor cult empties grapes into a machine, their hands clad in yellow rubber gloves. Somewhere Luca Sandrone doodles his own vineyard into the corner of the clipboard. Replaces the pencil behind his ear.

But here, Sandrone standing hands on hips, his face glowing with diabolism, I push my nose mere inches from the pulsing red mash and take an inhale that would have made Dizzy Gillespie proud. The alcoholic steam rushes into my nostrils, hot condensation envelopes my face, and *ZING!* I am clubbed and stung, punched full force, nasal passages and eyes, ears and throat swabbed as if before inoculation. My body shoots backward and my shoulders smack the wall behind us, knocking the wind from my lungs. The raw, fermenting alcohol. It attacks me. I remember those tavern-born legends of a drink so strong it could blind you. Light-headed, I feel something evil grow in my nose, petunia cross-bred with piranha.

This stuff shouldn't be above radar; it should be relegated to clandestine stills, attics and basements, garages and bad dreams. In fact, Italian law dictates that home makers of grappa are limited to a production of three liters per year. A law that Sandrone stresses is habitually broken, absurd and outdated like the banning of a cow on a roof in Virginia, the prohibition on dancing on a Michigan bridge.

The sound of a gas jet igniting comes from beneath us. I'm afraid this entire chemistry set is going to blow up. Sandrone erupts into laughter, taking the cheroot from his mouth and holding it low in his hand. He steps forward, belting deep, throaty pirate guffaws, and pats me on the back. My head is spinning, my eyes drippy, snot collecting at the backs of my stinging throat and nose. Every breath is a wheeze. I try laughing back, to join Sandrone in his joke as the good-natured butt thereof, but my attempt is so liquid that I stop myself midway, afraid that I will cough and then, in turn, hawk a lunger into his Nebbiolo.

While I'm certain his finished product is refined and smooth, possessing soft things like *body* and *bouquet,* the mash at this stage is, politely, *coarse.* I take some tissue from my pocket, wipe my eyes, blow my nose.

"Ivo!" Sandrone calls, and the man — chest, overalls — comes at a slow jog, yellow rubber gloves shuddering over his hands.

Ivo cocks his head, looks up at us ornaments on the scaffolding.

"Per favore," Sandrone says to him, pointing to the mash tank, asking him, I think, to cover the top.

"He did it to you," Ivo says, wafting the air to his nose. "The, uh . . ."

"Fumes," I manage.

"Fumes? Smells," Ivo says. "He does this. He likes to do this."

Sandrone laughs again, his billy-goat call echoing from the ceiling.

"Unbelievable," I say. "I think I'm crying."

Ivo tells me how Sandrone just exacted the same hazing on Indiano.

"He's new, you know," Ivo says, climbing the scaffolding stairs.

Apparently, Indiano replaced a long-standing member of the tractor cult, a man Sandrone nicknamed "PeMol" because of his prosthetic right leg. "PeMol," which loosely translates into English as "Peg Leg," later became the fantasy label name of Sandrone's red wine blend (40 percent Nebbiolo and 60 percent Barbera grape).

"He likes to think he is very funny," Ivo tells me as Sandrone playfully punches at his kidneys.

As Ivo fumbles with a control board on the wall, pressing a button that will surely re-cover the mash tank, Sandrone leads me past him and down the stairs. We stand at the archway, and through the windows I can see the dusk of the Langhe—moony, starry—and apparitions of trees—oak, poplar, chestnut, fig. Under this earth, truffles. Upon it, grapes.

We shake hands, his palm dwarfing mine in thickness and grape-feel, and he laughs again. I chuckle a bit and pat him on the back. It seems Ivo has sealed the tank, taken the wine thief for a proper cleaning. My stomach begins to scream for some food to complement the wine.

Sandrone says, "Aspeta."

He reaches to a shelf above us, a shelf holding old bottles of local wine—labels white and brown, beige and green, red letters, black letters, letters sheened in gold. Bottles dusty and sealed with red wax, ripped labels stained rose with ancient splatter. So many vintages, so many dates. While my grandmother was gumming her first taste of bread crust, Barolo was being made.

Sandrone retrieves a bottle of his own 1990 Le Vigne Barolo. He holds it to me. The red square on the label promises something—a four-sided drinking experience perhaps. This is a wine that is next to impossible to purchase commercially today (save for a few Japanese Internet auctions, where I've seen it selling for upward of a thousand dollars), most of it already having been drunk or aging in some lucky gourmet's profound cellar. This is a wine that critic and connoisseur Robert Parker dubbed one of the best wines of all time, bestowing upon it his elusive 100 rating at the time of its bottling. This is one of the last magnificent "blend-style" Barolos in existence. Nebbiolo grapes from four different vineyards (in the eastern portion of the Barolo zone) are blended together; the grapes of all four vineyards feed off of one another in this blissful union. Like my grandparents, married until death.

"Questo vino é il mio favorito," Sandrone says.

This is his favorite.

I take this bottle into my hands. The minimalist white label, its faded red square, its black block letters spelling the name of the man before me, engages me in a stare-down, and I know that I have to look away first. When I do, I look up.

"No, no," I tell him, that generational guilt reasserting itself in my throat. "The experience was all I wanted, I mean, the . . ."

"Prego," Sandrone cuts off firmly, giving me an order. "Mille grazie," he says. "Ciao, ciao."

And with that he turns and walks back toward his tanks as if escaping another pat on the back. It seems I am to walk back to Il Gioco dell'Oca. My stomach protests, but my hands are happy. I rotate the bottle in them. I double-check. It's real.

"Grazie, Sandrone," I call to him.

"Luciano," he says, turning to face me.

"Luciano," I nod.

He narrows his eyes.

"Sì," I reply, not quite sure what I'm saying *yes* to.

He smiles, then disappears through the far doorway. I look at the bottle in my hands, watch as the words on the label stack themselves before me to become this cantina, this man, this region, these spring-loaded clippers and pain-in-the-ass scissors, these tanks, and this rubber-gloved crew. It is medicinal in my hands, smooth. In this gift, this bottle, Sandrone has offered me a chance of some kind. A knowledge. And so I clutch the bottle to my chest, knowingly begin the three kilometer twilit walk to my dinner with Raffaella and her family.

6

All You Have to Do Is Say "Sì"

Walking the narrow lip of grass that divides the vineyards of the
Piedmont from Via Crosia, clutching Sandrone's 1990 Le Vigne
Barolo to my chest like the Grail, like a child, like a surrogate heart,
fixing my gaze on the orange lights of Il Gioco dell'Oca half a mile
away and farther into my forthcoming dinner with Raffaella and
her family, I unearth an exhilarated exhale each time a car speeds
by, mere inches from my legs. My breath shoots into the night like
a mist, and I quicken my pace and walk through it face-first. It feels
ancient and damp as stone — chilled, marble — and my chest is tight
with the exhaustion of a full day's grape picking, tight in the face
of this country's generosity, manifesting itself as the bottle in my
arms, the dinner that will soon be in front of me. For the first time
in my life I feel like saying grace. In her grave Grandma Ruth rolls
the other way.

I turn to see the eleventh-century castle of Barolo lit up preserved
yellow, a beacon on the cliff face presiding over the closed and gated
shopfronts: the *macelleria* with its dormant red meats, waxed wagon
wheels of cheese, the *panetteria* with its cornmeal-dusted breads
sheathed in greasy white paper, the *bottiglieria* holding the history
of this region beneath countless stained corks. Stop. Breathe. Face
forward again.

The sky is dark, the air chilled enough to break glass. The wind
howls in a cluster of poplar trees. The fig trees stand flat topped as if
the wind has scalped them. Abandoned barrels upturned streetside,
battered in this nightbreeze. Lank wires of scrubgrass breaking into
cracks in the road, the blades falling to the cooling stone. The land

refereeing its own metamorphosis into myth. The smell of wine everywhere.

My feet are crunching the white stones of Raffaella's driveway. I one-arm the black gate, nod at the two peach brick pillars flanking it as its keepers, and step toward the farmhouse. Pongo shifts in his doghouse. I am, still, filthy.

She is in the kitchen, working the foot pump at the sink, copper hands running themselves over the face of a white dish. The kitchen walls are painted a faded yellow, the shelves graced with expensive cookware and ceramic roosters. Niccolo, her terror of a son, was thankfully dumped off at her brother's house in Alba.

"You are back," Raffaella says, setting the dish at sink's bottom and drying her hands on a blue towel. "How was the picking up the grapes?"

We sit across from one another at the dining room table, the thick wood surface pressing our palms. The stone floor is cold. The white cast-iron radiator, an old columnar behemoth, switches on at the head of the table with a horrible clanking. Soon it will be too hot to touch.

I tell her of the day, of the cantina tour, of Sandrone's gift. She takes the bottle from me, examines the label for a long time as if attempting to uncover its subtext, its taste, or perhaps Sandrone's rationale for bestowing such a treasure on some frivolous American passerby. She putters her lips.

"I think it is one of the best," she says.

The bottle will soon become the first installment in the intended wine cellar at the corner of my tent, but here, at the table, it serves as a silent focus for both Raffaella and me, mutually captivated, a frozen moment on film. Raffaella, the bottle, and I are stuck—a glorious pause. We sit together in prolonged silence, neither one of us able to take our eyes from the Sandrone Le Vigne. The radiator puffs with steam or oil, changing gears in raw eructations.

Raffaella is about to say something when a thunderous stampede echoes along the adjacent stairwell, sound bouncing from the living room walls. I swear I hear the throat-born cluckings of a formidable hen interrupted by the vibratory lowing of a steer on speed. As if in a mutual hurdle over a limp electric fence, Raffaella's mother and father spring from the stairwell and into the living room. They hush when they see Raffaella and me, smiles glued to their faces like wallpaper, and I can't decide whether their grins want to serve as function or decoration. They sway shoulder to shoulder, analyzing, waiting to be analyzed.

Michele, the lanky, chiseled ex-butcher, stands clad entirely in black — shoes, socks, shirt, pants, tie, sport coat — his shock of white hair topping the ensemble like the afterimage of a burnt match. Gothic scarecrow. Pallbearer. His long-fingered hands run over his thighs and down to his knees as if waking his legs for a marathon. His smile continues to gape, adding light to the room.

I return the smile, and Adriana, always waiting for the tiniest excuse to erupt into laughter, erupts into laughter, pointing and cooing a string of motherly Italian. She shakes her massive arms over her head, their peach undersides shuddering like pelican mouthbags. Her white costume jewelry spits rattlesnake warnings from her wrists. She also is clad in black, dyed red hair teetering back and forth atop her head. She stops laughing and Michele begins as she shakes me by the shoulders and urges me, in earth-shattering Italian, into a shower and a change of clothes.

"L'uomo fangoso!" she cries, turning my griminess into exclamation.

The bathwater is barely warm. Outside, the trees scratch the house.

Four people crammed into a Fiat Cinquecento Rosso mini indicates a desire to tempt madness, trick space, break records, and we seem to pull off all three feats without so much as a groan or a fidget. We fill the car with body heat, the sweet chalk of Adriana's heavy makeup. Michele spins along the vineyard roads in typical Italian fashion, twisting the wheel and pumping the pedals as if a child deliberately coloring outside the lines. The grapes whip by outside in our speed. Adriana shouts to Raffaella from the passenger seat,

Raffaella shouts back, and I stare out the window as we careen past Sandrone's darkened cantina.

"She say she is so hungry she can eat Sandrone," Raffaella says to me, pulling me from the window. "His whole body!"

Adriana bellows "Sì, sì, sì" from the front seat like an air-raid siren, Michele turns from the road to slap me on the knee, the car jerks wildly right, Raffaella winks, and I hold onto the headrest for dear life.

"Mia mamma italiana," I muster, daring to mess the tight nest of Adriana's hair.

She bursts with laughter yet again and shoots an extended paragraph of Italian machine gun fire. She readjusts her hairdo with both hands.

The moon is near full tonight, haunting the Piedmont, the rolling vineyards, and, just out of sight, the Alps. Michele tosses the wheel to the left, and the moon tucks itself behind a hillside town. Outside the confines of Barolo the town we launch into La Cantinetta's parking lot, gravel billowing over the car like water. He tugs the parking brake skyward, and we pop from the car spring-loaded, this four-headed jack-in-the-box with a ravenous matriarch. The white facade of the restaurant extends its thick arms to us, the orange lantern-lit interior containing its secrets, if only for a final moment.

Inside, La Cantinetta is all purple flowers, green leaves, white vases, stone walls. Dark wood tables. Dark wood chairs, red cushions, patterned tablecloths. Each place setting marked with four wineglasses — one flute, one white, two red. Voices hushed, voices effusive, meld together into unified din. Candlelight animates the walls. A small fire fills the fireplace.

We are led to our table by a short round hunchbacked man, a crescent smile carved into his face. His arms pull our chairs with a practiced flair, his normal speaking voice seems a shout, and even his baldness, like Luca's, is exaggerated, an illusory addition to his meager height. Here the restaurant industry is staffed by professionals, respected by their customers, not merely a refuge for bookish ex-cons and starving artists. Hedonism is important business, and everyone knows it.

Raffaella and I sit across from her parents, and my heart swells like a persimmon when I notice that, within the confines of this legendary twelve-table restaurant, there is no such thing as a menu. Raffaella leans to me, explaining that La Cantinetta is run by three brothers and that, before the Alba white truffle and popularization of the Piedmontese wines brought the keener of the European tourists, not a single restaurant in the area allowed the customers menus.

"Every place make something different every night — whatever will look the best in the market, you know," she says, "and they only serve what they make. But the tourists complain, uh, they don't have the choice. So now some places make the regular menu. Stupid."

"Catering to the masses," I say.

"Yes, like the caterer. Boring. Terrible," she affirms.

"Remember that restaurant I was telling you about, Raffaella? Charlie Trotter's in Chicago?"

"Sì. I remember."

"Well, he doesn't give his customers a choice either. He offers a pair of fixed-price degustations of his own choosing, which apparently stirred some complaints among the more unenlightened of Chicago's diners."

Raffaella smiles and slaps my hand. "You are a snob, too," she says.

"In an interview the interviewer asked him why, despite these numerous complaints, he would still refuse to offer his customers a typical menu, a choice. And you know what he said?"

"What?"

"He said, 'You don't go to the symphony and tell them what to play.'"

"Mmm," Raffaella hums. "I like that."

And here our waiter, the only one of the three brothers with hair on his head (according to Raffaella), fills our red wineglasses with a 1995 Bartolo Mascarello Barolo and our white wineglasses with a Ceretto Blange, both highly respected local bottlings. The Blange is made from the rare white Arneis grape, which thrives in the atmosphere of the Piedmont. Raffaella explains that the Ceretto family stirs controversy in the region; their winery is an ultramodern all-glass cube perched on an otherwise medieval hillside in the hamlet of Castiglione Falletto.

"They say they are the, uh, uh, antipioneer," she says, hoisting her glass of the hay-colored liquid.

We toast *cin cin,* our white wineglasses meeting over the table's single candle like the beat of a gong, and, glassy aftershocks encircling us, we sip. Cow tastes: soil and grass. Ceretto Blange.

"Oh," I moan. "Wow."

"*Wow,*" Michele mimics and laughs, wrapping the snakes of his fingers over my wrist and shaking.

Adriana throws her head back and pumps laughs from her stomach.

Raffaella says, "Yes."

The hunchbacked host doubles as a server, roves like a gymnast among the tables, balancing trays of food and wine, vaulting the wild gestures of the customers.

And then: the food.

The waiter emerges from the kitchen with an expansive white plate, tiny mounds of various antipasti, dabbled paints of meat-and-cheese. We lean backward in unison, making room on the table, thrusting ourselves into the underlying din of the restaurant: overlapping murmurs and shouts of Italian, glass tinkling against glass, silverware tapping plates, groans of delight and submission, and, scoring it all, the tinsel of laughter. Simultaneously raucous and serene, the interior of La Cantinetta shines with utensil and revelry.

Adriana, with a luscious disregard for her silverware, begins snatching at the bits of food with her doughnut hands. Then Michele, his hands pecking at the plate like a bird for ants. And Raffaella, taking up her fork and slithering it among the whites and yellows of the cheese, the purple disks of salami speckled with diamonds of fat, the prosciutto silks spun pink into half-open roses, the flesh-colored mound of bagna caoda.

The cheeses alone play like the Piedmont's greatest hits: the Toma (that lovely lowland cow-goat hybrid Sandrone provided to his crew in the vineyards), the barely solid Robiola (a creamy goat cheese), Fontina (a high-fat cow's milk cheese typically aged in ventilated stone buildings at elevations exceeding 10,000 feet), Castelmagno (a hard cheese that combines barely skimmed cow's milk with the milk of goat or sheep), and Braciuk (an unpasteurized hard cow's milk cheese ripened in grapeskins) frame the antipasti platter.

The bagna caoda (which translates as "hot bath") is the nucleus of the spread. This Piedmontese relish, served with crostini, is a hot combination of butter and olive oil, blessed with an abundance of garlic, anchovy, red and yellow pepper, sunchokes (also known as Jerusalem artichokes), and cardoons (an edible thistle and a local favorite). Today the bagna caoda is topped with the Alba white truffle, that royal fungus, tempering the acidity with a measure of earth.

Also adorning the plate is carne cruda, elevating the simplicity of raw chopped beef by topping it with white truffle oil, unfiltered olive oil, arugula, and shavings of Parmesan. To the left of this dressed-up beef is vitello tonnato: thin slices of roasted veal topped with a tuna mayonnaise — the Piedmontese version of "surf and turf."

As I reach with my fingers for a gleaming sliver of Toma and a dark brown circle of salami, Michele leans across the table and whispers, complicitly, "Salame degli asini."

I turn to Raffaella. "What did he say? 'Salami of *what?*'"

"It is the . . . uh . . . asini . . . how do you say . . . uh, the ass. The ass salami."

I can't help but laugh. "The ass salami?" I chuckle.

The hunchbacked host subverts my chair with a sway that would make a belly dancer blush.

"Yes," stresses Raffaella, slapping my shoulder. "Is that wrong?"

She presses her fingers together — here is the church, here is the steeple . . .

"What, from the ass of the pig?" I ask.

"No. Not the pig. The ass. I tell you."

Illumination.

"Oh, like the donkey," I say, moving the salami closer to my mouth. "The animal."

"Yes. The donkey. The ass. Asino. Asini."

"Bello," Michele smiles, kissing his fingertips.

A handsome salami, he says. I believe him.

Chewing, the natural spice of the salame degli asini sits me back in my chair, penetrates my nose, the moist jewels of fat dissolving in my mouth like cotton candy. It's not funny anymore. I follow it with the indigenous Toma, musk upon musk, the lowlands dropping lower.

"Oh my god," I croon, eyes rolling toward my brain. "This is amazing."

"Just wait," Raffaella coos.

And I do, but not for long. The waiter slithers among the tables pouring a new round of wines, and soon he produces his brother, the chef, even rounder than the host, even more disarmingly bald. The chef cradles a massive communal bowl of pasta and strolls from table to table, grunting under its weight and chatting to the guests as if they were neighbors. The waiter spoons four plump ravioli onto each plate. The steam snakes upward, escaping. The restaurant takes on a haze, a nebbia of its own, brought on by the billowing plates, the effects of the wine, the way the candlelight bounces from the walls. Adriana grasps Michele's hands in delight, her costume jewelry further calving the light. Michele laughs and kisses her flush on the mouth, reemerging smeared with her lipstick, which he proceeds to wipe onto a cloth napkin. I shake my head, gallivanting dazed through the best of food dreams, and Raffaella whispers in my ear, "They are famous all over Piemonte for this ravioli."

"Is it the plin?" I ask.

"Better," Raffaella says.

Ravioli al plin, a Piedmontese specialty, can be filled and sauced with almost anything—cheese and nutmeg, spinach, prosciutto, truffle cream, wild boar. Often dubbed agnolotti al plin (agnolotti refers to a smaller ravioli with a higher ratio of filling to dough — there is just enough dough to wrap the filling), this dish graces the menus of many Piedmontese restaurants. The word *plin*, or "pinch," references the pinching of two sheets of dough together over and around the filling. Agnolotti al plin is typically filled with cheese and sauced simply with butter and sage; or, for an added bonus that my meat-loving family would applaud, it can be filled with veal and cheese, then sauced with butter, sage, and a veal stock reduction.

But Raffaella repeats, "This is better than the typical plin."

The pasta dough wears its yellow proudly, overstuffed and bursting with the egg yolks that created it. I lift my fork when Raffaella calls, "Wait," yet again. The waiter, after dishing the restaurant's plates, sprints to the kitchen and breathlessly emerges holding an Alba white truffle to the light. Larger than his fist, resembling a stone, the truffle at first silences the dining room. In this silence the lower lips of the uninitiated drop, knowing smiles grow across the faces of La Cantinetta veterans. Raffaella takes my hand. Warm. Woozy. Then the diners bellow as one, some clapping, some shaking their arms in the air. Raffaella lets go of my hand, and we follow suit.

The waiter jogs through the restaurant, shaving slivers of the truffle over everybody's plate, his wooden truffle slicer rigid with arrogance, having been created for this sole purpose. He approaches our table, his fingernails perfectly groomed, the backs of his hands devoid of hair or blemish, and shaves, shaves . . . Adriana kisses the air with her sloppy lipstick, Michele holds his hands to his cheeks, Raffaella says something that makes the waiter laugh. I don't know what to do. After a mound of slivered white truffle has been shaved over my plate, Raffaella nods, "Now is okay."

I sink my fork into the bloated center of one ravioli and recoil in surprise. From the cut I make into the dough a thin burst of barely cooked egg yolk streams onto the plate. Egg-dough ravioli stuffed with another egg yolk and smothered with white truffles and butter. *Egg-dough ravioli stuffed with another egg yolk and smothered with white truffles and butter*. So simple. So divine. Such integrity. The

wet of the egg meshing with the slight give of the ravioli dough calling to the pure earthiness of the truffle feeding the quiet sweetness
of the butter sends my hands, like Michele's, on a trip to my face.

I want to tell Ivo about this, ask him if he's ever been here. I
picture him at a corner table in his harvesting uniform, the clasps
of his overalls catching the candlelight, his bare chest beading with
sweat. We devour the ravioli quickly, our lips sheened with yolk,
goofy grins hanging on our faces. And the meat and dessert courses
still remain.

We find ourselves with beef tenderloin on our plates, poached in
Barolo wine, sauced with the poaching liquid, and buried beneath a
spread of porcini mushrooms. The heady, steaklike porcini sprouts
in the northwestern reaches of the Piedmont, where it borders the
Valle d'Aosta region. With a white stalk thick as a baby's arm and a
deep brown sunhat of a cap, these fresh porcini threaten to suffocate
the tenderloin.

The steak rests in the center of the plate, a small, contained island;
we surround it, oceanic, the four of us drained of our solidity. We
eat. We drink. We laugh and touch hands. We shake each other.

When the waiter brings the plates of dessert, I am stuffed and
dizzy, half-drunk and enamored. "Oh, no," I say, shaking my head.
"I don't think I can."

Raffaella, Adriana, and Michele collectively sigh, "Panna cotta."

Ubiquitous in the Piedmont, this dessert consists of cooked
cream, which can be infused with a variety of ingredients — vanilla,
orange, honey. The cream is then chilled and lightly gelled. The
waiter rotates the dessert plate in front of me, panna cotta the color
of copper.

"It is made with the hazelnut," Raffaella explains.

"It looks amazing, but I don't think I can cram it in," I tell her, rubbing my hands over my stomach, feeling for any available space.

Moderation must have been burned up in the candle flame.

The waiter, as if to top the many surprises of the evening, bends
to my ear and says in very broken English, "All you have to do is say
'Sì.'"

I nod. The m-word has no place here.

"Sì," I say and scarf the hazelnut panna cotta in four bites. I am in pain. I rinse the sweet nuttiness of the cooked cream from my mouth with a Perdaudin Passito 1985, a thick pumpkin oil of an amber dessert wine, glossing my lips. The Passito wines decorate many Piedmontese menus. Amber, honey sweet, and a little viscous, Passito is traditionally made from the Erbaluce, or "grass of light," grape. The grapes are left on the vines until mid-November, then picked, trellised, and dried in the sun, which generates a high concentration of sugar. Pressed in the winter, the juice ferments six to seven months in oak. La Cantinetta's Passito helps ease my discomfort, dissolves the pile of food with its hints of pear, red current, vanilla, chestnut, tobacco, licorice, aniseed . . .

The night progresses in a blur of evening gown sequins, ruffled tuxedo shirts, polished leather shoes. The only way to confront such a dinner it seems is with an ironed sense of the cosmopolitan. At this point in the night the straps of the evening gowns slip off the shoulders, the top two tuxedo shirt studs come undone. At midnight a well-dressed man at a corner table produces an acoustic guitar. He and the chef sing and sway together, crooning Italian ballads. Adriana encourages Michele to join them, but he shakes his head, then dives face-first into her cleavage. Raffaella slaps at them both, rolling her eyes at me.

We sit talking with each other, with the other patrons, with the three brothers (who grow their own herbs and produce for the restaurant) until one in the morning, Michele nodding in and out of consciousness at the table, hopefully resting and sobering up for the drive home. Finally, we lift ourselves from the chairs, our backs stiff. Somehow we make it through the door, the three brothers shaking our hands, demanding we return tomorrow and the next day and the next . . .

We collapse into the Cinquecento, and the car sinks with our weight.

We are carried along the vineyard roads back to Il Gioco dell'Oca, Adriana at the wheel. We ride in silence, Raffaella's eyes closed at my side, her head leaning toward me. A soft string of drool. A muffled snore. Looking out the window at the darkened vineyards and the stars that watch over them, at the grapes waiting to be harvested, my mouth full of Italy's flavors, I am anointed with a vision of how I want to live my life. And it is overwhelming and perfect, earthbound and traditional, steaming, bloody, a sensual color gradient, a succulent medium-rare.

7

Grape-Shaped Ball of Light

Waking with the now-stale but still-spiced taste of salame degli asini on one's tongue must surely be indicative of Italian rural living in both its nonchalant elegance and crackerjack rusticity, no matter how foreign, no matter how gamey.

I unzip the tent screen, jeweled with dew, and the tent door, jeweled with the same, and, clad in yesterday's Cantinetta clothes, walk for Il Gioco dell'Oca's heavy front door. In grasping its black steel handle, still cool from the night, I feel a jolt of electricity (Beppe Fenoglio's ghost?) and connection via my belly, sagging with Barolo and white truffles.

As the inside air wraps its inside warmth over the back of my neck, I feel more outside than if I were still in the tent, and I sense, from either the sound or the smell of the foyer, that Raffaella is not home. She often leaves for early morning Alba runs — groceries, espresso, pastry — and I picture her in the Cinquecento, lips closing around a lit Merit, tooling recklessly over the Piedmont's dips and curves. Her blonde hair would be fanning toward the barely open window, wind calling the strands into the air. Her hands on the wheel in a loose grip, the color of a penny, Lincoln's faded profile, and as I step into her darkened kitchen, she surely pitches around a pedestrian, and all I can think is *emancipate*.

And so I do: free my parched throat with a cup of Lavazza coffee, send the ass salami to a better place with a single crostino and butter. Pongo the Pyrenees scratches at the door, and I drown the sound with my next bite. Adriana must have come early to feed the animals — Pongo, cats, chickens — and returned home to Alba. In the early mornings, still dark, I often hear her from my tent, calling the animals with a high-pitched *Mi-mi-mi-mi-mi-mi-mi!* before distributing a stockpot concoction of fat, gristle, carrot, stale bread, and water into their respective troughs. (The chickens are limited to the carrot and feed.)

I listen for the sound of Michele's hammer or circular saw, but I hear only silence. He's forever engaged in some project involving wood and a blade. The tourists have checked out, the next wave not due until this afternoon (so Raffaella told me last night). I have the day off today — no picking, no mopping. Alone in Il Gioco dell'Oca. The stone walls, the piano, the thermostat. But I leave all in place — shelter, music, temperature: all beyond my control. I will eat bread. I will drink coffee. I will not check the time.

Soon I will debate whether or not to stroll by Sandrone's cantina, decide that the man needs at least a one-day break from my American face, and wait at the bus stop for the increasingly unreliable Satti blue and yellow to pick me up for Alba, the rose-cobblestoned hamlet of vegetable, pasta, fruit, truffle, of wine markets, of white-walled cafés dripping yellow chandelier light, the big — it seems to me now — city.

Across Via Crosia from Il Gioco dell'Oca, the driveway of the Borgogno cantina meets the dusty white stones of the six inch road shoulder. Borgogno is a common name in the Piedmont, but Lodovico Borgogno, to whom this cantina belongs, has a unique reputation. Raffaella has warned me, "He might be a little crazy." Like his father, Enrico, before him, Lodovico began to head production in 1950. His florid personality enabled him to market his wine extensively for the time simply via his incantation-like sales pitches, which Raffaella describes as "church sermons." He constructed this cantina in 1970 in the shadow of the Cannubi hill. Many vintners own parcels on the Cannubi hill, but only two possess vineyards on the coveted Cannubi Boschis subplot — Luciano Sandrone and Lodovico Borgogno.

Borgogno's water barrel splats its consistent wet argument next to me, a strange, seemingly nonfunctional contraption constructed from a defunct wine barrel and a recycling water pump of some kind. Water fills the barrel, spills over its sides, and somehow shoots from the bottom in a cane-shaped spray through the center and into the air.

I love it. I love this barrel and its function (or nonfunction) because I've only seen it here. Perhaps Lodovico Borgogno dreamt of this fountain—both ugly and beautiful—as a child and finally envisioned that a life of producing wine would lead him, as an old man, to the dream's realization.

And perhaps Lodovico Borgogno, while meditating over his morning coffee, watches from his front window as this stocky American, his shirt too tight at the armpits, strays thirty feet along Via Crosia from the stoicism of the Satti bus stop sign to the squat squabbling of his rickety fountain. Something, my trespasses or otherwise, stirs him from his mug and his kitchen to approach me, and not so stealthily, from behind. I whirl at his bellow.

"Ciao, regazzo!"

The double z struggles to come off his seventy-year-old tongue in a disaster of lisp and spittle. Seventy, perhaps, but strong, most certainly. He strides to my side, an Army jeep coasting to a breathless stop, bare arms coated in a thicket of tiny gray hairs, swinging like caveman clubs at least a foot from either side of his ribs. His glasses are thick, humpback whale thick, eyes barely open as if papercut into his head, nose almost aggressive in its abstraction, a treebark tumor, tongue trapped between his smiling teeth, pitching like a hooked fish tearing itself for water. Rings of sweat edge his sleeves and collar. With his shape and his cross-eyed glare he confirms his "a little crazy" reputation.

I can't tell if his victorious bellow of "Ciao, regazzo!" ("Hey, guy!") is the product of genuine delight or genuine stupor.

"Ciao, Lodovico," I manage.

He leans in close, suspicious that I knew his name, the burst blood vessels dancing on his nose, tiny red threads. His glasses held onto his head with a black elastic band, attached to the earpieces. The lenses stained with old food and saliva. His hair tattered by the wind. Behind him the wind ravages the grapevines, their expanse stretching to the horizon, and above them the lifting fog. The fig trees lose their balance. And driving it all, the splutter of Lodovico's water barrel fountain, his wet surrealist manifesto.

"Ah! Ah! Andiamo! Andiamo!" He beckons me to follow him back into his house.

He reaches above his head, beefy hands clasping at some invisible firmament upon which he draws his blueprints for future useless inventions.

"No, no, Lodovico. Io, uh, e necesario che, uh, il pullman Satti per Alba, e . . ."

I try, I try, but . . .

"No! No pullman. Andiamo."

I try to tell him about the bus and Alba and, and . . . well, this is Barolo. Andiamo.

I follow the man, his back threatening to breach the off-purple threads that hold it and its probable gray thicket at bay. Lodovico spews a string of liquid Italian as I step inside. He is what he builds — his water contraption: makeshift, haphazard, the stuff of sleep. I sniff at the air and can't tell if I'm smelling wine or sauerkraut.

His front tasting room is dim, leech-dark and suctioning. I can make out a line of bottles on a white-clothed table, a wineglass standing in front of each. A crooked set of shelves presses into my left side, swaggering with the braggadocio of what it holds: stained and dusty bottles, sealed at the necks in red wax, boasting impossible numbers, vintages long thought dead, but no, no, just resting. These 750 milliliter Jimmy Hoffas are indeed intact but hiding, waiting to be discovered: 1897, 1902, 1927, 1941, 1962, 1964, 1970, 1979, 1985, 1989.

And at the top shelf's left corner a black-and-white portrait of a man with a hauntingly Lodovicoesque smile, shaded in a corduroy hat, squatting in a vineyard, and cradling in his hand a tight and tapered bunch of grapes. The sun, hanging paternal over the man, caught the grapes at a certain angle in conjunction with the hidden camera, bursting them into a ball of light. In supporting these grapes this man was indeed supporting the sun's offspring, and I know immediately that this is, or was, Lodovico's father. In another string of his patented river-Italian, Lodovico rushes me to the white-clothed table, uncorks a half-empty bottle of his own 1985, and pours two half-full glasses. The photograph asserts its energy behind us, the voices of the dead leaking through the frame.

Eyes now adjusted, I notice that even his bottles, boasting the Borgogno name in black block right-slanting letters, are disproportionate and liquid, as if pulled from the fire half-finished. Frozen while melting. My glass is the only perfectly shaped thing in Lodovico's house of tricks. I lift it by its stem to my nose. Strawberry, rose, hay, and soil. The entire backroad drive from upstate New York to the Nebraska-Colorado border. Farms and fruit stands. Tomato plants and maple syrup. I lift the glass to my mouth and: charcoal, molasses, Sandrone in rags. The essence of Lodovico's Barolo singes my mouth in a rougher way than a Sandrone, but here in the Langhe the jester and executioner are just as important to the solidarity of the court as the king.

Windowless, Lodovico's tasting room is the essence of *interior*. Library stacks. Research station. The outdoors a dream. Fig trees forgotten, fictional. As we progress from 1985 through 1989, 1990, 1991, 1992, 1995, and 1996, Lodovico's Italian somehow begins to make sense, his wild gestures, bobbing white hair, slipping glasses pressing his words beyond language into something already known. He becomes prerecorded, holographic.

Proudly, he stresses that his Barolo is bottled without filtration. This choice adds an unrefined muskiness to the wine, wearing the rough edges of the region proudly. While many contemporary producers are aiming to smooth out and rein in Barolo's untamable nature, Lodovico explains that he exalts the wine's peculiarities and shadows, showcasing the holiness of its imperfections and gradations. He paces his tasting room, bumping into furniture, his heavy feet stomping, arms flailing, voice carrying forth like some medicine show megaphone, a "Guess-Your-Weight" pitch-daddy. He tells me

of the fierce competition among Barolo's vintners but also of their
love for one another. He tells me of four other Borgogno families in
the region ("No relation," he insists. "No relation!"), all of whose
wine is inferior to his — especially Francesco Borgogno, his rival in
women and wine since their teenage years.

"Francesco Borgogno: sempre jeloso," Lodovico spews, his *s*'s
deflating like basketballs on asphalt.

"Always jealous of what?" I ask.

"Tutti!" Lodovico shouts, indicating everything with his arms,
now lifted over his head into the wet orange light of the chandelier.

Headache encroaching, stomach empty of all but wine and crostino, I am still able to register that Francesco Borgogno lives behind
Il Gioco dell'Oca and that I am a man who is not above fostering a
little rivalry. Tomorrow, I decide, I will visit the other Borgogno.

When Lodovico finally drops his arms, he caresses his bottles,
picks up a pen, and writes something in a leather-bound notebook
of cryptography. Flying machines and catapults. The Dada da Vinci.
He spins the page to me, and I expect to witness the stuff of invention
and equation. Instead, I see a shaky drawing of two stick figures,
one considerably larger than the other, standing on opposite sides
of a table lined with irregular wine bottles. He nods his head and
smiles, spanks the tabletop twice, and snaps the notebook shut.

"Eh? Eh?" he asks.

When in doubt, *va bene.*

"Va bene," I say.

"Va bene!" Lodovico shouts. "Ah, regazzo!"

I try to explain to him that I need food and a bus ride to Alba.
My blood sugar is on the floor.

"Va bene, va bene," Lodovico says.

As I reach to shake his hand, Lodovico grabs my shirt collar,
twists it into a black cotton ball, and snaps his other hand into a fist.
Seven glasses of wine or not, I swear I feel my feet lifting from the
floor. He curls his mouth and seems about to punch me. Spit strings,
wine stained, join his upper and lower lips. I look around frantically, half-expecting that Ivo will appear and, with his arm-wrestling

prowess, free me from Lodovico's grip. But there's only Lodovico's father, trapped in a photograph, palming his ball of light. I pray to him. Lodovico exhales an inch from my face. Garlic. Grape. Boiled milk. Sourdough.

"After a glass of my Barolo," he barks in Italian, "and a big piece of steak, you can beat up anybody in the world."

I feel the saliva collecting at the back of my throat and I swallow, audibly.

Lodovico throws his head back and percolates four sharp laughs, glasses shooting upward to slam his hairline, then down again to slam his nose. Only the elastic band keeps them on his face. He releases me, and I don't know whether I'm smiling or drooling. I think I'm smiling.

Then "Ciao, regazzo!" and a mallet-smack pat on the back.

The outdoor light, the fatherly sun leaps into my eyes, and they begin to water. I suddenly crave the dimness of Lodovico's home, the stone under which the frog inevitably needs to crawl for sanctuary and secret.

I am amazed to see that I am still just across the street from Il Gioco dell'Oca. For god's sake, I can see my tent behind the fence. Shaking my head, temples beating with blood, I walk to the foot of Lodovico's barrel and dunk my head to the ears. In the rush of water, as in a conch shell, I swear I can hear another place: America, perhaps. Maybe, 1897. I lift my head and breathe hard. My back is soaked. Lodovico is not at his window. The bus should be here any minute now.

8

Between the Bell Beats

Deposited in Alba's Piazza Garibaldi a mere 102 minutes behind my printed and fading bus schedule, I begin a search for the perfect bready sponge with which to soak up Lodovico Borgogno's seven-course, preafternoon Barolo degustation. The rain has started, clouds leaping Alba's orange-tiled roofs, alternately burying and exhuming the sun.

I come to Via Vittorio Emanuele, trace the narrow street, heated, starving, an accelerating strand of mercury reaching for the dead-end thermometer bubble that is Piazza del Duomo. Every storefront window holds in large letters — often black, often gold etched — the word *tartufi*, or truffles. As anxious as I am to get to Piazza del Duomo and its outdoor market and superb cafés, I can't help slowing my pace to engage in the only window-shopping I think I've ever done: silver platters of black and white truffles stacked like pyramids beneath glass lids, truffle cream, truffle butter, truffle oil, fresh porcini mushrooms, hand-spun *tagliatelle* twisted into single-serving nests, rabbit terrines, duck salami, and, undercutting it all, the musky smell of grape and basement.

I blink rain, hugging the storefronts so as not to be harpooned by the whitewater rush of umbrellas: multicolored, leopard skinned, bounding, bobbing, a collective canopy, nylon ice floes; and I rove among them, the wet, umbrellaless white American polar bear, hunting for a breathe-hole and my seal dinner.

Cool on the outside but stomach burning, fanned by Alba's mouth-friendly wares, I duck my head beneath the maze of umbrellas and charge forward in a blurred netherworld of Italian shirt collar and lapel, cleavage and pearl necklace. The street opens into Piazza del Duomo, the steaming covered stands of roast chicken, pork, veal, the wagon wheels of Parmigiano-Reggiano tickling my desire to buy the best and devour it with a minimum of chewing. My father's passed-on genes, the desire to inhale troughs of rib tips and chicken wings, assert themselves here. On the orange cobblestone of Piazza del Duomo, so many food stands. I wind up in front of an aproned man peddling roast half-chickens, the crowd shaking their bills as if in a Wall Street pit.

On a brick ledge in the red shadow of the Duomo I press both thumbs into the chicken half, tearing the hot meat from the bone in white and dark strands. Steam kicks into the air. A craven spirit escaping. Countless raindrops, once packed back to front in cloud-limbo, are released into the air. This chicken, this pollo arrosto, while not the bread-based sobriety I initially envisioned, leads me into my needed, full-stomached center. The rain soaks the chicken, but what the hell; it only makes it easier to swallow.

The sycamores spit their yellow leaves over the ledge in a rainbow arc, dropping to the earth. The Duomo bell sobs twice, and with the first, the marketplace crowd elbows one another, with the last, everyone finds his or her place in line. Something happens between the bell beats, the same thing perhaps, as between an inhale and an exhale: the calming of the lungs, a dusty realization that every umbrella is in the same boat. We all deserve our hot pollo arrosto in the rain.

I am docked at this chicken, nearly finished except for the rib bones. I separate them and teethe on the sail-thin meat in between. Still chewing, I wrap the carcass in a stained sheet of newspaper. The headline says something about a thunderstorm.

It's only after I finish the bird that I see them — conigli arrosti, spinning, fished from their flame by a large woman in a red hair-net — these roasting skinned rabbits, heads still on, teeth charred, eye sockets going black. Porcelain dolls trapped in a housefire. The door closes on moderation.

More rain. In my hands now the white greased paper that once held the entire rotisserie rabbit. Its bones clack together like hooves, a horse in the distance. I clutch this paper coffin to my chest as if for warmth and scan the piazza for a garbage can. My hunt for refuse carries me into the covered pulse of the marketplace, and I have to blink to focus. Now unburdened by my desire to eat a whole animal, I am able to assimilate this lovely chaos. There are hundreds of vendors—fruit stands, fish stands, meats and cheeses; rounds, bricks, entire civilizations of cheese, octopus, persimmon. I toss my trash in a can beneath a string of blood sausage.

"Hey! Hey!" I hear someone shout.

The voice opens like the lid of an ancient hope chest, rides its dusty remnants and long-dead dreams on the rain. If I were to look inside this voice, I'd expect to find centuries-old taxidermy, owls with shellacked eyes and sawdust in their feathers. I hear it again, this time in triplicate.

"Hey! Hey! Hey!"

I have no reason to think it's directed at me, but I turn to face a tiny knuckle of a man, dressed all in white, head so perfectly circular it could have been designed with a compass.

"Hey! Viene qua!" the frump calls from behind his fruit stand.

I turn and point behind me, my forehead certainly a mess of wrinkles. People cascade in circles, not one of them standing still. I turn back and touch my chest.

"Io?" I ask.

"Sì, sì," he creaks. "Tu."

I move forward and, as if stepping on a hidden button in the cobblestone, I activate this man to produce a baseball-size fig from his fruit pile, bust it in half with his thumbs, and shove both bowled sides into his mouth at once. As if a magician waiting for applause, he, less than a second later, waves the cleaned purple fig skins at me like theater curtains.

"Wow" is all I can muster.

He holds a fat palm open to me. I freeze into position. He turns and retrieves another intact fig, this one even larger. Again, with his cigar-stub fingers, he breaks the fruit in two, its swampy sweet cilia waving yellow at my nose like a sea anemone. Soon his hands are in mine, wet with warm rain, rolling the fig halves into my drenched palms.

"Prego," he offers, but it could easily have been "Abracadabra."

I want to match his magic, so I shove both halves into my mouth. The music of the fruit shrieks soprano with cherry and yeast, the texture of limp comb teeth. This is a fig to resurrect the dreams of a great-great-grandmother. This is a fig to make her a little girl again, stretch her hair from stiff gray to blonde braided pigtails. I think of the tango and pull the stripped skins from my mouth. The frump actually applauds, laughing.

"Bravo! Bravo!" he bellows.

I laugh knowingly with him, having shared in his secret bag of wizard's tricks.

I reach into my pocket, expecting a string of scarves, but produce only my wallet. When I flash a few coins, he shakes his head, a bowling ball on shoulders, and turns to help another customer, a middle-aged woman with a faux-snakeskin umbrella.

I feel large and somehow filled out, rounded, fat handed, aged, and neckless. This is a market without illusion. The magic here is real. Over the reptilian umbrella I watch the man hoist a watermelon into the air.

9

Red-Beard's Silent Deal

I run my hand over my hair, spitting mist like cracked carbonation, and make for the indoors. The indoors takes the form of Alba's Caffé Calissano, its cream awnings and shrub-lined exterior nearly kissing the orange stones of the Duomo. Raffaella has insisted that I frequent this café.

"Very local," she described it.

The café indeed has been "very local" since the middle of the nineteenth century, though the space has been used as a communal meeting place since the fifth century. Alba resident Luigi Calissano was a talented producer of vermouth who originally peddled his product to the locals at the café. Soon I am drying off at a mother-of-pearl table, a snifter of rosolio reflecting its oval pinkness in the white-tiled ceiling as if assuring itself of its own existence before I pour it down my throat. This liqueur, which I've found only in Italy, wears its rose-petal roots proudly in both smell and taste.

No one recipe exists for rosolio. Some historians purport that it was invented in 1332 by a Padua-based doctor named Michele Savonarola when he macerated rose petals in a fruit-and-spice-infused alcohol. Others claim the drink originated in the fourteenth century in Torino as a variation on vermouth, fortified with wine, cinnamon, cloves, tangerine, orange blossoms, and various herbs, barks, and flowers. Most beverage scholars agree that rosolio was first distilled from the strange leaves of the sundew, an insect-eating bog plant famous for its aphrodisiac and curative properties. (Catherine de' Medici was said to have bathed regularly in rosolio.) The sundew's leaves produce a tangle of red hairs whose glands secrete honey-scented, dewlike droplets. Rosolio was originally called rosa solis, Latin for "dew sun."

The original sundew-derived liqueur was then infused with rose petals and various exotic spices, including cubeb and the aptly named grains of paradise. Originally, rosolio bore a slightly floral bitter taste reminiscent of hazelnut, jasmine, citrus, ginger, cardamom, and butter. As the drink evolved, various attempts were made to "improve" it, and the ingredient list grew and grew — countless honeys, flowers, herbs, fruits, spices, and oils can include a residency in rosolio on their résumés.

I sip and, petal tongued, watch two raindrops race down Calissano's window. I bet on the one on the right. It has a fatter bottom. It wins. Out the window a helmetless boy passes on a rickety moped, disappears around the Duomo's flank. Then an elderly woman in a blue plastic kerchief limps past grasping an armful of rolled bathmats to her chest. A young waitress, twenty-something, curly brown hair, green butterfly barrettes, sets a small white plate of meat and mushrooms in front of me. She has a full face and short fingers. I didn't order this.

"Um," I say, "io no . . . uh . . ."

"You are American, yes?" she says in a voice steeped as if in rosolio.

"I wear it like an overcoat, huh?"

"Aah," she says. "This is salami with the, uh, truffle and the porcini in the, uh, vinegar."

"Truffled salami?" I say on an inhale, my words sputtering as if spoken through a floor fan on high.

"Yes, this here," she says, the face of her left pointer hovering dovewise over the plate.

"And these . . ." I say, sniffing the smell of delicacy eight inches above the plate. "Pickled porcini?"

"Yes. Uh, you cannot have a drink and, uh, not have something to eat. This is a rule."

"Really? Just here, or in all of Italy?"

"Oh, everywhere."

"Well, these are the best bar snacks I've ever seen," I say. "This is a good law."

She laughs, I think, because she feels she should.

"Mille grazie," I say.

"Prego," she says and turns away.

Northern Italy is a region of wine and chandeliers, and I sit beneath yet another dangling mobile of crystal, shedding a cottony orange light. I imagine that Beppe Fenoglio and Cesare Pavese often sat beneath Calissano's chandeliers with other local artists, eating, drinking, forging World War II's partisan movement before playing bocce ball in the piazza. If the rabbit wasn't kicking so violently in my belly, I'm sure I would be able to hear their ghosts.

Now the Cinzano mirrors reflect the mostly business-suited patrons and waitstaff clad in tuxedo shirts, loose bowties, black pants, and black aprons. The bar, stretching the length of the north wall, is patrolled by a young blonde man, forever pacing its expanse, playing guard to the thousands of light-spitting bottles filled with elixirs of red, white, clear, green, rose, yellow. The ceiling's thick white tiles are carved with oak leaves and wine grapes, fish flanks, and the occasional seraph. Calissano indeed seems a museum-turned-café, and the staff roves among its tables so cleanly as if curators, sculptures come to life. Their hands and feet trace the nooks and bottles of their home.

I know, mouth now greased with truffle salami, cheeks aglow with a postporcini sting, that this is going to be my place in Alba. I raise my snifter to an especially chubby ceiling angel, swear I see it wink, and swallow the thick last. At the bar the young blonde man rolls a raw porcini mushroom to the center of a wooden cutting board and hacks it in half with a meat cleaver. Even split, its stem is as thick as an arm.

Back in the rain my wet hair flattens against my skull. Hugging the shopfronts of Via Vittorio Emanuele, I see a white triangular peak in the distance. It could be anything—a downed mountain bowing to commune with this street, the cobblestone river that carved it—except, glowing with rain, it looks to be made of canvas. Raffaella told me, rather, *warned* me about this. It is October. This is Alba. Simple arithmetic: October + Alba = Truffle Fair. Gustatory mathematics. This peak in the distance is the demure cap to Alba's famed truffle tent. Once again polar, once again bearish, the fur on the back of my neck stands up.

Dueling with Barolo wine for the region's gustatory crown, the truffle is an underground fungus found beneath the bases of oak, linden, poplar, elder, willow, and wild hazelnut, where it establishes a symbiotic relationship with the tree. Though there are sixteen known species of truffle, the two most prized for the plate are black truffles (*Tuber melanosporum*) and white truffles (*T. magantum*). The black have a stronger flavor of pure earth than do their white counterparts. The white truffle is latticed with hay-colored veins, its earthy flavor tempered with hints of violet, vanilla, and honey.

Alba is the undisputed epicenter of this elusive white truffle. Ranging in color from ivory to tan to gray to pink, the white truffle, once formed below ground, begins absorbing sap from the tree roots. A famous Piedmontese tale claims that truffles make their homes in the graves of dissipated gnomes and that their often-irregular shape is a result of the "heartbeats of plants about to fall asleep."

Soon I am at the tent's entrance and, ducking my head as if about to Fosbury flop over a highbar, leap inside. Somehow, with my compact burst into the tent, doorway swishing drenched over my shoulders, I think Lodovico Borgogno would be proud.

Rumors of this clandestine truffle fair, initially launched in 1929, spread beyond the Piedmont's borders when Giacomo Morra (founder of the fair and innkeeper-restaurateur of Alba's Hotel Savona) envisioned a strange but successful promotional campaign. In 1949 Morra began shipping the "best truffle of the year" to famous international athletes, politicians, and actors. In 1949 the lucky recipient was Rita Hayworth; in 1951 it was then–U.S. president Harry Truman; in 1953 Winston Churchill had to buy his first truffle shaver; in 1954 Marilyn Monroe and Joe DiMaggio added some Piedmontese spice to their relationship; in 1955 Haile Selassie, Ethiopia's emperor, was introduced to an empire of taste; in 1959 U.S. president Dwight Eisenhower found out what he was missing; in 1965 Pope Paul VI thought about moving the Vatican to Alba.

In the fair's first year the white truffles were already selling for two hundred lire per kilogram (about ten cents for just over two pounds). At the time this was a teacher's average monthly salary. By 1932 the festival officially became known as the Fiera Nazionale di Tartufo Bianco d'Alba, or Truffle Fair, pairing these delicacies with glasses of local wine. Rendered defunct at the outset of World War II, the Truffle Fair crept back into existence in 1945 — this was seen as a political move in partisan-oriented Alba, a desire to reinstitute indigenous values and practices. The Truffle Fair of 1945 was an enormous success. Spanning three days, it saw the price of the white truffle reach £3,000 — about $3 — per kilogram. Today, since the price of truffles breaches the astronomical — white truffles can run anywhere from $1,500 to $2,500 a pound; black truffles, cheaper, can run $350 to $650 a pound — connoisseurs pride themselves on careful selection. I hope at least to pretend I know what I'm doing.

The tent canvas quakes. Umbrellas whoosh open and closed, people entering, people leaving. I shudder from the waist up, a dog shedding its rain-sheen, and survey this white vacuum of aroma and taste and commerce. Row after row of truffle vendors chat with a clamorous array of buyers, displaying their wares, which they dug from tree bases with the aid of their sniffing dogs.

These truffle hunters, or *trifolau,* have always had their quirks and secrets and their own fair share of lore. Often disguised as a man and his dog patrolling an autumn hill at night, the trifolau are reputed to walk with lighter steps than the rest of us and speak only necessary words. The truffle-sniffing dog, or *tabui,* is calmer at night (hence, the typical night hunt); also, the night protects the trifolau and tabui from the imploring eyes of others. (Pigs can also be used to detect truffles, but dogs are preferred, since they are less likely to eat the reward.)

These modern-day Santa Clauses and Rudolphs arm themselves with their professional tools: ancient calendars (often passed among generations), dictating specific places and on which days to dig there, and a hoe. Tabui, like racehorses, tend to descend from other tabui, typically nonpedigree country dogs. The training of a tabui is, like domesticating a wild horse, rigorous.

These rigors pay off here in this tent, where the black and white delicacies, the essence of earth and epitome of fungus, lie platter-lit under glass containers, exhumed by the merchants to be held, like their children, to the noses of probable patrons. This is the second coming through a kaleidoscope. The dirty gray rocklike truffles, like Lodovico, like the Fig Man, like the figs themselves, play their cards close to their chests until the glass container is lifted and aroma spills into the room like oil.

Their scent is the scent of history and religion and politics and poetry. In the Bible Job was described as an eater of the "dudaim," which is thought to be the truffle. The ancient Greeks called them *ydnon,* a word that later gave birth to "idnology" in the early nineteenth century. Perhaps the tastiest of all "ologies," idnology refers to "the science of truffles."

So affecting was the truffle's aroma and flavor that Plutarch described its taste as "a mix of rain, heat, and the ground."

"A jewel of the ground," Pliny said, "a miracle of nature."

Juvenal described it as "the son of lightning."

The truffle became a tool of Aphrodite, the ancient cultures realizing that those special postdinner stirrings originated closer to Hades than to Zeus. It is said that it was his appetite for white truffles that sent King Vittorio Emanuele II, after whom this truffle tent street is named, into the open arms of his mistress, Bela Rosin.

There is something in the contained stoicism of a red-bearded man in the tent's west corner that makes me want to buy a truffle from him. He, unlike the operatically effusive majority, seems to share the wise hermit nature of the truffle itself, the stereotypical reputation of the original trifolau.

I walk to him, the sea of people, downward-pointing umbrellas rushing from my heels like jet smoke. His red face, unearthed just this morning perhaps, spreads in a bread-and-butter grin. Wordless, he reaches for his platter, left hand bracing its bottom, right hand poised on the container lid. This is potential energy as it should be. The orange sodium lights buzz at the tent's ceiling. The canvas begins to sag under the weight of the rain. Red-Beard opens his hand. The lid is off, the sweet white truffle smell of soil and mushroom, corn husk and asphalt gift-wraps itself bowless over the back of my head, grabs me by the ears like a schoolyard bully. I am thrown face-first into this silver platter's playground dirt. This is not fair. I'm telling on you. I want my mom.

"Quanto per uno?" I ask.

He waves his chapped hand over the pile, indicating that I choose my favorite. A champion of the underdog, I choose the second one from the top, a battered golf ball of a tartufo. Red-Beard, with a thumb and forefinger, lifts it from its family litter. It wriggles, wags like a puppy. The next thing I know, it's in my hand. Its touch is gold and scab, bottlecap and skipping stone.

Once a white truffle touches your skin, a strange thing happens. The world goes affirmative. A purchase is inevitable, even for those with psychotic regard for self-denial. Rough, dimpled, irregular, geologic, its bloom waits for contact with a truffle shaver and a quail egg, a plate of ravioli, a loin of venison.

And just like that, he picks it from my palm like a poppy, weighs it, and writes £80,000 on a slip of blue paper. Forty dollars for an entire white truffle, for a tongue's meditation stone that will span a week's worth of dinners. Weep. Pray. Hand him the money, and he proceeds to wrap the truffle in a fan of white tissue paper, places it into a tiny paper bag. I hold the bag to my face and breathe as if hyperventilating, like a horse licking the first oats from its feed-bag.

Then Red-Beard, perhaps as penance for his namesake's pirating, removes a plum-size black truffle from another platter, wraps it, and hands it to me without so much as a "Prego." I match his silence, my hands go numb, my hair most assuredly turns white. This is a place where the purchase of a white truffle gets a black truffle thrown in for free. Somewhere, hidden in the stitches of the tent canvas, Marilyn Monroe and Haile Selassie couple beneath an oak tree. Talk, philosophically, about death. This place is Alba. Three easy payments and $19.95 be damned. I reach my bagless hand to Red-Beard, and he shakes it, his palm rough as cornflakes, eyelids drooping nearly to the corners of his mouth. He says nothing.

I retreat to the tent's entrance, the other merchants thrusting, then cradling their truffles under my nose, offering their perfume. My eyes begin to water, my breath shortens, my head spins in a wild vertigo. This is sensory overload, the ripe fungal blossom of the tent tattooing itself into my nostrils. I need to take a breath of rain.

And in a step, stutter, step I am back in it, iron pencil sky relentless in its spewing. I worry about Sandrone's grapes, the picking crew surely having been dismissed for the day. Seeking a dry spot, I tuck the truffle bag into my Eagle Crest jacket's inside pocket and make for the bus back to Il Gioco dell'Oca, where the kitchen will hopefully be empty and my tent, most certainly, saturated.

10

Dixieland Basement

Rivalry doesn't always wait until you're done with dinner. Rain dissipating, tent dripping, white truffle napping next to its shaver, sky now dark, the second side of the Borgogno vs. Borgogno feud refuses to hold.

I just finish dicing three cloves of garlic when I hear it: the jangling of live Dixieland music traces its way through Raffaella's half-open front door, over the lip of the dining room table, and into the fluorescent yellow of the kitchen. *Where could it possibly be coming from? In the middle of vineyards . . .* I turn from the cutting board toward this burst of sound, the garlic's smell-energy delivered from my fingertips to my legs.

And I can't help myself. Maybe it has to do with the vision of oneself as a child again, tearing through parks, backyards, and back-streets — any available shortcut, the fastest possible speed — after the faint tinkling of the ice cream truck. Since I've been in Italy I've had to loosen my belt two notches. In response to this belly and this music I tear from the kitchen in what is for me a mad sprint, for most of the world a slow jog. I skid on the white stones of Raffaella's driveway, still empty of her Cinquecento. Pongo eyes me with all the morbid fascination a dog can muster, gaping jowls, and I arc past the blue and yellow picnic tables for the backyard fence. Over the cold iron rim is a nine-piece band standing under a white canopy the next yard over, the yard belonging to Francesco "Sempre Jeloso" Borgogno. Lodovico's enemy. Lodovico's muse.

I turn from the fence and run again, the blue and yellow tables whizzing past in a whipped green stripe, then Pongo looking up from an infected paw, the entire white and peach facade of Il Gioco dell'Oca, the front gate sliding right, then the carless street, Via Crosia's curve to the left, vineyards, vineyards, and Francesco Borgogno's front yard. Sweat lines up along my hairline. I lurch forward, my hands on my knees. My chest is dry. Breathe and breathe. Feel an acid vomit rise and fall. The flavors of Barolo and rosolio, pickled porcini and salami, the smells of the truffle tent and grape. Privileged indigestion. Gourmet nausea. I look up.

On Francesco Borgogno's driveway I join four other onlookers, three gray-headed old men, one middle-aged red-headed woman. The musicians are lined up in two single-file rows on the red cobblestones, blasting into their instruments. The old clarinet player jumps from his line, round glasses falling to his nose-tip with a storm of sweat, stamping his feet and bird-calling a solo to the nest-heavens. The overalled bass player, arms fully outstretched to reach the strings due to the displacement of a magnificent gut, plucks his chords as if they were feathers from a chicken, rotates the massive instrument on its spike, and nods at the cascading brown hair of the trumpeter. Bass and trumpet duel at opposite ends of the scale, the clarinet bridging the two instruments somewhere in the middle. The drummer, snare strung around his neck with an orange utility belt, barks a nonsense vocable from the diaphragm, the clarinet man jumps back in line, and the song crescendos into the upper registers with an ear-challenging, high-frequency trumpet blast. Then the drummer shouts, "Yaaaah!" and all falls silent.

The onlookers pause for a hiccup of quiet, then shatter into claps and whistles. Then they turn to me and ask questions in Italian: Where am I from? How long have I been here? How long am I staying? Where am I staying? What brought me here? I answer everything truthfully. The middle-aged woman is about to ask another question when the band begins their next number, led by the thirty-something tenor sax player in a lime green button-down.

It's here that a skinny old man emerges from inside the house, arms and legs frail and irregular, fingers dangling, copper wire from rooster-bone wrists, eyes heavy beneath the weight of Martin Scorsese eyebrows. His anchors. If not for those eyebrows, he would surely blow away. He steps toward me, trips over the trumpet case, and miraculously rights himself with a quickness reserved for the lanky. He bends forward at the waist, flexible as a rubber band, and coils his fingers over my forearm. His gray hair is thinner than onion skin.

"Me chiamo Francesco Borgogno," he says into my ear, spittle misting over my lobe.

What is it about the Borgognos and their saliva?

The band erupts into "When the Saints Go Marching In."

So this is the unlikely man who drives the Mack truck–shouldered Lodovico to the heights of loving disdain. If Lodovico is an 18-wheeler, Francesco is a mare. I begin telling him about my staying at Il Gioco dell'Oca.

"Sì, sì," Francesco mutters in a deep, turtle-slow wheeze. "Resta a Raffaella. In una tenda, no?"

"Sì. In una tenda," I say, picturing the rain cover of my tent hugging its inner walls.

Francesco leans forward, chin in the cave of his sternum, and begins a laugh so slow I swear two seconds pass between each "ha."

"Americani," he says, shaking his head, wiping his nose. "Andiamo."

Another Borgogno. Another andiamo.

He, not having let go of my arm throughout the exchange, leads me to his heavy front door. My stomach is growling, but I'm compelled to follow. Behind us the sax player belts a crazy solo. Dissonant exit music. Francesco's foyer is riddled with houseplants as unruly as his eyebrows; stray leaves and branches have been staple-gunned to the walls and ceiling. Somewhere I hear a woman's voice on a telephone. A daughter? A wife? Lodovico's former love?

Francesco tucks me into a rounded stairwell, the woman's voice drifts away, and we are heading to the belly of his home and cantina. I'm exhausted. I'm hungry. I think about the three diced garlic cloves drying out in Raffaella's kitchen. But what can I do? Damn

Dixieland! Francesco pushes his lips close to my ear, tells me that winemaking has been in his family since the early 1930s. He launched his own cantina in 1954 with the help of his wife, Guiseppina, and has now passed the majority of his business responsibilities to his sons. But, he assures me, he is still the cornerstone of his cantina, forever present to provide guidance and enthusiasm.

He drags his fingers along the wall, nearly kissing my ear now, and explains how he didn't experience his first major commercial success until 1971, when he released his version of the now-mythical Barolo vintage. His wines now, as they were then, are fiercely traditional. He pulls his lips away and descends a flight of stairs. Smells of fruit and plaster, a strange mechanical humming, broken glass being swept up. We arrive in the warm acid air of his basement, lined with Lodovico-sized barrels, steel holding tanks for the budding Barolo, and a forest of wax-topped bottles. Nobody else. Who was sweeping up the glass? I begin to distrust my ears, even as they listen to Francesco Borgogno crack a knuckle, bite a nail.

"Questa è la mia vita," he says, declaring his purpose in life with a violent stamp of his foot that should collapse his skeleton like a house of cards but doesn't.

He marches to a steel tank and throws his arms around its base. He musses the hair of a barrel-top and caresses the swell of its hip. He hugs a row of four tasting bottles to his chest, rolling each back and forth over his heart as he tells me in winter-molasses Italian, "These are my favorite travel companions."

I drink from all four bottles with this man, his wine bursting with bluefoot mushroom and hazelnut, glycerin and pine: 1990, 1991, 1993, 1995 captured in paper-thin crystal. Though starving, I succumb to Francesco, and we talk for nearly four hours. I know Raffaella will now be asleep, and I'll have to save my truffle dinner for tomorrow in exchange for two cups of yogurt and a gargantuan slice of Adriana's apple cake. In these basement walls — white going to yellow — Francesco details his philosophy on winemaking, a holistic approach to existence that benefits bacteria, ant, and human alike, a process he calls "the natural life." He speaks of Lodovico ("He has never been quite right") and marketing his wine in foreign countries.

When he mentions Japan, he reaches to his feet and produces a rolled and rubber banded poster, a prop seemingly placed there for our conversation's convenience. He shakes it from its binding as if dusting a doormat and reveals a picture of a scantily clad underage Japanese girl looking suggestively at the camera in what appears to be a B-movie ad. Francesco curls his gatekeeper pointer to the bottom right-hand corner of the poster, and I'm stunned to see his own wine label logo and multiple pictures of his Barolo bottles.

He points to his temple, winks, and says, "Ah, ah."

I finally realize that Francesco is just as mad as Lodovico but at a much slower pace. I buy two bottles of his 1993 at about seven dollars apiece and shake his hand. His fingers bunch together like a pearl necklace. Francesco turns to recap the tasting bottles, and I walk, unled this time, up the stairs. The house is quiet and dark. I open the front door, so heavy I can't imagine Francesco opening it without help, and step into the air. The night is cool and quiet, the band having long ago dispersed. The wind stirs the vineyards, the leaves rubbing together like the legs of cockroaches, and this is it — that sound of broom over glass — it's the vineyards, in wind, at night.

When I get to my tent, still dripping at about 11:00 or so, I set Francesco's Barolo next to a bottle of Lodovico's and turn the labels to face one another, finally friends.

11

Pruning

The pruning today must be meticulous. The clippers and scissors exhausted, so many split grapes. After yesterday's rain Sandrone's forehead seems to have sprouted a few wrinkles, his eyes, dark circles. But the sun cleaves the nebbia today, and the harvest should be all right.

"At least we have no hail," Ivo said this morning. "The hail, in ten minutes, can ruin everything. The whole harvest. Bad. I've seen it happen."

Sandrone last night must have made a plan in his nightstand notebook, Mariuccia groaning beside him. My hands are looser today, able now to take the sharp metal of the pruning tools without reddening. Indeed, there are many broken grapes, and we have been instructed to snip them away, one by one, retaining the best of each bunch. This is slow work, surgery. For the time being the sweaty woman, again sharing my row, holds her sweat inside her.

The ants of the Piedmont have come out today, threading the sparse grass at our feet, their hills possibly flooded or their hunger piqued by the spilt Nebbiolo juice. I imagine them pouring up through the drains of the bathtubs of Barolo. In one of these homes someone will be washing for work — maybe the hunchbacked host of La Cantinetta or the full-faced waitress of Caffé Calissano, dreading the sight of leatherbound menu and silver tray. By the time the ants reach the white-green tile, this person, whoever he is, will recall his breakfast if only with his throat, the buckwheat flour, egg, and water gelling inside him to spawn something entirely new.

But here in Sandrone's vineyard the temperature drops one degree over the grapevines and the wind brushes them into hair. The last of the ant colony, having just dined on a drop of juice, folds full and thoraxfirst into the drying-out anthill. Signaled from the front of the line, the last ant knows that in a distant tub someone is afraid to bathe, can't afford to fix the hole in her tile. This person, whoever she is, cannot wash away breakfast's hold, lest the ants, with the water, rise from the drain like palm fronds, slow in destroying the foundation but surely building something — the spindle-laddered metaphysica of the flightless insect perhaps. Yes: they rise, craving the mask of spiders, a banana tree sprouting in fast forward, to bite cactuslike at the soft dough ends of Italian toes.

Breakfast will reassert itself with the fundamentals. Everything must evolve: the eggs, the hens that laid them, the naked stomach snapping back on its food, and fear. That too.

"Watch what you're doing!" Ivo shouts from Tractor Alley, and I see that I am overfilling the red crate at my feet, the topmost bunches tumbling to the grass, feeding the ants and their penchant for hypnosis. This is slow work. Lulling work. The mind wanders. Notices the little things too much. First an individual grape. Next the forelegs of an ant. The sun warms the wind.

"Sorry," I say, carrying the crate to the flatbed, the sweaty woman not even damp. "Daydreaming."

"Leave that for Indiano," Ivo says and gestures behind him with his giant thumb.

Indiano is watching the sky, some bird there I can't see, and Ivo stealthily takes off his shoe. Before I can say "Don't" it's in the air, white laces flapping like wings. It hits Indiano in his back, between his shoulder blades. He elicits a feeble grunt, the wind forced from his lungs, his palms falling to his knees. I can see his ribs through his clothes. Ivo scolds him in Italian, and Indiano, welled with surprise, picks up Ivo's shoe and launches it in perfect outfielder form downslope. Then he drops his pants and moons Ivo, his ass sunken in at the sides as if it had spit out its dentures. The clubhopper boys see this and hoot from their rows, calling for a fight, the nieces attempting to shut them up.

For a second I don't know if Ivo's going to tackle Indiano or laugh. His body poised in his coveralls, beefy chest gleaming with hairlessness, lunges forward. Indiano yanks up his pants, and I get my answer. Ivo laughs, then runs to Indiano and throws his arm around him. Indiano laughs too, and for the first time they start talking as if they were old friends.

In the sound of a coming engine we all go back to work. Beppe pulls up on his tractor, his jacks at home in his coveralls pouch, Sandrone riding the now-empty flatbed. Apparently, the man is examining every bunch brought back to his cantina. Part of his notebook plan. We pick, prune. Hours. The Alps come out, distinguishing themselves from the haze. The peak of Monte Bianco pokes forth, invigorating the chatter of the crew. Rarely is it visible here. While virtually every square inch of the Piedmont's rolling hills has been analyzed for its wine-producing capabilities—quality of the soil, kinship with the sun—the Alps rest uncharted and imposing, and there is an undercurrent of fear in the cooing voices of the clubhoppers, nieces, grandparents. Only the children look out serenely, able to absorb the mountains, their snow. But everything must evolve, and we do, from awed sightseers into pickers, trimmers, carriers, employees of Luciano Sandrone. The man himself takes his beret from his head and holds it against his hip. He regards Monte Bianco for one second, then leaps onto Ivo's flatbed and makes of himself the centerpiece of his grapes. They drive down Tractor Alley to the cantina, Ivo retrieving his shoe along the way.

About an hour before sundown Sandrone makes good on his mopping promise. He dismisses most of the crew from the fields and summons me to his cantina. As Ivo, Indiano, and Beppe load the grapes into the rotofermentors, I drag the mop across the cantina floor, the concrete absorbing the water and old wine. We work without speaking, save for Beppe's occasional belch. Luca twines the steel tanks with his clipboard, checking the gauges.

I yawn and begin to feel settled in. Part of the crew. Comfortable silence. The wind outside rinsing the windowpanes. Getting dark. Machines click on and off, sounds like threshers and blow-dryers.

A stomach settling. A portion of Italy's foreignness being pruned away.

Mopping Sandrone's cantina floor has only an immediate persistence. It becomes memory before it's over. Flawed, rich with pining, the stirs of classic rock DJs who are only voices, never faces. Until Sandrone pleads, "Va bene, va bene," after I've gone over the same wine stain for six minutes, swipe after swipe, blotting out or adding paint.

Evolution: from overseasoner to overmopper. Ivo, Indiano, and Beppe empty their last crate of the day, and Luca pencils his final checkmark. Sandrone's forehead has smoothed, the circles under his eyes have faded. The grapes have been salvaged. It is night in the Piedmont after hours of harvesting. Some kind of arrival that, under Sandrone's cedar ceiling, even the helicopters can't see. Not even with all their lights.

12

Follow the Steeple

The hamlets of the Langhe are thankfully, blissfully connected by shoestring hiking trails called *sentieri*, deviating sometimes through vineyard rows, sometimes through tangles of plum trees. Within walking distance of Barolo are Castiglione Falletto, home of Ceretto's glass house; Serralunga d'Alba, home to Luigi Pira, his sublime Barolos Marenca and Margheria, and a flat-faced burnt orange castle that always seems to angle toward you, no matter where you're standing; Grinzane Cavour, with its bulky castle and classic Nonna Genia Ristorante; Novello, with its stretch of persimmon trees and vineyard rows curving uphill, then downhill in perfect rainbow arcs; Annunziata, with its lack of working telephones and amenities, really, of any kind; Monforte d'Alba, replete with views of the Alps and narrow streets so steep, you crave a tow-line and a bottle of water to get you to the top of town (the towns here have tops). And La Morra: my destination for the day.

The morning after my mopping of Sandrone's floors I relaxed under Il Gioco dell'Oca's brick overhang in the middle of the yard between the farmhouse and my tent, sipping Lodovico's 1995. That night, with Raffaella, I ate a dinner of Barolo-stewed rabbit (hacked to pieces, bug-eyed head included) smothered with my white truffle. She spoke of Francesco (her friend, not Borgogno) and how she spent yesterday with him in Torino ("the big city"), about a forty-minute train ride northwest. I got the feeling there may be something between the two of them, though she insisted on their friendship and that marriage is a shackle she no longer wants to step into.

"Really? There's really nothing happening there, Raffaella?" I asked.

"With Francesco? Oh, he is a nice boy," she said about the man probably ten years her senior, "but he is very serious. The apartment in Torino — Piazza Castello — the bank work. He even has a *maid*."

"Ooh," I said. "Terrible."

"She is very attractive, too," Raffaella said, "so I don't know."

Between us rabbit steams, bright discs of carrot. The mysterious interruption of Francesco's attractive maid.

I didn't sleep well that night, my sleeping bag rain soaked through at the head and the feet. I was still tossing at about two in the morning, wet and cold on my pillow. The weather was a factor in this, of course, but there was something else. It was as implacable as 1986, as Bon Jovi and Big Macs without buns, the first time I noticed girls in short skirts and the virtue of the tomato. Hidden in the Piedmont's fog were things way beyond my range.

I lay awake on my side, legs outstretched, on top of my bag, weight on one elbow, feeling as if I was filled with gasoline. I reached for the upper corner of the tent where I set up my makeshift nightstand: a camping lantern perched atop my book, Saul Bellow's *Henderson the Rain King*. In the moonlight I could see the lion on the cover. I kept waiting for it to roar. To sleep tonight. But wakefulness and open eyes. A land that, like the Piedmont, holds castles, history that will not be demolished. Staring at the lion, I decided not to read. The wind rattled the tent canvas, then escaped into the night without so much as an *a-wimoweh*.

Raffaella told me during dinner that Francesco (Borgogno, now, not "the boy") raised hell when she wanted to add a floor to the farmhouse to accommodate a few more rooms.

"He said it will block his view, but he cannot see over the house anyway. Or through it. Stupid . . ."

The rooms went up nonetheless, but the neighborly tension was staked. History was added-on to. Tradition faces the advent of the parking lot. Francesco must have been livid. This was as bad as the barrique.

"Francesco Borgogno, he does not approve of divorce," Raffaella said, "and that Niccolo has a mother but no father in the house. This is every place. Italy is still about the man."

I sat up in the tent, remembering how I touched her shoulder, the small dime-sized scar there, remembering how she smiled with her eyes. Then we each took a bite of truffled rabbit, the tan-white shavings rippled like brains.

I rolled Francesco Borgogno's wine bottle toward me from the bottom tent corner, picturing his yellow script FB logo at the bottom of the illicit Japanese movie poster. This image was exactly the lung-swelling nonsense that I needed. I kept the poster and logo in my head until I fell asleep. Near the village, the peaceful village, the lion eats the sheep . . .

I woke early and decided to hike to La Morra, the highest town in the Langhe, reaching from the bottom of the Piedmont's bowl to the sloping sides of the Alps. La Morra produces the greatest amount of Barolo in the region. Its 750 vineyard hectares are responsible for 35 percent of all Barolo produced in the area. Long before its oenological renown, La Morra began its existence as a single castle. In the sixteenth century the French occupying army commanded the town's residents to destroy it. Fearing total pillage, the residents complied. Today the castle's bastions, fortified defense walls, are all that remain of the original construction. La Morra's hiking trail extends along these bastions, providing yet another inclusive view of the Langhe.

Based on Raffaella's purple-penned and toweringly crude map drawing of the region, I find myself on this dirt path, switchbacking over the ocean swells of vineyard: a steep incline, then down, then a steeper incline, a steeper down, until the long uphill leads me through a private farm. These vineyards are far steeper than Sandrone's, and my heart bleeds for the poor souls — the sweaty women, nieces, and clubhoppers of La Morra — who are charged with harvesting these fields. Can I still be on the right trail? Nebbiolo grapes brush my legs in encouragement. I walk carefully so as not to detach them from their stems. I sip from the water gallon I filled at Il Gioco's foot-pump kitchen sink and dump a splash over my head and back. Amazing that nights so cold could bleed into days so warm. I pull Raffaella's map from my shorts pocket, directions now running in purple streams over the wrinkled paper.

Even without Raffaella's map, La Morra, at its elevation, doesn't hide itself. Barolo is far below, streets and shopfronts and castles that once appeared larger than life now fold like algae into the rolling green quilt of vines and fruit trees — a train track oasis on an epicurean's model set. Switching back, lungs struggling, I look down on the famed Cannubi hill, a half-mile up Via Crosia from Il Gioco, and the grapes that will become Sandrone's Cannubi Boschis. Il Gioco itself has fallen into a rolling sinkhole of angle and altitude. In case of emergency, wine and truffles first.

As the elevation increases, so does the classic Piedmont haze that swaddles these towns in a force field against the rest of the world's supermarkets. The waves of vineyard, the smatterings of town, the region today are endless, bordered only by sky. At the crest of this uphill I find a spigot and flip it open to a belching release of rusted sulfur water. I stick my face in its stream, cold, wipe my eyes, cold, and see a warm roof poking its orange nose into the air. This is someone's yard, and I get moving again to avoid an encounter. I have set my sights on a quiet café.

The dirt path twines around an apple-treed hill and soon congeals into hard orange stone. A yellow aluminum sign waves like a whippoorwill shuddering under the weight of its two-word, black-lettered message: La Morra. Its entrance marked with a brown-faced church, modest steeple tilting slightly west, as if pointing a finger. I follow it to a tiny, black-awninged café-with-no-name and order an acqua minerale naturale (my water jug long empty) and a Barolo-salami panino from a blonde, thick-calved waitress in her sixties. She wears no glasses, but her eyes move in different directions as if searching for the one way out of their sockets. Sitting, I start to feel whole again, and grounded and light.

I breathe hard, sweat caking on my clothes, and scan the town: mostly closed shops, a person or couple occasionally walking past, and the church, its steeple . . . I sip my water and find religion in its molecules. Oxygen. Hydrogen. I catch my breath. My mouth a mess of crumbs and crust, bottled water and wine-fat, I pay the bill and wave to the waitress.

"Aaayyy," she returns in the raspiest voice I've ever heard—more so than the sensual growls of Patty Hays and Kitty Lowie—vocal cords surely knotted into rope ladders from years of abuse. Something vital but corrosive. Chain-smoking? Opera singing?

I wonder what Ivo, Beppe, and Indiano are doing today. Sandrone keeps me on as a part-timer due to his loyalty to Raffaella, but my presence in his fields surely stirs visions of the governmental helicopters and their steep fines. His cedar ceiling can't protect us forever. The work is thinning out. The grandparents and children don't show up every day. I miss the crew. The clubhoppers must be trying to woo the nieces over a spread of prosciutto at that wrought iron lunchtable. Ivo, Beppe, and Indiano must be playing a game of jacks on the cantina floor. Luca must be meditating on his clipboard. The sweaty woman must be sweating. And Sandrone must be lighting another cheroot, forever presiding. The sky is a cracking blue.

Full, I stride to the Cantina Comunale at the edge of the Belvedere, the viewpoint peak of this peak town. The Cantina Comunale is a "communal" wine cellar showcasing the wines of forty-six La Morra–based vintners, offering bottle sales and tastings. Legend has it that the Romans once built an array of villas in the Langhe and that Julius Caesar, when returning from France, insisted on stopping in La Morra to drink some of the local wines.

At the Cantina Comunale, in the tradition of bad puns, I *commune* with Caesar. I taste three different Barolos from La Morra, each one coniferous as a spruce grove, one Nebbiolo, and one Langhe (a blend of Nebbiolo, Barbera, and 5 percent Cabernet grapes), each sip like bubble gum, popping alternately with liquid raspberry and the earth's core. And one Dolcetto too, crying like a fat-cheeked toddler, wanting to be as tall and strong as the Barolos. From the delicate man pouring the wines, his nostrils flaring like bat-wings with each glass he fills, I purchase a Bartolo Mascarello 1993 Barolo for Raffaella's parents. It will be their fifty-second anniversary in less than a week. The man introduces himself as Lorenzo, his arms flailing also like wings, his thin shirt hugging his chest, the patterns of his chest hair pressing from beneath. His voice is more whistle than speech, and, as he tucks the wine bottle into a paper bag, his "Ciao" is like a mating call to the auks.

I walk from the Cantina Comunale to the Belvedere's stone-benched viewpoint and see, under the slight mask of haze and cloud, the effervescing wound of the Langhe, more healed than the rest of the world but closer to the blood. I try to make out the Cannubi hill, but from up here the region fits strangely together, each hill defining those that stem from it in one large blanket of texture — a moss river frozen over rounded stones. I look for a while, wondering if Raffaella is in Barolo or Torino, if she's ever tempted to look inside my tent while I'm gone, the place where I sleep and wake and store my bottles. I look and can't believe it's already starting to get dark.

13

Limbo on the Landscape

Descending from La Morra's Belvedere, the orange lights of the Cantina Comunale blinking out, I pass the town's bastions—the ancient defense walls—and try to imagine any motivation for attacking these people. Wine poaching? Truffle imperialism? The view? Raffaella has spoken of the region's historical violence, how the local town of Novello, also once a medieval defensive outpost, housed an impressive castle owned by the Del Carretto family, how medieval upstart Marchese Manfredo was murdered in the castle in 1340 by his grandsons.

The thought of towns so peaceful caught up in bloodlust and battle runs, oddly enough, from my brain to my knee-caps, aching in a downhill march, and ending in my left shoe sole, which responds by busting in half. In 1340 Manfredo's chest opens to the knife.

My father taught me at a young age to wrap a couple rubber bands around my wallet to prevent it from falling out of my pocket. This and meat. This and "I Am a Rock." While this rubber band practice earned me certain ridicule during the Bon Jovi years, I can proudly say that I've had the same wallet—never lost—for over a decade now and found that, in sticky situations, a rubber band is useful either as a weapon or as an adhesive. Defying pickpockets for years.

I fish into my right shorts pocket (my wallet pocket) and retrieve a thick purple band and a thinner beige one and twine them over the toe of my shoe, temporarily holding the sole in place. I hope it will last to Barolo. As I hike tenderly down through the vineyards, La Morra towers above me as a scattered yellow torch, a watchtower, a deity, and I can now imagine the ancient people of the lowlands staring up at it in jealousy and frustration. This cathedral of towns. Closer to God. I try to keep my eyes on the steeple city as I zigzag ... home?

I think of the house in which I grew up, the raised-ranch mock Tudor presiding over the cracked driveway like La Morra over the Langhe. I can see the driveway, its poking weeds, where I used to play when I was a kid — Running-Bases, Four-Square, Lightning-Basketball, any game with a hyphen — while my mother deboned chicken legs, boiled beef ribs, microwaved a loaf of ground chuck. I can see the driveway's concrete slowly cracking into tectonic plates beneath my mother's and father's tires, leaving early, then returning late from work six days a week. No time for cooking, really, for vegetables and good food. I see the basketball backboard cracking in half like a shoe sole when my sister's high school boyfriend tries to woo her with a two-handed dunk. Chicago: the sky never starry or completely dark but pink with pollution and city lights. I've read that when a sky is not permitted its darkness, when human lights obscure the stars, our visual turf remains truncated, igniting an adverse psychological effect, not unlike that resulting from a lack of sun.

Breathing heavily, I stop walking. I stare at Italy's sky, and the longer I look, the more the stars come out of their caves. Nothing moves. No sound. Under the influence of the sky, everything is frozen and untwitching: the grapes suspended in middangle, faraway car lights trapped in a flat-roaded neutral. Even the wind chimes of this vineyard path's rough-shod cantina seem to lie in a perfect diagonal, angling somehow east to Il Gioco, not yet wanting to pander to gravity and fall lawfully into a north-south orientation. This sea of night and vines dumbfounds the animate, clings to the slopes and sky with mere fingernails — an impossible act of balance and strength — protecting these grapes from overexertion, ensuring their sweetness in the mouth, their warming of countless chests, the applause of the world's ladies, gentlemen, children of all ages.

This limbo on the landscape must infect Il Gioco dell'Oca: Pongo paused in midrun and midbark along the fence near my tent, all four paws in the air, fur half-matted, half-windblown, tongue draped twisted and sideways from his mouth; Raffaella frozen like Pompeii into position at the sink, dinner's last swallow of pasta still in her mouth, foot poised above the water's pump. I see the pipes freeze, cold water having slowed her red hands and wrists and blood, having soaked the belly of her shirt in malign seduction. In this night I can't help wondering about Francesco, "the boy" in Torino, in what state he is frozen — rigor mortis or postcoital, sighing after making love with her, his racehorse hands in the copper small of her back as a Merit burns down to nothing over her lips.

And then the cosmos, having induced this Piedmontese freeze-frame, decides to break it. A star shoots lazily east, a cold breeze blows, then dies, and I want to ask someone, anyone, if she also saw the star. A leaf tumbles from its grapevine into the air. The earth, all space and time, sputters in its light ripple. A sound like silverware clinking the bottom of a china dish curdles my ears, and maybe it is the wind chimes, and maybe the death rattle of the limbo. At Il Gioco Pongo's forepaws surely thump the grass, the second half of his disrupted bark erupting toward some probable biker. Raffaella wipes her hands dry and puts the dishes away, closes, with a definitive click, a yellow cabinet door.

I look left and right and see no one but Italy. Illinois, like the valley floor to La Morra, fades into the ever-present haze. It is algae. Bioluminescence. The Langhe is quiet. The Langhe is dark. My ears are humming, and I'm struck with that peaking well in my lungs — a strange happiness, I think, or weeping. The kids of the Piedmont could be flying their bikes full speed over the vineyard grass in the pitch-black. The wind whipping their hair. Growing their revolutions, probably not culinary. To them I walk down. I walk into. The rubber bands, for the time being at least, hold.

14

Slow

Returning sweaty from La Morra, I unzip my tent flaps to retrieve a clean shirt from my backpack and switch out my broken hiking boots for a pair of gym shoes. I notice it immediately on my pillow, perfectly centered, not at all crooked, as if someone took her time placing it there, then righting it. It is the inch-thick guide for the Salone del Gusto in Torino, held in the city's Lingotto (the old Fiat factory), creeping into reality in less than two weeks.

I first read of the Salone del Gusto—the Salon of Taste—in Juneau at the Channel Bowl Café. During the customer lapse between greasy breakfast and greasier lunch, over a slow steaming cup of Heritage coffee, I began thumbing through *Harper's Magazine* and uncovered an article on Italy's Slow Food movement and its prize offspring, the Salone del Gusto. First, second, third paragraphs: a wild cheer grew in my chest, and it took all of my resolve not to yelp a spew of coffee over the Channel Bowl's puke green, gold-flecked counter. If good food is cool, the Salone del Gusto is Fonzie in mirrored shades.

Here is what I read then, and here is what I read now, brushing salt crystals from my hair and absentmindedly setting Adriana and Michele's Barolo next to the Francesco Borgogno. In two weeks, from Wednesday to Sunday, the Salone del Gusto will exhibit and offer, in lapidary comprehensiveness, the tastes of the world. The belly of the Lingotto will growl with a massive food and beverage market where small-scale purveyors and farmers, hunters and vintners, restaurateurs and cheese-makers, butchers and olive-pressers meet face-to-face with their admiring customers, having traveled to Torino from every continent save Antarctica. And then the workshops: sit-down tastings and studies of a particular ingredient or cuisine or chef or region or wine or vintage, information about the delights pumped through individual and multilingual headphones, the comparative consumption and analysis of ingestibles in a scholastic atmosphere, experts lecturing on the specific product, its narrative, its history, and the nature of its native territory. These are laboratory classrooms in which eating while learning is not only permitted but mandatory.

The Slow Food movement itself was born in response to a McDonald's infecting the traditional landscape of Rome. In 1986, when the McDonald's Corporation decided to spread its dumbed-down version of a meal (sorry, Dad, your bunless Big Macs) to Rome's Piazza di Spagna, a gustatory revolt ensued. Striving to uphold the "right to pleasure," the Slow Food movement chose as its headquarters the village of Bra, just west of Alba in the Langhe. The movement soon accumulated a massive following. Carlo Petrini, founder of Slow Food and original organizer of the protest against the Roman McDonald's, drew up a concise manifesto detailing the movement's aims. The manifesto denounces the insensate ideals perpetuated by the speeded-up McDonaldization of the world while attempting to raise public regard for fresh, seasonal foodstuffs and initiate a mass "education of taste." This concept fuses a local, natural element (quality of soil, elevation, weather) with a local human element (culinary and agricultural traditions and methods) in order to pinpoint the uniqueness of a particular region and its cuisine, from the farm (or forest or sea . . .) to the plate.

Toward the tail end of 1989 an international delegation convened in Paris's Opéra comique to officially sign and approve the Slow Food manifesto. The signatures represent the backing of Argentina, Austria, Brazil, Denmark, France, Germany, Holland, Hungary, Italy (of course), Japan, Spain, Sweden, Switzerland, the United States, and Venezuela. With this international backing the Salone del Gusto was inaugurated in 1996.

The first Salone del Gusto introduced the concept of the Ark, or "un'Arca del Gusto per salvare il pianeta dei sapori" (an Ark of

Taste to save the planet of flavors). Faced with the endangerment or extinction of various species of vegetable, fruit, grain, cheese, and meat and a zealous governmental health code that rendered certain traditional "farmhouse" methods of food production illegal, Slow Food teamed with scholars, historians, political scientists, sociologists, biologists, anthropologists, and flat-out gourmets to create a medium to safeguard the traditional production of quality foodstuffs. I wonder if the Ark is responsible for Lodovico Borgogno — for all of Barolo, really: the beautiful archaic stuff that should have long ago gone the way of the dinosaur.

Tent walls flapping, the Piedmont wind beginning to buck, I hold Lodovico up to the Ark's detailed rubric. To gain entry, a foodstuff (or, in this case, a man) must meet five criteria:

1. The foodstuff must be of optimal quality (locally debatable, but I'd argue for Lodovico).
2. It must be of a species, variety, plant ecotype, or animal population indigenous to a particular territory or made strictly of local ingredients and aged and prepared according to traditional local techniques (Lodovico).
3. It must be connected historically, environmentally, and socioeconomically to a particular territory (Lodovico).
4. It must be made in limited quantities and small batches (there's only one — those glasses, that spittle, that water barrel).
5. It must be at risk of potential or actual extinction (Lodovico writ large).

The wind is really blowing now. Sandrone's crew must be struggling against the slope. Tent protected, I flip through the workshop titles. Exhibitions of the world's coffees, ice creams, buffalo mozzarellas, balsamic vinegars of Modena of varying ages, olive oils of Abruzzo, Parmigiano-Reggianos, prosciutti, smoked meats, mid-African soups, potatoes, rices, American barbecue, American southwestern cuisine, vertical tastings of Barolo, Barbaresco, Champagne, Hungarian tokaji, rum, chocolates, oysters, beans, corns, teas, cigars, sometimes the salami of one specific farmer, sometimes the Pecorino of one cheese-maker, sometimes the Sicilian coffee of one grower, day in, day out, hundreds of events and dinners spell themselves into this tent, anchored with the opera of their Italian voweled endings. I read that on the Wednesday there is to be a workshop on foie gras from five countries—Italy, France, Germany, the United States, and Hungary—served with five different wines corresponding to each region. My mouth opens like a mail slot, thinking of all that fattened duck and goose liver, all those decadent semisweet wines that will wash it down. Dormant since my descent from La Morra, sweat resprouts from my forehead, beads resting unburdened in my eyebrows. I have always been somewhat of a sweaty man. In my catering days I would try to ignore the customers' low whispers of disgust as I dripped into their consommés. This time it's only the wind that whispers—shouts, really, inflaming indecision. At the same time as the foie gras workshop there is scheduled a tasting of the region's most profound Barolos: Paolo Scavino 1990 Cannubi, Giocomo Conterno 1991, Sandrone 1991 Le Vigne, Pira Marenca 1993, Elio Altare 1993, Elvio Cogno 1995. Oh, hell. My throat's closing up. This is only going to get harder. *Read on.*

On I read to find that at 3:00 that Wednesday Michel and Maryse Trama, famed chef-proprietors of Les Loges de l'Aubergade in Puymirol, France, are giving a cooking demonstration. I want to kiss these pages deep in the mouth. At Charlie Trotter's restaurant in Chicago, at one of my seminal fine-dining experiences that expelled me from the world of McDonald's for good, Charlie and guest chef Michel Trama engaged in a dueling night of culinary King of the Mountain, alternating courses in a tear-the-mouth-down chewed-and-swallowed extravaganza. Trama's potato blini. Trama's apple crème brûlée.

Then Thursday: oysters paired with various Veuve Cliquot Champagnes, chocolates paired with French Bordeaux, an eight-course risotto tasting. This must be a dream, my body having fallen asleep on La Morra's Belvedere bench or perhaps earlier, leaning into the mop handle in Sandrone's cantina, Ivo, Beppe, and Indiano sliding my hand into a goblet of warm water.

In an effort to wake myself, to not wet myself, I unzip the tent door. Stomach pursing like lips over lemon, I walk for Il Gioco's kitchen to see what I have left in the fridge. The wind is a cold shower. In it the smells of basement corners, ignored by all but the spiders.

The author harvests Nebbiolo grapes for vintner Luciano Sandrone.

The author hikes along the vineyards of the
Langhe and finds a downed persimmon.

Pasta fresca smothered with shaved Alba white truffle.

A fresh pasta demonstration at the Salone del Gusto in Torino.

(*above*) The Nebbiolo grapes.

(*below*) The table, postdinner, at Il Gioco dell'Oca.

(*opposite*) An Alba white truffle, a truffle slicer, and a glass of Barolo.

A bottle of 1964 Boschis Barolo.

15

Halves

I pull the Salone del Gusto guide from under my pillow the next morning, sheepish as a twelve-year-old boy reaching into his *Playboy*'s hiding place. It is early. I have slept well, dreaming oddly of American steakhouses, massive sixty-four-ounce porterhouses calling from the T-bone to be smothered in white truffles. Over the slabs of beef overstuffed Manhattan socialites calling for diamonds.

The air ruffling the tent screen is heavy with dust and attic, somehow higher — at least two stories above — and lighter than last evening's basement air. Overnight the Piedmont has moved upstairs. Propping myself on one elbow, wakefulness running downhill from brain to belly to feet, I turn to page 14 in the guide and read an article on the world's salts.

Roving from sel gris to the elusive fleur de sel, I want to return to America if for no other reason than to bury my cardboard cylinder of Morton's iodized in my garden, forever closing the book on my former and illiterate cooking practices. So many unexcellent meals.

This morning hunger begins to peak with a low wheezing growl from just below my sternum. Surely, there must be at least one plain yogurt cup left in Raffaella's fridge, just enough to carry me the two kilometers into Barolo's tiny, labyrinthine *centro*. I am walking today, my desire to rely on the bus system — though it brought me to Lodovico Borgogno — snuffed like a candle flame in a monsoon. In India. In August.

I yank a clean set of clothes from the netherworld of my backpack. The tent's storage corner is beginning to reek of mildew. I resolve to leave the back screen open. The Salone del Gusto brochure, carrying with it all the excitement and wary guilt of adolescence, beckons to be put back into its under-the-pillow cocoon. All things in their places, I step from my tent, skid on the mud-puddle doormat, busy drying out in the early sun, and, eight steps later, listen to the familiar crunch of the white driveway stones. Pongo shakes the night off his back, and my heart shakes with him when I see the Fiat parked by the front door. I hear Raffaella coughing inside, her footsteps sliding over the stone floor as if sanding wood, moving at that exact pace that tells me she's about to leave the house.

Something goes cold in my fingers, tells me to run back to my tent. I don't know why I'm nervous about seeing her. Perhaps because I now know that she has been inside my tent, delivering the Salone del Gusto guide on top of my sleeping bag, smelling its smells, its own attic-basement stench part of a poorer house than the one she's used to.

Reaching for the door, Raffaella foot-sanding the floor into what must be marble by now, I half-expect an electric current to snake from the iron handle and drop me, dead, to the stones. The wind unfurls a wild gust, I pull my hand back to my side, and I swear it's a ghost warning from Beppe Fenoglio, the door's original owner trying to blow one last stanza of cautionary wartime poetry from the great beyond before all fades into his own personal non-Italy.

Inside a loud crash and Raffaella's voice driving frustrated and doubtless obscene Italian to the other side of this still-closed door. My hand once again finds the handle, fingers coiling loosely around it. Beppe Fenoglio keeps quiet this time, but I'm sure he's looking down, shaking his head. *Coffee,* I think and depress the handle's steel button. Fenoglio's door swings inward, heavy and creakless. The indoor air rushes through the crack.

Raffaella in a beige pantsuit squats next to the dining room table, wiping with a white and yellow dishtowel what appears to be blood from the floor. Barely green shards of glass are scattered from her feet to mine. I can make out, in the piece closest to my toe, the shape of what was once a bottle neck. She's still muttering as she looks into the light I've shed, all by opening the door.

"What happened?" I ask. "Are you okay?"

"Ah," she grumbles, disgusted, "I have to go to Niccolo's school. He make trouble again, and I drop the wine. All this hurry. And Altare 1995. Terrible."

She shakes her head at herself, clicks her tongue against the roof of her mouth, the sound echoing from the ceiling in muscular detail.

"If you're in a rush, I'll finish cleaning this up."

"Oh," she says, tossing the dishtowel to the table, "you are good to do this."

"Usually not before my morning coffee," I say, half-hoping she will tell me there's a half-pot still left on the stovetop.

I'm not yet in the mood to create. I only want to rewarm.

She half-laughs, half-coughs, and picks up a brown purse.

Tucking her hair neatly behind her ears, she rises to menacing height, legs stilt-straight, and says, "You see about the Salone del Gusto?"

I exhale. I nod. I say nothing. I don't stop nodding. I feel battery-operated. Now she laughs without the cough.

"Wonderful," she says.

I manage a "Yes, wonderful," and she walks for the half-open door and the full outdoors, which I, tranced, am still blocking.

"I will help you to translate later," she says.

"Thank you," I say. "I get the gist of it." Then: "Don't be too hard on Niccolo."

"Ah," she grumbles again, exactly like the first time.

She grabs my shoulders, her thumbs pressing strong into the muscles, the things that landed on so many plush mats after so many high-jumps. Her current runs over my torso, ends at my waistline, and rests there, waiting for something: a completion or a snapping-out-of. She swings her hips to the left, beige jacket flying from her body like a wing, and rounds me. It takes the grinding sputter of the Fiat's engine to move my feet across the floor.

Her jacket, Barolo's centro, the hidden Gusto guide, and coffee — all achieving a random lightness on the brain, tickling it with their pastel tissue. Walking to the wine stain on the stone, spread into the shape of a long-necked peacock, I step hungry and excited to get to Barolo. That strange guilty excitement leaps in me again like a flame while I clean up the mess, as if I am soaking someone else's life into someone else's dishtowel.

When I step into the kitchen's fluorescence, Raffaella's coffeepot is on the range, filled to the brim and still warm.

16

Luca Sandrone Enters Shakedown Street

I walk to Barolo. Hard, strong. As if to banjo music. The coffee
sloshes loud enough in my stomach for me to hear it. It sounds like
the ocean from a mile away. My yogurt cup — my meager breakfast — is drowned like a sliver of seaweed.

The path of flat land between Via Crosia and its infrequent but
maniac minicars and the ditch edging the vineyards is only shoe-
wide. I walk it as if performing a feat. Green tightrope. Vineyard net.
The bored gutturals of tractor, not even a mutter of wind. Somehow, though, the vines rustle themselves as if driven by some inside
force — an animal or a heart. I wouldn't be surprised at all to discover
these vineyards run on blood.

Somewhere, beyond one of these hills, Niccolo is getting yelled at
and Raffaella is wringing her hands red. The tractors rumble the air
behind the vines, releasing it thick and rich. Ivo? Beppe? Indiano?
I walk against traffic, the matted, traveled grass just wide enough to
keep the cars from taking out my knees. There is no slowing here.
The Italians have either an inborn eye for distance perception or
a decreased value for the use of one's legs. Every so often I don't
trust the perception theory and lean away from the street, left foot
dragging mud at ditch-bottom. My shoes since I've arrived in Italy
are either destroyed or always caked with sludge. I pass the entrance
to I Cannubi restaurant, then the Cannubi hill, its swell and fertility
shooting the growl of my stomach downward into my shorts. I'm
hungry and feeling a little crude. I wait for this to pass, and it does
as Sandrone's cantina lifts its blush shingling from behind the hill.

It's been a few days since I picked the Nebbiolo for the man, and I wonder if today he's wearing the same burgundy suspenders. When the sun catches a window near the roof, it looks exactly like a wink. I kick a white rock hard, and it bullets into the ditch, sticks lengthwise in the mud. It angles straight at Sandrone's cantina.

Turning left onto the small dirt road that continues to Sandrone's garage, I hope not to find the cantina empty. I've got some serious beret and cheroot withdrawal. I want an arm-wrestling rematch with Ivo. The cantina bursts with damp and dungeon. All is silent save the low kazoo chorus of the rotofermentors, the washers, the temperature-controlled holding tanks. The harmony of these machines is impossible and enviable. Communicating with one another telepathically. Undercutting the machines is the expanding rhythm of dripping water and the cracking smell of grape mash and noble rot. I step once, then twice, and my footsteps are the loudest thing in here. I feel as if I'm in the belly of a whale.

"Ciao?" I call in a normal speaking voice, and it rises to the thirty-foot cedar ceiling, spreads its echo like cream over the white lights.

At the far wall faint music comes from behind a single closed door. The knob, gold, flickers. A dare. I scratch my chest, and my stomach fires a line of acid hunger to meet my hand. I consider turning around when the music frantically jumps in volume. Jumping with it, I muster a louder "Ciao?" Nothing. The gold knob narrows its eyes.

I step closer to the door and hear that the music, be-bopping with bass and a shooka-shooka guitar line, is the Grateful Dead's "Shakedown Street." I've never been a fan of the band, never heard their song titles spoken in the sweet radio gruff of Patty Hays or Kitty Lowie, but, overhearing their song in Sandrone's cantina, I get the feeling that, despite their other successes, they have finally arrived.

I envision the bulldog members of the tractor crew returning early from the fields to unload the red grape crates, kicking on a little music while they do their work, amoebas of sweat ringing their white shirtbacks, breaking the two-lane boundaries of their coveralls.

I want to say hello. I want to commune with those who know what it's like to stand on a Sandrone hill in waning orange light with aching hands stained mythical purple.

So, calling the knob's bluff, I palm it hard and twist. The music rushes through the door crack like revolutionaries. The air on the other side is warmer than this air. Over the curves of caravan barrels I see a short but obviously strong man, bald head bursting the confines of his black hair and splitting it to either ridge over his tremendous ears. His scalp is wrinkled and sun reddened. Luca Sandrone. He is alone in this room, and he is dancing. He is dancing in a white undershirt and pink swimming trunks. This is not just a moderate and mellow collection of steps. Not just dancing but DANCING! Sweat runs down his face like rain.

Luca, forty yards away and unaware of me, thrusts both arms out to his sides like a wannabe Moses, parting this sea of barrels. With a violent step and spin he kicks his clipboard across the floor. It ricochets from the wall. His shoes are white. Cymbals and vocals and Luca's legs curving inward. His cheeks are vibrating. Light from one of the many raised house-tall windows shoots from Luca's head like a star. The glass elevator watches in disbelief. His fingers jut, stabbing out the eyes of the wine-ghosts. I half-expect the barrels to lift from the floor and, lofty, uprooted, spin in the air above him.

Like Luciano, it seems Luca has found his mastery. Is this how he blows off steam after grape picking? After recording the cantina's many numbers onto the clipboard sheets? Is this how he emerges from beneath Luciano's famed shadow? Is this empty cantina his sanctuary away from his wife and kids?

His baldness rattles from side to side as if on a spring about to snap. I imagine his head coming loose, rolling between the barrels to my feet, and staring me down bug-eyed, angered at my intrusion. What could make a man dance like this? *Only love.*

As the song crescendos, preparing for its own end, Luca's body sparrow-twitters across the floor, and it seems this dance isn't his escape but his celebration. He must adore his work, his brother, his family. He must have something amazing to go back to.

Before the song ends I close the door. Walk through the empty room back to daylight. No tractor crew. The mop missing. The machines whir and switch gears. Before I get to the double entrance doors I make up a song. Maybe it's hunger delirium, maybe something else.

Luca Sandrone enters Shakedown Street, yeah,
Luca Sandrone loves her all the wayyy home . . .

My hands are dirty. I open the right side of the double doors, and, as if on cue, a navy Fiat pulls up fast and cuts its engine. This is the car that first picked me up at Raffaella's, brought me to these vineyards. The hatch. The bucket-seated outer space. Through the window I see, walled in its own shadow, the cumulous hairdo of Mariuccia, Sandrone's wife. Before I can blink she is in my face, kissing my cheeks. She pulls back, rubs her lipstick stains from me.

"Come va? Come va?" she clucks, slapping my face with both hands as if closing an encyclopedia. This is a country of tough facial love.

"Bene, bene," I decide, envisioning Luca, still dancing. "Dov'è Luciano?"

"Ah," she lilts, giving her voice to the newly developed wind. "Sempre lavoro."

Sempre. This is also a country of *always.* And Luciano Sandrone is always working.

"Andiamo, andiamo," she says.

I'm getting used to this.

I follow her waddle into the cantina. Luca is now in the front machine room, recovering, polishing a steel holding tank. He is flushed. He doesn't suspect a thing. To him this is our first meeting today.

"Oh, ciao, ciao," he breathes hard, voice thin as paper.

I smile and reach for his hand. I want to touch him. I hope some of it will rub off.

"Ciao," I say.

When he thrusts his hand into mine, I expect sparks.

Sandrone's wife lifts a clipboard from a nail in the wall and calls to me again in the "Andiamo" refrain. I love this. I should be on a leash. I follow her, always the good boy, to the double doors. Behind us, Luca is catching his breath.

The doors close, and Sandrone's wife is ten steps ahead, reaching for the car. Even before she waves me toward her and bellows yet another wonderful "Andiamo" I know I will be getting into her car. This is a country of long morning hungers. I open the door and sit down for somewhere. She stamps the gas pedal so hard, my back bounces against the passenger seat like a drumbeat.

17

Chandelier, Carpet, Mariuccia

My stomach is building up calluses. It is getting used to mornings like this, starting to expect wine before food. Tearing over dirt roads so narrow an oncoming car has to bury half of itself in the grapevines, Sandrone's wife, Mariuccia, and I speak of the Salone del Gusto.

"Oh, è come paradiso," she flutters in a pitch-perfect clucking that I expect her to follow with a few vigorous chicken-wing flaps. I wonder if she is consciously attempting to out-hen Adriana. She tells me that she and Sandrone are going to the Salone on its Friday.

"Oh, sì? Venerdì?" I reply.

Mariuccia blinks two fat stars and flies around a blind curve, sending an oncoming Subaru slushing into the foliage. I can't imagine an American tire taking this sort of beating. The Romans constructed roads in the Piedmont in the second century BC — helter-skelter, uphill-downhill pathways — in order to connect the region with coastal Liguria, where they had economic aims. It appears the infrastructure has changed little since then. Here speed limit signs remain a rarity. We twist uphill, driving a braided rope, the road alternating dirt, gravel, pavement. Tires spewing dust, crunching, whistling. The earth pitches a fit around the car, on the verge of violence, and this is not the type of earth with which you want to argue. The soil here is serious. The vineyards, ever-green and rippling, draw their leaves over their eyes.

The Salone del Gusto rests in the air between us, hovering just over the gear-shift box, and it takes all of my hungry energy to turn from it and Mariuccia's multiringed hand to the passenger window. We pass an old man with a shovel. He is wearing a green-and-black flannel shirt, and when I check the side-view mirror to see if he's moved on, I watch as he steps into the middle of the dirt road and angles his shovel toward the car like a jousting pole. I watch him until he blurs green into the landscape.

We hit a rough section of road, the car vibrating like a cheap motel quarter-fed bed. Up the road a clearing waits like finish-line tape, and when we hit it, shoot through it, I look downslope and see Barolo's red-orange castle hanging on a hillside at least a hundred yards below us. And somewhere below that countless hands harvesting Nebbiolo.

Mariuccia turns to me, says, "Ah," and slams the brakes in front of a large, beige-bricked house. Sandrone's house. This is where the man sleeps, where he dreams of his methods and modes of perfection, where he writes in his midnight notebook, red digits of his nightstand clock threatening to burn all vision from his eyes. The afterimage of late numbers.

A tree bearing orange fruit, fruit big as softballs, bobbing like lures in water from fish-hook branches, dangles teasingly over the car. Every foxwise instinct I've ever had roars into my belly at once. I ache to devour, but Mariuccia claps me from my fairy tale, right between the shoulder blades with the beaking peck of her jeweled hand.

"Andiamo," she says.

The word sounds so comfortable in her mouth, carries all the warmth of memory, all the times it's been spoken. I can't help but follow. She's got a grip on me. I am walked up a flight of huge stone stairs, so steep I nearly knee myself in the chin with each step, with a massive front door at the crest. This is a country of elephantine doorways so impressive and imposing that you feel as if you've completed a ridiculous feat simply by walking through one.

Exhaling hard, Mariuccia teetering a couple steps ahead, I wonder about a historical race of Italian giants that actually required doors of this size, and as the people evolved and shrunk, the doors remained. Ivo must be one of their descendants.

I shake my head. *Italian giants? You need food bad.*

The door skulks inward, slow as a whale's mouth, and as I step over the stone threshold, Mariuccia wrapped in doily silhouette, I again think of Pinocchio, the patron saint of Italian woodwork. He must surely be lying three-quarters digested on the rose tile of the Sandrones' foyer.

The inside air is cool, fan-spun, new, old, a perfect domestic complement to Sandrone's cantina. Just as my body relaxes into this air and this room, its wicker furniture and sliding glass door giving way to a back porch of vineyard and sky, Mariuccia leads me around a white-pillared corner to yet another astronomical stairwell. This one goes down. Pebbles of sweat push through my forehead in protest, my stomach lets out a strained yelp, and soon my feet find themselves cliff diving into the bowels of Sandrone's lair.

The corridor is gray stone, cold, damp, rounded as the front door, and lined with dim orange lanterns. Maybe it's only the hunger, but my body, six stairs down, suddenly goes light, and my brain spins in my skull like a record. A frazzled music plays, as if accompanying a mouse fleeing a cat. An unsettling dirge. A broken trumpet. If Lodovico's cantina held the spirit of Jimmy Hoffa, Sandrone's basement must have in it the chained bones of Miles Davis.

That Subaru we ran off the road. I wonder if we actually hit it, if I have been transported to some basement afterlife where the Sandrones will lift their green wizardly heads and decide where and when I will go next.

In a flicking snap of light switch and the white illumination of an arresting chandelier, weight runs back into my shoes. My stomach bucks like a shot horse, then lies still. Sandrone's basement, darkly ornate, is carpeted in thick rouge, the color of Roman blood. The walls hold photos of vineyard and grape and family. In one photo stands a young Luca, hands on hips, prebaldness, pre–that dance. He looks so strong, as tough to open as the front door. At least one person in every photo is wearing glasses, a testament to their own vision. In fact, this whole basement is a testament, the storage room of a museum. Cardboard boxes of tyrannosaur skulls yet to be untaped.

Like a neighboring gargoyle, Mariuccia stands stoic, wings at her sides, staring down a table of wine. I can't believe that I have to follow her gaze to notice it: a plain fold-out card table, clothed in white, supporting a ballerina row of Sandrone's bottles. What a morning.

Soon I am sitting, and Mariuccia, uttering the words "Barbera 1998," is pouring. The Barbera grape is incredibly versatile. Some Barberas, like Sandrones, can be aged five to six years, often challenging the Nebbiolo to a bar fight. Half of all Piedmontese reds are Barberas (it's known as the region's "country" wine), and when enjoyed young, they can exhibit a bright, tart, red fruit flavor and an almost bubbly nature. The thin tapered glass fills with the Sandrone Barbera, the faded rose square on the label pointing its four corners respectively to chandelier, carpet, Mariuccia, and me. Knights at a long table. The wine is dark in my glass, almost brown in this light, and its woody acid spice spills from the rim. Chewing on the roots of a weeping willow. She pours one for herself and raises her glass. I match her pose.

"Mille grazie," she says, "per la vendemmia."

She tells me that Sandrone was incessantly preaching about bringing me here, about sharing his wines in thanks for my work. As if his other bottles and the experience weren't enough. Excess. Wonderful, healthy excess. Away from microwaves and preservatives, away from kitchens with televisions, there is such a thing. I can't believe this language has a word for *enough*.

We ring our glasses together like bells and sip. The wine bursts on the tongue with lemon, grapefruit, orange, then calms with the swallow as if tempered with cream. Nothing, not a marathon runner, not a life fully realized, finishes like a Sandrone. Mariuccia runs a hand over her neck as if smoothing the wine down. She speaks with exasperated love of how crazy she thinks her husband is for wanting to go all the way to New Zealand to pick wine grapes.

"Sempre lavoro," she says, "sempre vino. A Luciano, vino e vita è la stessa cosa."

Wine and life is the same thing.

I put my hand on her shoulder. It sinks into her flesh, a small stone in big water. She is nodding, barely containing her love for Luciano.

"Sì," she manages.

After 1995 and 1996 Barolos — Le Vigne and Cannubi Boschis — my mouth saturated with antediluvian sin and virtue, with forest and beach, snow-peak and earth-mantle, stream and wishing well, Mariuccia leads me back upstairs. I feel I have died and come back, lucky and stunned. Defibrillated. The stairs, this time, are easy.

We return to the foyer. Before she opens the door, before we are regurgitated into the outdoors, she slips a 100,000-lire note (about fifty dollars) into my palm. I am confused for a second, thinking it is a coupon or ticket or letter or scroll.

"Per favore," she implores, "per il tuo buono lavoro."

How many times can I get paid for the same job? I try to hand it back to her, but she turns and, Raffaellaesque, rounds me. She is out the front door and starting the car to drive me back to the cantina and my walk to Barolo.

The massive orange fruits sway in the tree. They seem to have doubled in size. They rise and set, dozens of suns. I imagine the ride into Barolo, the roads shaking us along, a speck of dust on a cracked whip. I can tell by the sky that it's still early. The money in my hand is already damp with sweat. I am going to use it to buy the biggest breakfast I've had since I've gotten here. I think eggs and bacon and ham and sausage and hash browns and know I'm not going to find them. So: salami and cheese and bread. Just as my brain starts sinking into a thick, crusty loaf, into the herbs and seeds and crumbs, Mariuccia, already in the car, roars the horn like a lion. The fruit waves wildly in the wind.

"Andiamo!" she says.

18

Orange

The classic Piedmont wind blows my shirt collar nearly to my ears as I take my first bite. It's a rabbit breakfast in Barolo. I have returned to La Cantinetta for brunch, to flatten my bellyful of Sandrone's wine into a Nebbiolo pancake with the sweet bony meat of coniglio brasato al Barolo. After traveling to hell and back this morning with Mariuccia, the rabbit grounds me, fiercely.

Hypnotized by the orange fruits, I walked, having just been flung from Mariuccia's still-moving car, that familiar narrow strip of grass that bridges the road into Barolo and the slack-jawed ditch riding beside it. She sped off, trailing cartoon dust behind her, and the road seemed endless.

Stomach burning with heat and alcohol, twitching in its emptiness like a nervous tick, I took my steps toward restaurant and salvation. Barolo's castle loomed in the distance. This castle now houses a wine cellar that I urged myself to avoid until I ate something. In 1970 the castle was acquired by the Comune di Barolo and converted into a museum and wine cellar. The cellar, known today as L'Enoteca Regionale di Barolo (the Regional Wine Cellar of Barolo), showcases and sells the region's wines. The castle still houses Juliette Colbert's original furniture and ceilings decorated with the Falletti family coat of arms, while the Enoteca exhibits ancient Barolo farming tools.

Presently run by eleven of the Langhe's towns and headed by its "president," Luigi Cabutto, the Enoteca's purpose is to promote an array of Barolo wines from all corners of its production zone and to protect the image of both the wine and the territory. The Enoteca offers the wines of 180 producers in three forms: as a collection of not-for-sale bottles (basically a wine museum—look but don't drink), as a series of tastings, and as a commercial exchange, the bottle's "second" purchase price established not by the Enoteca but by the wine's producer.

Stomach burning, climbing the steep streets, I came to the castle's base but resisted going in. The mantra: *food first, food first* . . . As if still dreaming in Mariuccia's car, I stomped the cobblestone streets past the tiny gated shopfronts, windows full of meats hanging like gourmet suicides. Everything closed. *Oh, no. Can it really be siesta time already?*

La Cantinetta's openness shocked me, wrapped me so completely like a hug from a massive aunt—an aunt only seen on the holidays—and the short toad of a host remembered me with both hands. He touched my back with one of them, fat fingers spreading over my spine, and my arm with the other. He led me to the cool black iron of an outdoor table.

To sit was divine, legs chattering like teeth. Sun lazy, I watched a well-dressed father and his two children—a boy and a girl—walking along the street. Their shoes clapped the cobblestone like tranquilized horses. The girl, five or six, was running ahead, and the father called angrily after her. He held his son by the hand. The boy wore a white beanie and couldn't walk on his own. Laughing and spinning, the girl made her way back and took her father's other hand. He seemed to rely on these two younger, blonder crutches.

Across the street a middle-aged man with broomstick hair limped to a shopfront. He wore a supportive brace on one arm. Very carefully, as if balancing a tray of martini glasses, he took keys from his belt loop and unlocked the wrought iron gate. With his unbraced arm, he lifted it in a sound like waking, eyes opening for the first time today. As he struggled inside and disappeared into the glare, the sun caught a wall of wine bottles lined up like library books behind him. I closed my eyes. My face went warm. I didn't hear a single plane. Soon the rabbit, and now a pile of bones. If I could floss my teeth with one of them, I would. I drink my water, stomach sighing, and my thirst for wine returns. An Elvio Cogno 1993 later (by the glass, of course), the host hops tableside and ribbits, "Come va Raffaella?"

"Bene, bene," I say, picturing her hands squeezing Niccolo's neck blue.

I smile at this thought. The host, misunderstanding, or understanding perfectly, runs his thumb downward over his cheek.

"Raffaella . . . che bella."

"Sì," I say too quickly, my words an overeager adolescent in spring visiting the public pool for the first time this season.

I picture Raffaella bending over Niccolo, her forehead knotted with concentration, her fingers curving like strands of sugarcane. Even when she is murdering she is beautiful.

"Ha, haaa," the host bellows, throwing his hands into the air. His fingers spread abnormally wide. His cheeks rise like bread dough.

"E Adriana e Michele? Bene?"

I haven't seen Raffaella's parents since we've eaten here, though I've heard Adriana from the tent, presunrise, talking to the chickens while she feeds them, telling them to eat more, eat more, that bigger, for the love of God, is better. Her shrill breakfast call to the animals — that insane *Mi mi-mi-mi-mi-mi-mi-mi!* A dawn alarm both intolerable and hilarious.

"Sì," I answer, "tutto bene."

Taking his hands from the air and pressing them into his apron, the host nods and laughs again, takes a step for the restaurant's entrance. He pauses and takes my plate, staring into it as if it were a crystal ball. I have lined the rabbit bones in circular fashion along the plate's rim. It looks like a voodoo picture frame.

He shakes his head, chin wobbling like a rooster's, and says, "Come un cimitero."

He walks away with my cemetery of a plate. As a din of unintelligible Italian meanders from the kitchen to the street, my legs stir, once again ready to move. Pay the bill with Mariuccia's lire. Take the last sip of wine standing up.

19

The Bleary Music of Wineshop Franco

Walking across the street, I swear I can feel the rabbit hopping in my belly. Maybe my glass of wine spawned some sort of unholy resurrection. The unmarked wineshop beckons with its green awning. The cobblestone street is devoid of people, fighting for its river-narrow space with the tight hulks of an attached macelleria (butcher shop), a rec center, a panetteria (bakery). The sun renders their glass-windowed facades opaque, concealing the sights and smells of their interiors.

My heart beats. Opening these wineshop doors seems an inhuman leap of faith in a street devoid of human. When I twist the brass knob, silver bells ring at the top doorframe, and I look up at their breaking sound to see that they also catch the light. The sun here throws its glare like baseballs, and everything on this Barolo street has its mitts ready. Inside the damp must of saw-cut wine shelves and unnecessary air-conditioning, ancient cabinets and the click-step staccato of the shopkeeper shuffling toward me, arm brace extended. He mutters a string of sunny Italian, his face a tangle of smile and wrinkles, his speech slurred like a lawnmower struggling to start. His left leg drags behind him, the foot's instep sputtering along the gold carpet. The knot of his shoelace is perfectly tied.

"Ciao," I say.

"Ah, ciao, ciao," he returns, his mouth wracked with effort as if he is trying to talk through water.

At the rear shelves the Barolos: the Conternos, the Mascarellos, the Borgognos, the Sandrones — you know, the guys from the neighborhood. He has every Sandrone: the Dolcetto with the faded

purple square at its label, the Barbera with its rose square, the Nebbiolo with its off-evergreen, the Le Vigne Barolo with its stark red,
the Cannubi Boschis with its confident blue. The lights dim as if on
a timer, casting the wineshop in a library's glow. A burst of breath
paints my neck with its warmth, delightfully bereft of the typical
Borgogno spittle. A shoulder brushes my shoulder, and the shopkeeper is at me, wondering which bottles have captivated me so. I
turn to him, his head so close it could be my extra limb.

"Ah, Sandrone," he says with a lisp more pronounced and
strangely more practiced than Lodovico's. "Ah, il migliore."

Yes, I nod, yes, I agree. The best. "Sì," I say.

"Franco," he says, introducing himself, bowing, his unbraced
hand capping his heart like a nobleman.

"Ciao, Franco," I say, taking his hand, warm as leather, rich with
topography.

The rises and falls of his palm pucker together like a peach left to
dry in the sun, like a map of the Langhe. This hand has seen some
weather. This hand has been around. Up close, his face, wrinkled
as it is, seems much younger than it did at a distance. He must only
be in his fifties, but the years have been hard until they gifted him
this shop of local wine. He tells me that his shop, though unmarked
with a sign, is named Il Bacco, The Bacchus. Distinguishing itself
from all the other Bacchuses.

"Resta a Il Gioco dell'Oca?" Franco asks.

I don't know what to say. The resident swami has just guessed
my weight and birthdate down to the ounce and hour.

"Barolo," he says and narrows his forefinger to his thumb to
indicate an inch — the actual size, perhaps, of this very small small
town.

And Franco is its spokesperson, at least for today; he comes across
as familial and enterprising, an old friend, a new friend. Franco, like
a bartender, waitress, mailman, father, first girlfriend, long-dead pet,
and psychiatrist, nods with seven heads at once, then looks up to
the dark exposed beams of the ceiling. He studies something I can't

see — his past or a spider, spinning its wealthy web. His breathing wet and rhythmic, also practiced.

He clears his throat and pivots in two quick jerks, his back curved and broken. He tosses himself flour-sackwise behind his cash register and leans to the floor. I think he may be falling, however slowly, until he reemerges with a half-bottle of Macarini Barolo 1995, the gold label communing with the carpet beneath us. Deftly, like a man with three hands, let alone a man without a brace, he uncorks the bottle and begins a long, slow meditation in Italian, the words jumbling together into linked mantras. His words are the people of the world joining hands.

At first, my mind detaches from the content, solely interested in surrendering to the old record static of his speech. When certain instruments are played out and wheezy, dusty and restrained, they attain a greater lull and allure. Franco is that one accordion, that one electric piano. You can hear his keys and his strings working. The music bleary and luminous.

He fills two glasses. The wine shudders and catches the sun, then settles again. Franco's chest expands and relaxes so slowly he could be sleeping. My fingers curve beneath the glass and I lift it, marveling at the function of my own body. In the sip the wood of an old neighborhood fence, the one you climbed as a kid and tore your pants on, slats coming unnailed and offering passage to squirrel, rabbit, coyote, their fur and musk rubbing off on the splinters. Just enough so you know they've been there. And then the smashing juice of black plum, the tannin of cranberry skin, the postswallow breath of a brand-new dog.

Suddenly, content is everything, and music shuts up and waits its turn. Franco is talking of his car accident. It was almost ten years ago, near Torino, a Cinquecento Rosso.

"Come Raffaella," he tells me.

I pick up only shards of the story: a blue van planting itself into the driver's side door. The Cinquecento spinning over. The last sight before unconsciousness, so much of his blood.

"Ping-pong," Franco says and bounces his good hand along the black sheen of the cash register desktop.

"E questo," he sighs, gesturing to his legs, "Ah, niente."

He sighs again. He sips his wine. He is nodding, but slackly. He swallows. He smiles. His wine is good.

"Italia," he says to me, strained, and bites a fingernail. "Paradiso." We finish our glasses. He pours off the bottle, and we finish that. I tell him of my time here so far—the Borgognos, the truffle tent, Sandrone—and he listens quietly, eyes more closed than open. He stays in his chair as I pick another Macarini half-bottle from the shelf and ask him, "Quanto?"

After handing him four thousand lire, the equivalent of two bucks, he shakes an enormous paper bag from its folded state. The bag puffs its gut and swallows my half-bottle and Franco's business card. Il Bacco, it says simply in red letters with an address, phone number, and a logo of a tipped wine bottle, liquid pouring down the side of the card. He takes my bagless hand, his good palm burning into mine like a brand.

"A presto," Franco says. "Grazie."

"A presto," I echo and hope that I do see him soon.

Outside the air warms my forearms. The smell of the vineyards rises from behind the castle. Inside Il Bacco the doorframe bells stop ringing. I stare into the depths of the brown paper. The half-bottle seems so small, the pea on the mattress. I wonder, still nodding, if this fairy tale of a day will have a moral at the end. The bag nods back, patronizing, impatient, waiting to be filled.

20

Breadstick Hydra

The front room is filled with fresh pastas and truffle emulsions, meter-long grissini breadsticks and lady's-kiss baci di dama cookies. Franco's paper bag crackles at my feet, begging for a taste. I am in Barolo's panetteria, the sole local bakery, and am enjoying its silence, its farmland smells, the sight of three shadowed heads work-bobbing behind the kitchen's glass door. They don't see me yet, and I'm glad for this. I'm tempted even to hide between the shelves of olive oil and the shelves of vinegar, becoming the bridge that brings the two ingredients together into a nebulous vinaigrette.

I squat to examine the pastries in their glass cases — hazelnut buns, chocolate-fruit truffles, and again those stretched, cat-after-a-nap breadsticks, the grissini dusted in what appear to be flakes of semolina. My eyes stray upward over the lip of the counter, and I hold them open with my fingers, water them into focus.

The three-headed kitchen monster whirls about in obvious oven-heat, sputtering with rolling-pin effort, palms surely greased with butter, egg, oil, flour, salt, dough. Two of the heads boast long, grassy, tied-up hair. The loose-strand shadows burst from their rubber bands and dance airily about the heads. The third head is what frightens me most, slides me back under my bedroom covers, flashlight tight in hand. It is the squarest head I've ever seen, made even more angular by the fact that it sits featureless in heat-shadow. It is as if the sharp squares of Sandrone's wine labels lifted themselves from their bottles, joined together, and spawned a body beneath them. The square-headed figure — male in shape alone — carries a continuous army of trays first into, then out of, a smoke-spewing hole in the wall.

With each added tray I can hear this brick animal inhaling, then exhaling, doing its job of cooking, rising, browning, melting, toasting, crisping, finishing, each removed tray wearing the label DONE. I breathe with it, trying to inflame my own coals into a large-enough glow to summon one of these frantic heads from its lair. I want a stick of grissini as long as my arm and two sweet baci di dama to kiss it down.

My eyes turn back to the front door, see the street corner beyond the glass. The cobblestone curves left, and I know that, just beyond this curve, Franco sits in his wineshop, waiting to tell the next foreign customer a part of his story. This door also has the silver bells lying dormant at its top frame. I inhale again, the wheatfield air rinsing me, taking me, car windows down, at peak speed through western Nebraska, then eastern Colorado — the breadbasket before the mountains. But there is something different here, not just the smell of flour but the smell of floured mushrooms.

I spin to face the kitchen again and see that the Hydra has lost two heads. Only the square remains. Before I can tear my eyes from the kitchen door I hear, in angelic choral unison, in an identical-twin hum, a luscious, lady-kiss of a "Ciao." Each voice extends the vowel at the end for just a second too long, then cuts out all at once as if some hidden conductor had waved a rod of grissini in a downward swipe through this fresh-baked air. I swear I see granules of yeast sputter all around me. They are standing side by side behind the glass-case counter in matching white aprons, greased in all the same places. Smiles threatening to burst the confines of their faces, they are shoulder to shoulder, wayward blonde hairs maning their forty-something faces, strands locking them together as if they were Siamese twins. There is something of their abundant mouths that reminds me of Franco. They are obviously sisters, richly identical, each defining the other as not one but two warm slaps across my face.

So, not to deny either one of them, I say, "Ciao," exactly twice.

In a ridiculous sideshow feat they break apart as if the air itself were a scalpel, and each walks to an opposing end of the counter for balance. They look like weights on the ends of a straight-from-the-oven barbell. My tongue rings in my mouth as I ask about the grissini.

"Oh, grissini," the woman on the left says.

"Grissini," the woman on the right overlaps.

It's now that I notice that the woman on the left (as opposed to the woman on the right) is wearing eyeliner. This tiny difference settles my heart. They go on to tell me, each interrupting the other midsentence, that the grissini dough is made simply from flour, yeast, egg, milk, water, olive oil, and salt. It is rolled by hand into meter-long narrow sticks, painted with a coat of egg-wash, then baked in the hearth. It is not semolina but cornmeal that gold-dusts the sticks after their removal from the oven to prevent them from sticking together while they cool.

The eyelinerless sister bends behind the counter, and I'm stunned to see just the one standing there. I've never seen a more solitary sight. She looks like an amputee. The sister rises from behind the counter with a stick of grissini in hand. I spread my arms to accept its length. The cornmeal sloughs from the crust, pushes beneath my fingernails, and falls to the floor. I look down and see that the floor is covered with it. Instinctively, like the desire to crush a beer can after the last sip, I break the grissini in half and am surprised to find its interior still soft, pliable, and barely warm. The simple smell of pure bread rushes at my nose, captures me like a cold stone plucked exhilarated from a river bottom. I moan even before I taste.

And the taste . . . My teeth break through the outside crust like a dessert spoon through caramelized crème brûlée sugar, the brown shards dissolving on my tongue and bragging the cornmeal coarseness that so arouses the roof of my mouth. The interior of the grissini, still warm with oven-memory, goes porous and gummy as I chew, its saltiness, earthy as soil, oceanic as brain coral, brings all hemispheres of my mouth together into one smooth swallow. I remember Henry

Miller's manifesto on bread — "The Staff of Life" — and wonder if he ever experienced grissini like this. I can eat this stuff until I die.

"Mamma mia," I quake, already embarking on my second, third, ninth bite.

The sisters laugh as one. In the kitchen Square-Head evicts a spray of sweat from his brow with both hands. The entire meter goes down as easy as an inch.

"Dove resta?" Eyeliner asks.

"Sì, dove resta?" Eyelinerless echoes.

The kitchen breathes hard behind them as if stifling a laugh.

"A Il Gioco dell'Oca," I say, "per uno mese, due mese, tre mese . . ." I shrug and smile.

"Una camera," Eyeliner says, forehead wrinkling, fingers rubbing together to indicate the expensiveness of a room for one or two or three months.

"No, no," I say. "Io resta in una tenda."

"In una tenda?" they bellow in unison, smiles cracking their cheeks into fault lines.

Together they descend into laughter. I laugh too, picturing the dark greens of my tent: my home, my bed, my wine cellar.

They speak to each other so rapidly; their mouths careen like unmuffled cars around a tight curve. Mariuccia at the wheel. They crash beautifully again into laughter, and I think I hear one of them mutter the word "Franco." I wonder if this is Square-Head's name or if they have noticed my paper bag.

"Franco?" I ask. "Di Il Bacco?"

I point to the front door and curve my arm left.

"Sì," both answer, unsurprised.

Then Eyelinerless: "Nostre fratello."

"Fratello?" I say.

Franco is their brother.

Disintegrating into coughs, the sisters notice me staring through the kitchen door's window at Square-Head.

"E lui, un altro fratello," Eyeliner says and points to the kitchen.

He also is their brother. The Hydra is a family.

Before I can ask for a bunch of grissini, before I can point to the baci di dama, the two sisters turn for the kitchen and their square-headed brother and disappear behind the door. I am alone again in the front room and confused. Was it something I said? Was it the way I chewed? Have they decided not to associate with this unshaven American — beard sprouting like wheat — who lives in a tent? I touch the glass case of pastries, my fingerprints staying there to do my begging for me. As I reach for my paper bag the kitchen door swings open; a plume of warmth and grain billows into the room.

It is Square-Head. He is shorter than he looked in the kitchen, in his fifties, and topped with gray hair. His white undershirt is drenched in sweat, and his arms burst willow-wise with salt-and-pepper hair. His glasses, each lens as wide as a wine coaster, match the shape of his head. He is holding a cluster of grissini in one hand like a nuclear family of magic wands. Without a word, with only a rhinoceros grunt, he waves me toward the open kitchen door with his grissini-less hand.

Grissini began its life as a reaction to royal illness. In Torino in 1666 Duke Vittorio Amedeo di Savoia was born. (The duke would later, in 1713, be crowned the first Savoy king.) Vittorio Amedeo was an extremely feeble and sickly child and began to decline rapidly. His mother, Madama Reale II, at her wit's end, summoned to the court the best-known physician of the area, Don Baldo Pecchio from Lanzo Torinese. Soon after his arrival Don Baldo detected that the child was suffering from an inability to digest bread known as ghessa or grissia, which was traditionally undercooked and improperly stored.

When Don Baldo was a child, he had also suffered from Vittorio Amedeo's malady. He recalled how his own mother had prepared him a very thin, twice-baked version of bread in order to improve its digestibility. Don Baldo called upon the court's resident master baker, Antonio Brunetto, to prepare this type of bread. It was this bread that resulted in the first historical citation of grissino (or "little grissia") and the subsequent cure of Duke Vittorio Amedeo.

When the duke grew to become the first Savoy king, he spawned the rise to power of the Savoy dynasty, which many historians claim would not have been possible without the advent of grissini. Torino, the city of its origin, became affectionately known as Grissinopoli. The widespread embracing of grissini helped to booster Torino's socioeconomic climate, turning it into an ornate and stylish city. Grissini's imperialist ideals eventually seduced Napoleon, who affectionately dubbed the bread "Le petit bâton de Turin."

I wish Napoleon and the duke could smell this. The air dense with cow and flower, bread and coffee: an elixir so intoxicating I feel I am breathing not underwater but underliqueur. I barely realize that I've abandoned my wine package in the front room. Part of me wants to go for it, but the circus of Eyeliner, Eyelinerless, and Square-Head calls me into a silent barbershop trio of sweat and flour and a better life.

Dimes of sweat push from beneath my skin for their first breaths of air since my waking. And as Square-Head, with a hairy right-angled wink, calls me, "Viene, viene qua," to a stainless steel surface coated in a flour-and-egg sheen, I know my hands will not leave unsatisfied.

Heart beats, forehead sweats, hands touch. And I touch a voluptuous mound of dough, yellow as a lemon, big as a cantaloupe. I swear I am grasping the culinary world's spirit animal, its orb, its crystal ball, and if I can somehow squint right, I can tell the future; I am only on the antipasto, sure, but with this circular soft immortal in my hands I have the power to see the dolce. In it is surely the answer to getting my father to eat a tomato, dealing with the militancy of the restaurant kitchen, learning how not to overwhelm a catered party with cumin.

Square-Head plucks at his apron strings, and I expect to hear a symphony in C. He pulls the white oiled cloth over his head and holds it to me: the uniform, the armor, the grissini-baton. Hands absorbing the dough's clairvoyant energy, I know he's going to say "Prego" before he does. And before he does, I wink at the dough and wonder if it knows where it is going, if it knows it is only in its adolescence — from flour to dough to oven to mouth. I breathe hard, yeasty air sweetening me like syrup all the way down.

"Prego," he says and unfurls the white apron like a shroud.

I loop the straps over my neck, lace the ties around my waist, and feel like a knight: impermeable, sword wielding, shining like Sandrone's soil. Square-Head pinches a section of dough and pulls it from its whole with a thumb and three fingers. His pinky, it seems, wants to remain innocent. Square-Head, shaking his head in ecstasy or showmanship, lets loose a cirrus cloud of flour from his hair and teaches me the art of grissini. It is in the hands. He rolls the smaller dough piece between both palms — there is no escape now — until a forearm-length snake dangles just millimeters above the floor. It is sheepish, a hesitant toe reaching to test cold, cold water. It knows it will eventually recoil. As Square-Head then takes the other end, looping the snake into a chest-high oval, shaking the dough into full extension, demonstrating its impossible elasticity, I wonder if I'm trapped in a Bible story. Surely, there is a first moral to be found in this kitchen and this dough. Surely, the twins mean something, don't they?

"Prego, prego," Square-Head says, rolling the raw grissini in cornmeal and setting it on an oiled baking sheet.

I pinch a piece of dough between my fingers, expect the ball to scream like a boiling lobster, but . . . nothing — no sound at all — just a soft easy give. Rolling the dough between my hands, palms going the way of oatmeal, Eyeliner sings "Sì," Eyelinerless echoes "Sì," and Square-Head undertones it all with an I'll-be-damned "Sì" of his own. Today, I am making grissini. Tomorrow, the world.

The hearth hushes us all with its awaiting whisper. I am lulled into a rhythm: pluck, roll, breathe, pluck, roll, breathe, wipe the forehead, smile at the siblings, pluck, roll, breathe. Soon I have made an entire tray of grissini, dusting the dozing dough strings with a grainy blanket of cornmeal. *Go to sleep, go to sleep, close your big egg-yolk eyes.*

Square-Head, knowing obviously when to take matters into his own hands, slides a wooden paddle under the baking sheet and carries it to the 600-degree oven. When it goes in, the fire leaps to embrace it and gives up, at the same time, a sheet of finished grissini to Square-Head's reaching paddle. The hot grissini (don't you dare call them breadsticks, Square-Head warns) lie cooling, coppered armbands unrolled, waiting patiently for the proper ceremony. Square-Head tells me that he and his sisters purvey their grissini to restaurants all over Italy, the remainder of Europe, the United States, and beyond. After ten minutes of baking he removes our tray from the oven. I am drenched in sweat, covered in cornmeal, gritty as a swimmer going straight from ocean to sand. And I do smell a slight sea-saltiness rising from the hot, hardening grissini. For what must be the ten-thousandth time since I've been in Italy I kiss my fingertips.

"Sale della terra," I say to them all, the twins now unwrapping brand new dough balls — the grissini mothers — from their plastic wraps, Square-Head nodding with his hands on his hips, admiring his craft.

Salt of the earth. When the twins lead me back to the front of the store, my hands full of grissini — some mine, some theirs — I feel as if I'm stepping not only into a meat locker but into the nineteenth century. Time and temperature unspool around me. I am shocked that three hours have passed since I entered the panetteria. I wonder if the crystal dough ball somehow transported me, somehow anticipated the synchronous "Ciaos" from the twins, the vicious wave good-bye from Square-Head in the kitchen.

The good old Il Bacco wine bag crinkles at my feet like a refugee. Somehow it too has slipped through space, found its way back to me. The front door's silver bells throw their light. When I open the door, those crazy, fantastic bells ring above me. The cobblestones are new and old all at once. The spell is breaking, but it's not broken. When I turn back into the store, before I allow the door to close, I am somehow not surprised to see that the twins' good-bye waves are not identical at all.

21

Raw Meat and Barry White

I can't believe it, but I'm hungry again. Dusk settling like purple ter-
rycloth over my shoulders, I once again find myself on that bridge
of raised earth between street and ditch, my path from Il Gioco to
Barolo, and, walking it for the second time today, I feel again like a
bar-regular. The paper bag, housing wine and grissini, grows heavy
in my left arm, so I switch it to my right. Then it grows heavy in my
right, so I switch it back to my left. Aaah . . .

The swell of the Cannubi hill defines itself across the street,
presses itself from the earth like a child trapped beneath a bedsheet.
On my right is the narrow stone path that leads between the trees to
I Cannubi restaurant. I've passed it so many times but have never
ventured in. The sign at the street, plain white with black letters,
grabs me by the shirt collar, communes with my paper bag and all
of the people behind it: Franco, the twins, Square-Head. This is a
small-town conspiracy of the highest order, and when the pull of the
unknown drags me along the white-stitched path, the known gives
me an encouraging shove from behind. Whose brother or sister am
I going to meet now?

The fruit trees hug the path to their chests, obese persimmons
dancing along my shoulders. Am I really up for this? It's been enough
of a day so far. Really. I should just go back to Il Gioco dell'Oca,
listen to Raffaella complain about Niccolo, eat some panini, and go
to bed, but the persimmons have other ideas. Like a cautionary fable
protecting its moral, if only for the time being, the round orange
fruits close off the path behind me and whisper, *forward, forward.*
The fright is wonderful, welcome, almost ticklish. I grasp my paper

bag like a broken sword. The leaves spread in a wake before me, the rich, damp foliage inflaming my nostrils into an oncoming sneeze. I try to hold it back, not wanting to give myself away, but . . . I let loose with a full-blown sneeze that nearly knocks out my wind with its violence, nearly drops the bag from my hand.

I see her spider tattoo before I see her face. It's on the back of her right hand, a fat-bodied, camouflage-green spider crawling along a web that covers wrist, knuckles, all five fingers. For a second I think she's going to throw it at me.

"Ciao, ciao. Salute," she says from far back in the throat in a rasp usually reserved for the dying.

I run my eyes from her hand to her face and am arrested by her worn beauty. She must be forty or so, long black paintbrush hair going gray at the tips. She has the face of an old house, the only one in the neighborhood that survived that fire all those years ago. Her skin is more olive pit than olive but leathery, somehow soft and impenetrable at the same time. There are those rare times when you can tell the texture of something just by looking at it. It works with a few species of cacti, and it works with this woman's face. She is dressed all in black, and her body seems assembled from the discarded broomsticks in some wicked witch's dumpster. When she wraps her fingers around a red velvet menu, I can almost hear her bones click. She is the most beautiful corpse I've ever seen.

"Ciao," I say. "Non ho una prenotazione. Ho bisogno di una tavola per uno."

"You do not need reservation for this night," she rasps, and my heart jumps hopscotch in my chest.

"You speak English," I say, stating the obvious aloud.

"A little," she says. "Your Italian sound very American."

My laugh is so dry it becomes a cough, and I sneeze again.

She leads me out the back end of the tree tunnel, the persimmons spreading themselves into an open outdoor courtyard with clay-potted plants spilling white flowers. Low, bass-driven music pumps like diesel from the speakers, rattles the tables' glassware. She seats me at the table closest to the restaurant's entrance. I peer inside to the yellow walls lined with wine bottles and sit in the wooden chair. As she sets the menu on the table a frenzied voice bellows from inside, "Loredana!"

I look to the right of the entrance and see two small open windows near the roof of the restaurant. They are lit cave-white, and from them I hear the banging of skillets, the chop of knife through vegetable, the simmering of stock, the opening and closing of an oven door, and the wild mating call, "Loredana!"

"Uno momento, Ercole!" she shouts to the windows.

In the kitchen lights I can see the shadow of someone shaking his head and probably throwing his hands in the air.

"The chef," Loredana says to me, "is a little crazy."

I laugh and, despite the crazy chef's insistence, we talk a bit. I tell her about Il Gioco dell'Oca and Sandrone, and she tells me that she knows Raffaella and Luciano.

Taking the unread menu from my hands, she says, "I bring you something nice."

She walks into the light of I Cannubi's interior, and I expect her to fade like a ghost. An inside realm of yellow-tinted walls and chandeliers, of pseudo-Mayan design. Only two other courtyard tables are occupied: an old man in square glasses and brown brimmed hat hunches over a demitasse cup of espresso; on the other side of him a young couple takes turns feeding each other spoonfuls of orange custard. I watch them and wonder what it would feel like to be fed in a courtyard like this. My eavesdropping is scored by I Cannubi's strange dance music, a shrill woman's voice struggling to be heard over the swollen bass, shrieking, in accented-English refrain, *I'm horny, I'm horny . . .* Where am I?

A muffled argument sneaks through the kitchen windows. The sky goes dark. By the time the music switches to Barry White, Loredana has brought me a 1990 Marchesi di Barolo.

"This is very good, uh, year. Very full of, uh, the mouth. You understand?"

"Sì. I think so," I say.

She pours my glass half-full. I bring it to my nose and am taken to a scene of which I've never been a part — not in this life, anyway. I imagine myself as a child thrown into a burlap sack that once held potatoes or onions or both. The smell assaults my nose, chases any further sneeze back into the recesses of my brain. I sip and the sack opens. I look to the sky and expect it to rain needles of rosemary. This wine is, indeed, full of the mouth.

"It is good," Loredana rasps, wiping her forehead with the spider side of her hand.

I swallow. The stars come out.

"Yes," I say. "Sì," I say again.

"Good. I tell Ercole. It is his selection, the wine. I tell him about you."

"The chef," I say.

"Yes," she says. "He is crazy, but he know the wines."

As she turns to go inside I am struck with the desire to have her back at the table. It's not loneliness per se, but I feel as if her presence supports my own, like a fourth table leg.

"Loredana," I call after her.

She twists around like a ribbon. "Yes?"

"Will you have a glass of wine with me?"

She smiles, reaches to some hidden shelf at the inside right of the entrance. I expect her to retrieve a brass jar containing her own soul, or her ashes. I expect to have a campfire story to tell. It's not a testament to her own death that she retrieves and holds out toward me but a tight and shiny red can of Coke. Her smile drops closer to her mouth.

"You drink Cannubi Barolo," she says, "I drink Coca-Cola."

With that she disappears into the restaurant, and I sip the wine without her, awaiting the first course. Barry White's voice pulls at the back of my neck like a shot of rum, and I hear the two voices dueling in the kitchen. Loredana and Ercole jab at one another with an array of sì's and no's. I sip the wine. The old man in the brimmed hat stands to leave, then loses his balance and falls into his chair again. He succeeds in his second attempt and tips his hat to me as he passes. His eyes are as wide and blue as a baby's.

Leaves rustling, persimmons dancing like light on water, the kitchen quiets just enough for me to hear Barry White croon, "Oohhhhh, yeaahh . . ."

For a while I sit and smell the herbs in the air, finger a white petal curling from a clay pot. I am about to doze off, about to drool, when Loredana's footsteps patter across I Cannubi's wooden floor. Stepping from in to out, she holds one plate in her hand, but the contents, like the grapes in Lodovico Borgogno's picture of his father, are obscured in the light. Hope running from my eyes, I look to her as a woman about to toss me an edible life raft. Strangely, the colors of the plate define themselves only in the dark of the outdoors. In the plate's center: jewels of rose stacked and folded over one another as if they were a napkin trick. At the plate's edge, scrambling for space: an inverted cone of gelled cream. At first it looks like a dessert.

"Carne cruda," Loredana announces from the great beyond, "with Parmigiano, uh, panna cotta, and the oil of tartufi bianchi."

As she sets the plate down with a dull bass thump, Barry White putters his lips, and I am attacked with the desire to lean in and kiss her spider. Instead, I bow my head and sniff Ercole's invention. The raw beef comes at me first with the caress of blood, then the soil-rich syrup of the white truffle oil, and, cutting it all, the honeyed Parmesan flan.

"Oh, Loredana," I say, hand on my heart, "this looks amazing."

"Yes," she says, "the chef is very good. Ercole, he is invited to, uh, uh, food exhibit in Hong Kong in March. They know of him there. Very famous in Asia."

I shake my head, barely find my fork with my fingers.

"Amazing," I say.

Here in this speck of a town, in this tiny, contained utopia, in this restaurant at the base of the Cannubi hill, in the middle — dare I say — of nowhere lies a chef who is big in Asia. How, from Barolo, Italy, does the word get out?

"Have dinner now," Loredana says, fingernails tracing through her hair, "then Ercole want to meet you. He and Sandrone have, uh . . . great respect."

Thinking of Sandrone, of his glasses, his hands, his suspenders, I pick up my fork. The weight of the world is in my fingers like a pencil. I reach for the plate, Barry White vocally beds yet another perfect woman, and Loredana, huntress-cum-waitress, stalks back into the restaurant.

My fork falls into the Parmesan flan like a penny into a pool, settles to the bottom, and, miraculously, reemerges coated in cream. Rolling the forkful of flan over the beef and swathing the bite in a paint-streak of white truffle oil, I hear the young couple at the other end of the courtyard moaning over a plate of sugar cubes soaked in a green liqueur. I bite as they bite, our flavors commingling, coupling. In this bite of carne cruda with Parmesan flan — this pinnacle of earth and animal — I am one step closer to my fellow humans and the notion of being alive. *Oh, baby* . . .

On my last bite of my first course the couple kisses with sugared and exhausted mouths. Come midnight, they will surely float off to the heavens. Ercole and Loredana are finally silent in the kitchen, the only argument being between what I imagine to be the caramelizing leeks and the shellfish stock. I wonder what Ercole looks like. I wonder where this couple is going back to, the woman in her long black skirt and white blouse ruffled at the wrists, the man in his red sport coat with cowhide elbow patches. Are these their special-occasion clothes? Will I ever see them again? Were we all only meant to share one wordless evening of tastes?

I stare at my empty plate, baring itself wide open to the sky, its ribcage exposed, and I wonder . . .

Alone in I Cannubi's courtyard, awaiting Ercole's arrival at my table, the air temperature drops so quickly, it's as if the floor has collapsed beneath it. I wonder: how crazy can this crazy chef really be? Crazy enough to create for me, for no good reason, a spontaneous menu above and beyond what was printed between the set red velvet covers — carne cruda and Parmesan flan, fresh lasagnette with porcini slivers, pork fillets in peach-muscat gastrique, veal fillets in rosemary sauce, persimmon panna cotta (the fruits plucked straight from this courtyard), chocolate soufflé, almond, peach, and chocolate tarts with hazelnut cream . . .

I don't know what to say. I don't know what to do except lean back in my chair, stare the stars into hiding, and lick the slick graininess from my teeth. I consider for a second never brushing them again, never eating again, letting myself go the way of Loredana. This courtyard begins to become as cold as my tent until a small pocket of air behind me, as if heated with a small but intense campfire, wraps the back of my neck.

I straighten without thought, my hands grip the table, and I turn to see the source of heat as a pea-sized glow of perforated orange light, winking in a desperate tango. It is the cherry of Ercole's cigarette, dangling ashen from his lips. His hands are on his hips, hands far too large for his arms, flaring from his wrists like the persimmons from their branches. He is barrel-chested and young — early thirties, maybe — and he has the face of that one small-town boy who has never left home but somehow knows everything about the world. He is plainly intense, eyes squinted, nose perplexed from countless childhood fights; he lifts his giant hands to the capped blades of Loredana's shoulders, mysteriously materializing directly in front of him. I am both comfortable and uneasy, as if sleeping in my own bed but with a brand-new blanket.

"This," Loredana says, "is Ercole. The chef. He speak no English."

His hand flits forward, swallows my own hand as if it were the head of a lamb.

"Come va?" he says.

His voice is like gunfire, each word a tin can, bullet-plucked from a picket-fence top. He could say the word *surreptitious* and it would be an exercise in cacophony.

"Bene, Ercole," I say. "Mille grazie per la cena."

"Ay, ay, è niente," he fires, wiping sweat from his forehead. "America, sì?" he continues, his curly grenade of a hairdo threatening to explode from his scalp.

He turns his face to the light of the restaurant, and I notice a large scar on his cheek. I think of Ivo and his Rottweilers.

"Sì," I say.

"Ah, ah," he shouts, drowning out the technomusic blaring from the speakers and kissing the air six quick times, "bellisima!"

Shivering, I search the air around Ercole for lightning bolts, the source of his heat, and see that Loredana has disappeared into the nebula again. Ercole opens and closes his right hand.

With three quick hand movements, each movement corresponding to a syllable of his speech, he says, "Bill Clinton."

His *i*'s are extended as double, no, triple *e*'s, his *o* is longer than his fingers, and the name comes out as *Beeell Cleeentone*.

"Sì," I say.

"Ah!" Ercole cackles like a warlock finally successful in spawning Armageddon.

A waterfall of Italian streams from his throat, and he ends it not with a period but with the phrase "Billy, Billy! Billy, Billy Clinton!"

As his laughter deteriorates into a cough he takes one final and enormous drag from his cigarette and flicks the filter like a fastball fifty feet across the courtyard. He exhales a bodyful of smoke and in it, appearing as the magician's beautiful assistant, is Loredana, holding three half-full snifters on a brown bar tray. Ercole turns to her and shoots her in Italian. She shoots back, her rasp somehow matching his fire, and then turns to me.

"He want me to move more fast than I do."

I shrug. I smile. Again: comfortable and uneasy.

"Ercole make this himself. A, uh, not wine, but, uh, thicker with dessert . . . uh . . ."

"A liqueur," I say.

"Sì, sì," Loredana rasps, and I feel like I've answered the bonus question and am now eligible for the really big money, "of hazelnut."

I look at the brown liquid, a log cabin in a glass.

"Does he make everything himself?" I ask.

"Yes," she says, "he teach himself everything. To cook everything. He is the only person in the kitchen."

She looks at Ercole with big eyes. I look at him too. His arms are folded, his gaze fixed on me. Loredana sets the three snifters on the table, and the two of them pull up chairs. The sight of Ercole sitting shocks me. It is as incongruous as a roadrunner taking a nap.

Ercole snatches a snifter in his fingers and raises it nearly to the persimmons.

"Billy, Billy!" he shouts, and we clink glasses.

The sip is like rolling the finest tobacco in the Dead Sea scrolls and smoking it. This inky hazelnut liqueur—the mad genius invention of this mad genius chef—is intoxicating and informative all at once. It teaches my taste buds new things: to open like flowers, then lie down and accept their fate. Loredana swallows first.

"He is, uh, an obsession with Bill Clinton. He love how he, uh, do everything."

Ercole begins rapping on Loredana's shoulder, and I expect her to break. He is asking her what she said. She tells him and he laughs, shooting a string of sì's — "Sì, sì, sì, sì" — from his throat like a clogged faucet trying to expel its water.

I sip again and then again, and soon, in the combination of Ercole's vocal rapids, Loredana's mist hovering over it all, and the sweet hazelnut running through me, I feel I am immersed in the most tepid and happy of the oceans. I feel preborn.

I try, to the best of my Italian ability, to tell Ercole my story—how I got here, the tent, the grapes, Raffaella, Sandrone . . .

Ercole throws his head back with the mention of each name. With *Raffaella* he runs his thumb over his scarred cheek to indicate her beauty; with *Sandrone* he palms the air as if searching for a hidden doorknob and mutters, "Sandrone . . . uva, uva, uva. Che è *uva* in inglese?"

"Uva," I say, "in inglese? Uva è *grape*."

"Grape?!" Ercole exclaims as if it's the most preposterous word he's heard.

"Sì," I say.

"Grape?" Ercole questions, then pauses, thinks the word over, and says, "Oh, come *grappa!*" He pauses again, thinks about grappa, then says, "Desidera grappa?"

"Oh, no," Loredana sighs, her spider-hand over her eyes. "He want to give you the grappa now. This is how his mind work."

"Sì, sì," Ercole says and springs from his chair.

Loredana and I watch the stars. He returns a minute later with tiny crystal grappa glasses and a tall bottle. As I learned the hard way in Sandrone's cantina, grappa is made from the grape mash — skins, branches, seeds, that leftover steaming junk that attacked me from his holding tank, sending the man himself into cheroot-rattling hysterics. Like certain cultures that use all parts of an animal after the hunt (the fat for lamp oil, the skins for clothes), the Italians use all parts of the grape. I have never sipped so much in my life, and I sip again; this sip of Nebbiolo grappa is the smoothest of its kind, running into my belly like silk soaked in kerosene. If the earth were a grape, this would be the taste of its core.

The three of us talk long into the night, drink deep into the bottle of grappa. We talk of Chicago, of Hong Kong, of cooking and eating and drinking, we talk of the upcoming Salone del Gusto. They tell me to return to I Cannubi tomorrow night to apprentice for an hour or two in Ercole's kitchen. I can't believe it, or I'm too drunk to believe it, and when he pours me yet another glass of grappa, Loredana now sleeping or pretending to sleep on the table, I have to wait until he averts his eyes and dump my entire glassful into one of the neighboring clay pots. I can't take any more. I am filled from belly to brain. I'm not even close to cold. Somehow I don't believe my grappa discard could have flown under Ercole's radar, but he doesn't let on; he just continues to stroke Loredana's hair, fanned over the entire tablecloth, muttering, "Mia moglie, mia moglie . . ." *My wife, my wife . . .*

When She Draws It, She Draws It

I wake with too much light in my eyes. The dark green of my tent walls should block out more of the sun. Last night's grappa is waxed to my lips, my mouth is dry, and, as I blink my way into the morning, the grapevines outside make shadow-puppets on the canvas. I dress and unzip the tent flaps; mosquito screen, then vinyl outer door. The day is cool, damp, rank with grapes and the upcoming I Cannubi apprenticeship. With yesterday comes residual headache. Today, though, I want to wash the grappa from my mouth with coffee.

The white stones of the driveway rush beneath my shoes. Adriana is busy hanging wet blankets from a clothesline to the left of Il Gioco's doorway. I'm not sure if I'm ready yet to speak, but Adriana will be my test. Her massive arms shudder with each clothespin-snap, as if her bones are also lines, supporting their own down blankets. Her eyes squint in effort. She is a hen about to lay a golden egg. She empties her palms of blanket, throws them to the early morning heavens like handfuls of confetti, and exclaims from the throat, "Aaaa!"

"Buon giorno, Adriana," I say, throat caked in chalk.

My voice, as if it is the sure sound that will make Adriana laugh, sends her into hysterics. She spits her laughter hard, like the hyena that swallowed the hen. I'm wearing my brown and white plaid pants, holes at both knees, and the thin navy fleece shirt that saw me through two Alaskan springs. Adriana, laughs disappearing down her throat with a large swallow of the early air, eyes me, my wardrobe, and three disapproving wrinkles appear between her eyes.

"Hai roba?" she asks not as a question but as a test.

She is a mother painting her child into a corner. I expect her at any moment to pull a washcloth from her pocket and clean my face. She wants to know if I have clothes for her to wash.

"No, no," I say and touch her shoulder.

My hand sinks into her as if between couch cushions. I can only handle so much generosity. I envision the pile of dirty clothes at the foot of my tent. Adriana narrows her eyes. She's about to wag her finger but stops herself and laughs again.

"Ciao, Adriana," I say, rounding her.

"Ah, ciao-ciao," she clucks and returns to her laundry.

She shakes a big wet blanket at the sky. It obliterates the sun like a sail.

Raffaella is in the kitchen drinking coffee from a red mug and reading *La Stampa,* the newspaper. She has the windblown look of having left the house earlier this morning, having lived a portion of her day while I've slept. She doesn't see me yet, hanging in the doorway like a marionette, and I'm not sure if I should wait for someone else to pull the strings. Her eyes are focused on her mug. She is staring at her own reflection in the coffee. On the stove behind her a saucepan releases its steam into the white light. I watch it hover, then spread over the ceiling. At the table Raffaella sips. Her newspaper crackles like fire. It's time. I open my mouth. I want to tell her about yesterday. I want to ask her about yesterday.

The *buon* of *buon giorno, Raffaella, come va?* about to swan-step from my tongue, Raffaella, without looking from her mug, shocks me with a soft, "Niccolo is so . . . hard sometimes."

I feel as if she's cut me off, though I haven't yet spoken a word. Is she even talking to me?

"So it was a hard day yesterday?" I try.

She looks at me with bathtub eyes. My arms go feathery. My head goes cardinal. I want to dive-bomb her face and take a drink.

"Yes. Always trouble," she says slowly. "Never have children."

I laugh, and she manages a smile, those parenthesis-wrinkles carving moons beside her lips.

"Sit already," she says, and for the first time I can hear Adriana in her voice.

I comply, and we eat breakfast together. The crumbs of Adriana's apple cake soak the last of my moisture. The cake is good, but my mouth is not. I need to take a swallow of coffee to chase each bite down. I tell her of yesterday, the words *Franco, grissini, Ercole, Loredana* hovering in the air with the steam.

"Wonderful," Raffaella mutters throughout. "And today? What today?"

"I don't know yet," I say. "Sandrone hasn't yet summoned me back. I think I may hike over to another town."

"You have seen La Morra?" Raffaella asks.

"Yeah," I say, picturing the orange lights of the Cantina Comunale blinking out for the night.

"Then you must go to Monforte," she says. "I think it is one of the best."

The name of the town tumbles from her lips, gathers weight in the air. She proceeds to draw me a trail map in black ink. When she draws it, she draws it on the back of a Salone del Gusto brochure. Somehow I know, in this kitchen, in this white light and oven-steam dancing, that this map to Monforte will, decades from now, find its way into my coffin.

Stomach lined, armed with Raffaella's request to tell her about my upcoming I Cannubi apprenticeship, I step from Il Gioco and once again cross the stones. Adriana is nowhere to be seen, but her blankets still hang heavy from their lines like a legacy. When I unzip my tent, I find that my entire pile of dirty clothes is missing.

The Unfinished

The air is so crisp you can break it like a cracker. The Alps push from the Piedmont haze, and I open my arms to them. Adriana's day-old apple cake still sits crosswise on my teeth like concrete that refuses to dry. The vineyards are everywhere, pitching me over slopes less drastic but more numerous than those on the way to La Morra. The occasional residence asserts itself, pushing its washed-out white stone, cracked orange roof, rusted black gate from between the rows and then, just as quickly, disappears. I feel I am somehow being stalked by structure and, as always, barely escaping with my life.

Persimmon trees tower above the rows but hang still today, keeping their secrets. Somewhere around a curve, behind a slew of vineyards, Sandrone is commanding his crew, Ivo and company are loading the crates onto flatbeds, Ercole is washing leeks for a stock, Raffaella is smoothing sheets for the day's guests, raw grissini is getting its cornmeal dust, wine is being sold, the Borgognos are harboring their quiet, cross-eyed animosity, and Adriana is doing my laundry. But here, now, curving left around a profiled slope, Monforte pokes its rose-colored head from a distant hillside like a turtle testing for rain. Finding none, finding only clarity and windlessness, it remains, pushing shopfront after shopfront, terrace after terrace up from the dirt and into the air.

It is a vertical town, even more so than La Morra, stacked, switchbacked, and as the trail descends at my feet, Monforte disappears once again behind a swell of green earth. I stop. No sound. No wind. I drop my hands to my sides. The air cleans my mouth of breakfast. But there is no wind.

If there is no wind, why do I hear the grapevines rustling on the downslope? To the right the crops gather together like clouds. The vineyard is imploding in front of me, closing its leaves into a fist, a concentrated heart of green. I expect Nebbiolo grape juice to run like blood over my shoes. I expect it to open itself into a first beat. And when it does, leaves deafening as wings, the vineyard spreads its aorta wide open and belches at my feet not blood, not love but two hunchbacked old men.

They are more wrinkled than wrinkled. They are overwrinkled, über-wrinkled, sun-dried as a tomato. The liquid was cooked from their skin long ago. Will the circus of Italy never end? What next? Will I look to the sky and see a helmeted brown bear riding a unicycle along a tightrope? The men's noses come at me first, riding parallel in the air. They shake the vineyard leaves from their white hair, loose rooster necks shuddering. Their eyes find me, laser blue, and two steady smiles spread like jam across their faces.

"Ciao," the man on the left sings in a surprising and pinched soprano.

His voice reaches like an unoiled hinge: rusted, stiff, but still functioning.

"Ciao, ciao," I say.

He squints at me, studying the accent that laces my "Ciaos."

"Americano?" he asks.

"Sì," I say, smiling, nodding.

"Mi chiamo Giuseppe," he continues, fanning the hinge open, closed, open, closed. "Questo è mio fratello Renato."

Giuseppe holds a hand at his thick throat and covers his mouth, indicating that Renato cannot speak. Both men push their hands to me, and I shake them, each one heavier than it looks, grittier than granite. Renato takes a step back toward the vineyard that, not two minutes ago, birthed him onto this trail. His hands reach for his hips and find them, and, staring at the snarl of grapes, the wrinkles run from his face. He is so placid, I'm not sure if he can't talk or if he just doesn't need to. The pride in his newly smoothed face tells me that this vineyard belongs to him, or to both of them. But I have to ask.

"Queste uve . . ." I say, struggling with my Italian this morning, "le tue?"

"Oh, sì, sì." Giuseppe sings so much like Farinelli I expect his gray hair to tie itself into two waist-length castrato braids.

Renato looks from the grapes to me. His wrinkles are back. He kisses his fingertips and holds his hands to the sky. The gesture is saturated in so much drama and summoning power that I expect the weather to change at once.

"Desidera Barolo?" Giuseppe enunciates slowly, chasing the clouds away.

I should be surprised, but I'm not. Am I becoming desensitized to charity and luck? I should be chastised for this, but instead a sigh springs from my stomach to my throat. It is the sigh of the poolside lawn chair, of sipping lemonade through a straw. I shrug. I look toward Monforte. It remains in hiding behind the hillside. I wonder if it is still there. Barolo, Monforte, Barolo, Monforte? Barolo.

"Sì," I say.

Their cantina is tiny. If Sandrone's cantina is the penthouse, theirs is the broom closet. It is more ancient than their faces; it must be the entity that spawned these two gentlemen — the Alessandria brothers, as indicated by a wooden hand-carved sign over the cantina's doorway: Fratelli Alessandria. Indeed, the entire cantina seems constructed of wood and sawdust, a relic, a holdover, an unsafe roller coaster from three generations past. The cantina is rickety and dim. A single brown lightbulb shines as if from the bottom of a coffeepot. The whole place, including the brothers themselves, seems in the process of fermenting.

Medieval wheelbarrows line the walls, and I expect to see them full of bodies, crushed by catapult and plague, ruined by arrows and hot tar. Instead, they offer in both smell and sight the organ-meat tangle of flattened grapes, skins, branches. The brothers parade along the wheelbarrows, and Renato holds his hand to the wall behind me. I turn and am stunned to see steel. In the muddy, reflected light three tanks stand equipped not with scaffolding, as in Sandrone's cantina, but with makeshift ladders, crooked rungs, wooden to be sure. Giuseppe begins to pull thin scarf-strings of Italian from his throat, telling me about their business, how winemaking has been in their family for centuries. Renato punctuates Giuseppe not with voice but with gesture, often karate chopping upward to either dispute or emphasize his brother's statements. Only one is speaking, but these brothers interrupt each other like Abbott and Costello. They are *choreographed*.

Renato reaches for the ladder in the middle. His ancient knees gong against the steel as he fills three wineglasses. Renato hands first to Giuseppe, then to me. In this light the wine is black. Giuseppe offers his glass to the ceiling shadows. I hold mine to my nose and: hay, sawdust, slaughter; then: truffle, blackberry, pine; fruitcake baked in a coffin. Even here, even in the dungeons of Italy, elegance is fostered by four seventy-year-old hands. Giuseppe mutters his toast, some private prayer only Renato can understand.

"Bravo," I say and clink glasses with the brothers.

I sip and am immediately struck on the tongue by a sense of the unfinished. This wine seems to be in the process of coalescing, the elements intermingling for the first time. My mouth goes yeasty and robust, sticky almost with fat and marrow, oxtail and liver. Then, on the greasy swallow, the wine inexplicably sparkles like Champagne (an element I haven't yet experienced with a Barolo), leaves the mouth cleaned and ready for another sip.

Another sip leads to another sip and then another, the dark privacy of the cantina now bright enough, the outdoors fading into a morning dream, disappearing like Monforte behind a hillside. I sip the last of my third glass, and Renato, obviously trained to balk at empty crystal, grabs it from my hand and fills it a fourth time. The more he drinks, the more comfortable he seems on the ladders. He hands me my glass and climbs down quickly. He's becoming younger with each sip. I wonder if, after ten glasses, he will get his voice back. We toast again to Giuseppe's mystery prayer. We talk of Il Gioco dell'Oca and Sandrone. In midsip Giuseppe, dribbling wine from the corners of his mouth, invites me to stay at their house. He scowls at the idea of sleeping in a tent.

"No, no," I laugh. "Va bene, va bene."

Soon this glass has been vanquished like the others. The thought of the outdoors and Monforte returns. I buy a bottle of Barolo from the Alessandrias; Renato drops it into a paper bag, and they walk me to the front of the cantina. Giuseppe lays a hand on my left shoulder, Renato on the right. They are pressing a story into me that won't find its words until later. They say "Ciao" with their eyes.

The outside cool plays in my hair. I turn back to the cantina and see the brothers' faces poking like trolls from the doorway, which itself seems disguised in the pattern of a giant tree trunk. When the door closes, the world becomes relatively real again, the fable receding into the vineyards behind me. The air smells only of early afternoon, and, rolling my shoulders toward my cars, I am struck with the desire for words in any form.

Taking small steps toward Monforte, I pull the bottle of Barolo from the paper bag in the hope of simply reading the words *Fratelli Alessandria*. I am greeted instead with the final hammering of the brothers' rustic operation. An unusual joy expands from my chest to my ribs. Monforte lifts itself once again from behind the hillside and reflects the sun from its windowpanes to the bottle in my hands, which reclines in a lawn chair of its own: dusty, purple, entirely unlabeled.

24

Trust the Pear

The more I walk, the farther away this vertical village seems to be. Monforte is a bully, teasing, taunting, and the paper bag in my arms, my Alessandria baby, is beginning to cry. Monforte disappears just when it should show itself, shows itself just when I'm ready to give up. But I go on and on, past vineyards and fruit trees: plum, pear, persimmon — the best the *p*'s have to offer. The afternoon has overstayed its welcome, the light barely waning from white to yellow. Surely it should be evening by now. Surely I am destined to walk this path forever.

Monforte d'Alba is second only to La Morra in the total acreage of Nebbiolo-producing vineyards, so this strenuous walk should be worth it. Situated at the southern boundary of the Langhe, Monforte takes its historically strategic name from the Latin: *mons* (hill) and *fortis* (strong). Monforte was once, indeed, a "strong hill" due to its erection of a modest defensive fortress during ancient Roman times. A constant source of conflict between the village lords and the township of Alba, Monforte was forced to wear its fortress on its sleeve.

Italian legend dictates that in 1213 Saint Francis stopped over in Cairo, Italy, on his way to Spain. While there, he came upon Cairo feudal Lord Ottone and cured his deaf-mute daughter. This action was obviously well received, and apparently Saint Francis amassed a small caravan of amorous Cairese. Perhaps it was in this "amorous" fashion that Italy was later home to many marquises of Cairo. Monforte was no exception.

Resting at 480 meters above sea level and housing approximately two thousand residents, Monforte still boasts traces of the original fourteenth-century "old houses" from the era of the Marquis Scarampi del Cairo. A sudden warm breeze whips through the vineyards and washes over the trail, carrying with it something ancient and, perhaps, Egyptian. The marquis's pinky ring. The dream of the pyramids. This breeze is followed by one considerably colder.

The trail branches three ways before me like a chicken foot. I'm afraid to leave the leg. Fingers untangling from themselves, from the paper bag bottle-sweat of an eternity of carrying, I fish my hand into my pocket. The wine bottle bucks, seems to double its weight, and I swear I can hear Prometheus whisper *I told you so* from the great Alpine beyond. I stop walking. Pull Raffaella's map from my pants. Set the moaning bottle at my feet. Unfold the paper, the smiling Salone del Gusto logo winking yellow, red, green in the sun. A lone pear drops from a tree and lands brown onto the path's middle fork.

I'm not quite prepared to put my faith in such a sign, and I proceed to shake Raffaella's map from its slumber. Maybe it was sweat, maybe friction, but the black ink of her directions to Monforte has bled into two long-limbed amoebas locked into an illicit, molecular, and illegible embrace. The air shoots through me like an arrow. I refold the map and put it back into my pocket. I am going to have to trust the pear.

Fetching my wine bottle, I continue toward the three trail-forks. The left fork descends into a dark tree tunnel, the trail carpeted with leaves either dead or dying. The fork to the right swings abruptly downward between two vineyard rows, the surface dirty, bony, full of exposed rocks — the bodies of the half-decomposed trying for air. The center path goes up. It twists through some trees, and I swear I can see blue sky at its crest. I step over the pear and ascend.

The fruit in here is thick, as if ripening in the bottom of a well, and the grapevines drop away, give rise to apple, wild plum, peach, apricot. I consider picking a snack but fear tripping an alarm, biblical, electric, or otherwise. The path narrows, and I have to hold my elbows in to fit through. I look ahead. The sky expands its gut.

Sweat runs from my armpits over my ribs, drips forward into my hands, wetting the paper bag. The trail becomes loose soil, falling downhill with each step, shedding its skin.

The fruit trees unfold themselves from the trailsides, and I come to the mountain's crest. I blink the cooling sweat from my eyes. The sun threatens to throw me back downhill. A white mist hovers, and for a second I think I am standing in a low cloud. Heart punching its way through my chest, I turn from the sky to see my shoes resting on the gleaming white gravel of a primitive road. The winds kicks white dust over my head, and I squint to see narrow tire tracks, possibly made this morning, stretched along the road, just off-center. Monforte is nowhere to be seen.

I look left. I look right. The road trails off into the greenery on both sides. There are no signs of life. Not a single house is in view. This must be the secret path out of Eden. Somewhere else even God is surprised. The air temperature suddenly drops, and I shudder. The sweat beads beneath my shirt scurry like a swarm of insects for a roof of skin to hide under. I have to bite my tongue to keep from running.

This is Italy, I tell myself. *Everything is fine, this is Italy.*

Hopelessly lost and for no good reason, I turn left. The gravel dips and ascends, dips and ascends as if built over water, and the sky fluctuates with it, alternately squinting and bugging out its blue. I struggle to breathe, the white dust filling my mouth, crunching in my teeth. My tongue now longs for Adriana's day-old apple cake, sings a muscular rendition of "Don't Know What You Got till It's Gone" to my mouth-roof. Alps flank the entire scene like security guards. I feel subatomic. The sky bobs like a lure I know I shouldn't fish for, but for some reason, heart now audible, I keep swimming. I meditate on melon gelato and mineral water and close my eyes. The sun shadows flap faster.

Not a microwave within a hundred miles, I bet. Exhaling, I open my eyes and see, about a hundred yards up the road, a car idling at the edge of the gravel, red taillights burning. I blink. I rub my eyes, the paper bag crinkling in protest and disbelief. I look again. The car is still there. It is about to teeter off the side of the road, tumble end over end into the vineyards. I stop walking. Turn around and see no one, nothing but the path I have already walked. The temperature drops another degree.

I step once, and the car's color defines itself as faded blue. The taillights spew their red. The air smells like snow. The car pitches in my vision. I'm fifty yards from it, then forty, then thirty. Riding the wind, a faint, dusty music slips from the open driver's side window. The music's bass may very well be the wind's driving force; perhaps this is the secret control room where weather is made. A human shadow rests in the driver's seat, but I can't tell whether it's big or small, male or female. I can't tell if this person wants to be discovered.

The music is hot and lazy. I walk and make it out to be Elvis's "Blue Moon." His voice croons like a gander to its lover. My heart flaps south for an early winter. The car is right next to me. I clear my throat to alert the figure to my presence. No response. My heart on vacation, I have nothing to lose. I step to the window. The paper bag dies in its sleep.

The man is staring straight ahead through a pair of sunglasses, low on his nose, lenses so small they barely cover his eyes. His gray hair holds tightly to his head. His forehead is run through with wrinkles. His mouth is neutral and serious. His white tank top doesn't quite cover his breasts, and I see them spill from beneath the cloth like played-out catcher's mitts. His eyebrows reach for his eyeballs. "Blue Moon," as if an interrogation lamp, fills the air between us. I don't know if he sees me. I'm about to clear my throat again when his eyes snap away to the passenger seat. He stares at something on the floorboards. He seems on the verge of a killing spree. Maybe I caught him at a bad time. The click of "Blue Moon's" drums, like clickings of the tongue, rise slow, periodic from the open window. I am parched and washed out. I could be anywhere — someplace with cacti.

"Scusi," I force out. "Scusi, signore."

He jerks his gaze from the passenger seat and takes a deep breath.

He needs to calm himself down. As he turns toward me I watch his eyebrows rise with the music as if yanked upward by bass strings. His eyes, green as the vineyards, stretch over his sunglasses. He's looking right at me, drowning in an ocean of "Blue Moon." He says nothing, so I have to speak again.

I point along the road in the direction I have been walking and ask, "Barolo?"

He doesn't blink, the evil green eyes still casting their spell, cinematic, trapped on film — there must be a voice-over explaining this scene and this man to some audience, perhaps this man's own internal monologue, but I can't hear it. I look around for help, strain to hear the warnings of the audience, see nothing but the blank white stitch of road in both directions, hear nothing but "Blue Moon" and wind. I wonder if I will see Il Gioco dell'Oca again. I wonder who will be the one to contact my family. I readjust the wine bottle in my hand, hold it by its neck just in case. The man looks down at my bottle, then up at my eyes.

Then, in a voice so deep it seems to come from his shoes, in a voice that sounds prerecorded, he says, just over the music, "Barolo."

He raises one hand from the steering wheel and points forward. His finger is long, ringed in turquoise and silver.

"Grazie," I say, delirious. "Mille grazie."

The wine bag reclines like a rubber chicken in my arms. The man nods slowly in perfect tune with the music, and I step away from the car. I know I have tested something dangerous and, in its dry, sun-bleached, murderous calm, escaped. I continue walking, the music fading behind me, until I can't see the car at all, descending finally into an array of orange-roofed houses and weeds and flowers. The temperature rebounds, and my heart returns home with an even tan. Barolo's centro, about a mile away, pokes its nose into the air, and I know that when I get there a melon gelato and a bottle of water are going to join me.

I walk. I exhale more than I inhale. I'm starting to get hungry for pear. Somewhere, deep in its hiding place, Monforte d'Alba narrows its eyes.

25

Italian Butcher Shop Blues

Since Barolo's sole gelateria is closed during siesta, my cravings invariably stray to meat. The macelleria, thankfully, is open.

I step toward the counter, the butcher hidden from view in the back room behind the meat case. I hear the sound of a handsaw. I look to the walls, mostly blank save for a poster of a bikini-clad woman holding a porterhouse in the air. The poster is signed in silver ink by "Valentina" and addressed, oddly enough, to "Franco." This town is drowning in Borgognos, Francescos, Francos.

Next to Valentina, encased in a black frame, is a picture of Barolo's castle with a man-shaped shadow clinging to its east wall. I step closer and see that the man, like a comic book superhero, is adhered to the ancient orange stone at least fifty feet off the ground. The man is facing the camera, sun in his eyes. His head is enormous, too big for his body, as if he's been pieced together by Barolo's resident mad scientist. A thick black mustache, curving over the sides of his mouth, is spread nearly horizontal in the force of his grin. He's dressed in rock-climbing gear, leg muscles bursting in effort, his hands gripping a strange and bulbous rope. I step even closer to the picture, my nose nearly pasted to the wall, my breath fogging the frame's glass, and see that this man is rappelling down the facade of the Castello di Barolo on a fifty-foot string of salami.

Before I can laugh, before I can even exhale, I hear the sound of thick flesh behind me spreading into a massive smile. I turn. It is, of course, the man in the picture, Franco the Butcher, his mustache crawling over his face like a caterpillar on steroids. He wears brown-framed glasses that stretch from his eyebrows to his upper lip, from his black sideburns to the bridge of his boxer's nose. A billow of black hair shoots geyserwise from his head, calling to the fluorescent lights. His hands, strong enough to lift me by the top of my head, are streaked with blood. And yet — I never thought I'd describe someone like this — Franco the Butcher is *jolly*.

"Ciao," I say. "Franco?"

"Sì, sì, Franco," he replies in a quiet, gentle voice, a voice as hairy as he is. He rubs his hands together as if compressing the air into a pancake.

"Queste carne," I say, running my hand over the expanse of display case, "è bellisima."

"Grazie," Franco says, truly touched by the compliment to his meats.

I watch as he rounds the counter, kicking sawdust from his shoes, and joins the scales, knives, and cleavers on the back wall. I examine his wares, salamis of all kinds: white salamis, red ones, pink ones, purple; salamis that nearly stray to black; duck salami, donkey salami, Barolo salami, truffle; salami as long as my legs, salami as short as my thumb; and there, twisted into cylinders as thick as my forearm, salami di cinghiale. Wild boar. Wild boar salami. I repeat the word in my head like a cured and fatty mantra: "Salami, salami, salami, salami . . ." until I descend into a cow-pig meditation. I wonder which meat held him to the walls of Barolo's castle. I wonder if he celebrated his climb by eating his equipment. I smile and he sees it, his hands now on his hips, his white apron smeared with blood and fat.

"Americano?" Franco slurs.

"Sì, americano," I say. "Ma adesso, in questa macelleria, sono italiano."

Franco laughs at my wish to be Italian, then sighs, turns abruptly left, waves to me, and utters, "Viene, viene qua."

He leads me away from the salami display, and I watch reluctantly over my shoulder as these lovely jeweled life vests float farther and farther away. Franco stops in front of the fresh meats: tenderloins, strips, porterhouses, sausages, pork chops, whole chickens, whole ducks, feet intact and orange, webbed and clinical in the light, pigs' feet, pigs' ears, pigs' blood, veal chops, veal scallops, headcheese, and sweetbreads. And tripe, beautiful white tripe spread wide in its container like a Chinese fan, trippa, reclining like the aurora borealis on its lunch break. Franco reaches for the tripe with an ungloved finger. It yields like a lover to his touch. The tripe, for lack of a better word, is *kissable*.

I feel my feet slowly spinning across that high school dance floor, slowly building a tango confidence to ask the beckoning girl out for a cup of coffee.

"Ti piace trippa?" Franco asks.

I shrug. I've never had it before. But how can I not like tripe?

"Sì," I say.

"Ah," Franco smiles, "serio."

"Sì," I nod, "serio," and I feel more substantial for saying so. I feel like I could knock down buildings with my bare hands. I feel like I could keep up with Franco the Butcher.

He lifts the tripe from its tray, and, like delicate lingerie, it unravels in the air. I want to rub its texture between my fingers. I want to try it on for size. I imagine taking a few pieces home to Il Gioco dell'Oca's kitchen, asking Raffaella for preparation advice, and cooking a tripe dinner with her: soup, casserole, napoleon, whichever. I watch as Franco cuts a small piece the size of a finger joint. He holds the white gem to the light.

"Ah, trippa," he says and hands me the piece.

Amazing, I think, *amazing that he sensed my desire to experience its texture.*

The tripe coin is soft and perforated, rich and heady like a chunk of Styrofoam soaked in black tea. I, like Franco, hold it to the light and can almost see through it. I think I'm seeing ghosts. I think I can see my family back in Chicago. They're all still sitting in rush-hour traffic, car radios blaring classic rock. I allow them all to return home safe, then lower the tripe to the counter to give it back to Franco.

"No, no," he says, holding his bloody but innocent palms at me, "prego."

"Che?" I ask, not quite understanding.

"Sì, sì, prego," he offers again.

I'm confused. I think he wants me to keep the tripe. I'm not sure what to do with such a small piece. I reach to put it into my pocket; possibly I'll play with it like a rubber stress ball on the way back to Il Gioco.

"No, no," Franco says, and I raise the tripe again from my pocket to the counter, "prego."

I look at him and shrug. I shake my head. Somewhere behind me, Valentina in her golden bikini is comfortably holding her porterhouse. Franco opens his mouth. For a second I think he's going to take a bite out of me. I lean back, and he points to the tripe, then points to his mouth, and again says, "Prego."

I get it now, but that doesn't mean I believe it. He wants me to eat the tripe.

"Crudo?" I say.

"Sì," Franco says.

He wants me to eat the tripe raw.

What kind of culinary hazing is this? Why? Why? Don't get me wrong, I have nothing against the pig stomach, but the raw ingesting of such items sends my own organs into disarray; my once hungry stomach now closes in on itself like a fist. My mouth goes dry. I'm having trouble swallowing.

"Prego," Franco says again, and I feel there's no way around this.

My stomach recoils deeper into my ribs, and I want to cry. I hold the tripe to the light again, and it goes from beautiful to revolting in no time flat. Raw tripe, if it's going to be cooked, is one thing, but raw tripe that wants to stay raw is another.

I look at Franco. His eyes are wide, his cheeks are glowing red. Jolly never looked so evil. I stare at the tripe, wriggling in the toddler laughter of my little sister whenever I got into trouble with my parents. I look to Franco. I look for a way out. The fluorescents burn into me like a spotlight. The audience is waiting; there's no turning back now. After all, I told Franco I was "serious."

I close my eyes and bring my fingers to my mouth.

I smell it before it hits my tongue: dust, metal, morning saliva, bathroom tile, campfire. It squirms in my mouth like a goldfish fighting for its life, a miniature skinned bronco bucking against my teeth, surely stirring a cowboy-shaped splatter from my stomach.

Hold on, I think as the taste of pure gut struggles to pass over my taste buds. *Hold on.* I don't dare bite into it, don't dare explode the taste of unmentionable pig over my tongue.

So I swallow it whole, think of oysters, hold my breath, and wait.

"Bravo," Franco claps and laughs in descending octaves.

A sweat breaks from my forehead. I gag audibly but keep it down.

Opening my mouth to exhale, I know I have passed a hideous test and am surprised to find that the taste, if not the memory, has already faded. I rode the bull and returned a little trampled but ungored.

Franco pulls a necklace of wild boar salami from the wall and hands it to me as my reward, laughing all the way. I can't believe I'm going to thank this man.

"Grazie," I say.

All Franco does is laugh.

As I turn to leave the macelleria, paper bag shifting in my arms, Franco the Butcher raises a bloody, tight-fingered hand into the air and, smiling his biggest smile of the day, dangles another slice of tripe into the light.

"Domani," he says, pointing to the horrendous thing.

I shake my head. I wave.

Tomorrow, I think, opening the door to the street. *Tomorrow I'm not coming anywhere* near *this place.*

26

Instructions of Ercole

I Cannubi presses its light upward, stifled only by a haze of cigarette smoke, draping itself over the outdoor patio. Wild boar salami tumbling end over end in my belly, I examine tonight's diners. At my old table, hugging the clay-potted plants, are two gentlemen, one visibly older than the other, their legs hidden in the netherworld of dinner table and tablecloth. An array of young couples expands like a tornado from my old table to the edges of the patio, laughing, smoking, tasting Ercole's creations. A few stars make a final plea for attention before the patio, as if in a communal exhale, releases a storm of Italian cigarette smoke into the air, a signal to the rest of the world: *all is well, all is well . . .*

A performance well into its second act bursts from the roof-high kitchen windows. Pans clatter, pots simmer, wooden spoons dip into sauces, then raise themselves to Ercole's silent lips for scrutiny. I can't wait to see what the kitchen looks like. As if on eight legs, Loredana crawls across the floor, roving among the interior tables, her antennae reaching for the patio. She sees me. A quiet smile sidesteps over her face as her eyes return to the tables, her raspy Italian tracing the air, checking to see if everyone is satisfied. She's dressed tonight in an elegant black ankle-length skirt and white buttoned blouse. She has pushed a red rose into her hair above her left ear. *A gift from Ercole?* I wonder. Underscoring her voice is an Italian dance remix of "Perhaps, Perhaps, Perhaps." Loredana approaches and slides a snifter of Vecchia Romagna into my hand.

"Sit there," she says in a voice that hasn't been dusted in a decade, pointing to the patio's only open table. "You eat something first."

Then she is gone, having fallen off the earth to report back to the president of purgatory. But the afterimage of her spider tattoo remains, and I follow it to the small white-clothed table at the patio's corner. I am directly behind my old table, listening to the two men, the older one shaking a nub of a finger at the younger one. The younger man, though well into his forties, seems about to cry like a baby. He is dressed, I can now see, completely in black leather: motorcycle boots, pants, zipped-up jacket throwing the silver of its clasps to the stars. He is clearly a fallen angel who wants to return home.

The older man, gray hair rippling like a spit-in rain puddle, shakes his fists into the air, pink button-down shirt vibrating, calling to the Devil himself. Their plates are cloaked in rabbit. They have already gone through three different bottles of wine, displayed empty at their table's center. Not understanding why I'm suddenly competitive, I believe I have some catching up to do. I raise the snifter to my lips. The brown liquid sloshes in the glass, and it—the Vecchia Romagna—smells of the Italian Empire in its heyday: rich, decadent, bloodthirsty, as yet unaware of its impending fall. And fall it does, over my lips in a waterspout of wood and orange rind, soil and sparks.

Vecchia Romagna, the Italian version of Cognac, is currently the most commercially successful spirit in the country. In the thirteenth century Italy began to distill its own brandy, and in 1939, after years of technical refining, the Jean Bouton Distillery introduced Vecchia Romagna to the world. Distilled in "swan-neck" copper stills (used also by makers of French Cognacs), the brandy was created from a secret and highly coveted recipe once served solely in the Medici court.

My mouth glows with this Medici secret, contributes its own boozy smoke to the ceiling of cigarette. The haze ignites in the patio lantern light, dances over the bowed heads of I Cannubi's fortunate diners. Loredana appears tableside with two Champagne flutes. She sets them on the table, clearing the now-empty snifter.

"Drink both," she says.

I put my hand to my forehead.

"Shouldn't I be . . . somewhat . . . clearheaded for my apprenticeship?" I ask her.

"No," she answers, the rose winking from her hair. "Drink both. It is instructions of Ercole."

I exhale. She runs her fingers over my back. She once again fades away. I take the first glass quickly, plucking the Champagne from its flute like a feather from a chicken. It goes down easy, with a pop and very little flapping. At the patio table farthest from the kitchen a middle-aged woman in a blue-sequined evening gown tosses a blanket-sized Italian flag into the air. The red, white, and green unravel in the night, pushing the smoke aside, and poke a breathe-hole for the stars. The lantern light catches the flag, coats the *tricolore* in orange before it sucks in its middle and descends again into the woman's long-fingered hand. The patio's far half applauds as one, and she curtsies, takes a shot of some mystery orange liqueur, and sits back down. Her male companion is red-faced with laughter.

By the time I finish my second glass of Champagne I feel injected with hydrogen. Surely, I am watching this patio scene from above, this thimble of diners tucked into one seam of this vineyard quilt, their noise and reveling of consequence only to themselves. This tiny civilization of pleasure — how I wish to descend and rejoin them, anchor my Champagned stomach with a bite or two of solid food. I wonder if anyone will catch me.

As if on cue, Loredana steps from the restaurant with a single plate in hand and sets it on my table. I look down, wondering if it's the rabbit. Loredana looks up, finds me hovering in the nebula. Her hand reaches through the haze, opening like a snake's mouth. She closes her poison over my shirt collar, pulls me as easily as a balloon from a ceiling, into my chair. She sits me up.

"Risotto of the, uh, zucchini," Loredana says, barely breaking a whisper, gesturing to the plate. "Then to the kitchen."

She sets a glass of hardly red wine on the table, mutters "Freisa," and is gone.

A staff meal. A staff meal in Italy. The Freisa shifts in the glass like juiced violets. The risotto oozes cream and Parmigiano-Reggiano, releases a pearl firework of starch with each bite. My mouth goes pasty and full as if my tongue is filling with blood. Only then does the zucchini assert itself, tempering the rich with the fresh, a light planty crispiness that has the same effect as the Champagne. Every time the zucchini threatens to lift me into the air, the risotto is the hand that pulls me back down. My stomach relaxes, and I feel the olive hand of Loredana press against my back.

"It is good?" she slurs.

"Oh, yes," I say.

"You are ready for the cooking?"

I exhale. My heart leaps like the rabbit I never ate. I stand up on swaying legs.

"I am," I manage.

"Follow," she says.

And I do, into the bright white light of the restaurant's interior. She leads me curving right around a wine cabinet, and then I see it. It's straight ahead of me. The swinging door of the kitchen. Behind its one square window, Ercole's head bobs. I can sense another me still sitting at the patio table, ordering another glass of wine, then dessert. I can see that me finishing his plate (from here it looks like panna cotta), paying his bill, and returning to Il Gioco dell'Oca. He has an espresso with Raffaella, then returns to his tent and falls asleep before he means to. Dreams of a salt waterfall, colonial Big Macs, radio DJs in lingerie, a rock, an island . . .

But here I stand like a soldier about to cross the line into Ercole's kitchen. Loredana smiles and reaches for the door. For this me there will be no sleep. For this me the dream is wide awake.

The kitchen door swings open like a sweater-vest: comfortable, heavy, dated. I am stepping into the cockpit of a Roman orgy, all slack mouths and extremities and grapes, the blur of Ercole's self-propelled storm, his clouds knitting together at the kitchen ceiling. One moment he is whisking a saucepan on the range, another moment he is unstringing a rope of sausages and swinging them lasso-wise into a skillet-stockpot combo. My heart scampers across my chest like a mouse on a wooden floor when he looks up at me, blinking rapids of sweat from his eyes.

"Have a good time," Loredana rasps from somewhere back in the present, and then it hits me: *that's* where Loredana disappears to all the time.

She drinks Coca-Cola over Barolo, is rooted into the front of the restaurant as opposed to the back. She is perhaps the only soul in Barolo, Italy, to live in this century. It's not the land of the dead at all but the land of the present. Looking over my shoulder, I see her cloud of dust, the kitchen door flapping forward and back in its diminishing creaky refrain. When it comes to rest, Ercole grabs me by the shoulders and, without a word, invites me to watch. All of my reservations about working in a restaurant kitchen surface. In my experience it is a blend of ego, the yelling, the tattoos, the tears, a skillet flying at the head of a line cook, a cleaver thrown at the wall.

Ercole's apron is spattered with kitchen slaughter, and he descends into an opera of sound, the same opera that seemed so muffled through the roof-high courtyard windows. All I can do in this walk-in closet of a kitchen is press myself against the back wall, avoiding the saucepans hanging like stripped rabbits from their hind feet. All I can do is watch. Ercole leaps from the range, leaving a wooden spoon resting on the lip of a skillet, to a white cutting board. Faster than a sewing machine, he slices six cloves of garlic into even, paper-thin disks, throws them into the skillet, then pirouettes, his elbows brushing my ribs, to the sink, where he slices twelve leeks lengthwise and rinses them of their sand. The leeks open to him like accordions, then descend from his fingers into an awaiting stockpot.

"Prego, prego," he sprays at me, flashing his eyes upward.

I jump into action. I step to the range, the sink now to my right, Ercole's prep-work station behind me, and stir the leeks into a slather of butter at the stockpot's bottom. The burst of steam whispers the loudest secret in the world. Like a cowboy viciously tossing the dregs of his coffee mug into the dark of the desert, Ercole from the back saucepan wall tosses a coarse, stretched arc of gray salt over my shoulders and down into the stockpot. The leeks wail in protest, and I turn to Ercole, but he has no time to turn back. No time to yell or throw a cleaver. He parades with the sausage chain to a burner on the other end of the ten-burner range — the burner closest to those ceiling-high, quarter-open courtyard windows. As he winds the sausage over a skillet's circumference, then empties a bottle of Barolo over it, I shake my head at the decadence and strain to hear any signs of life on the other side of the windows.

I can envision the cool-night other side perfectly, but it is locked away into a dream of a false present. Somewhere people are eating. Somewhere there are stars. Somewhere Sandrone's vineyards go dark, unaware of this hectic kitchen life, their roots pulling old rain from the soil.

I picture myself on that narrow strip of grass that has taken me from Il Gioco into Barolo so many times: Ercole is now that speeding mini Cinquecento Rosso, missing my legs by inches, threatening me with eternal paraplegia. But somehow he's able to make the pass every time without causing damage, and perhaps this fact alone imbues him with the confidence to almost speak a full sentence.

"Salsiccia e Barolo," he exhales, indicating the sausage skillet, "per il risotto."

"Salsiccia e Barolo risotto?" I croon, my leek arm starting to cramp up.

"Ya," Ercole expels in affirmation as he throws his arms deep into the sink.

I half-expect him to pull out a piglet, delivering into this world, fresh from the sow, the potential for yet another great Italian salami. But no: he only washes a stainless steel colander and spins to the far reaches of the stove. He sets the colander on a metal work surface and opens the oven door.

"Viene. Viene qua," he summons.

I abandon the leeks, and he quickly slides my stockpot to the edge of its burner.

"Aaah," Ercole sighs, nodding into the oven.

I peer inside to a trayful of white ramekins, billowing with four different soufflés — orange and brown, yellow flecked with dark red, and toast gold. I cannot be convinced that Ercole runs this kitchen himself, no matter how wild his dance. How can he afford the time to show me his desserts, let alone put out the kind of food that allows him to be "big in Asia"? Who is this unmasked man? And how can I not feel faint, how can I believe it when he points into the hot cave, his finger roving among the ramekins, and says, "Vaniglia di Tahiti, cioccolato, caci, e nocciola"?

This is a quadruple threat of the highest last-course order, a street gang of soufflés: Tahitian vanilla bean, chocolate, persimmon, and hazelnut. I am about to lean too far inside when Loredana gallops into the kitchen, spewing a string of Italian coarser than the salt, longer than the sausages.

Ercole and I leap from the oven door, stand shoulder to shoulder as brothers about to get into deep, deep trouble. Loredana takes a step back and laughs. She says something to Ercole in a thin voice, and Ercole spews back like motor oil, laughing with his wife.

"Che?" I shrug.

Loredana runs her spider along her forehead.

"You look crazy like Ercole," she says.

I stare down at my chest and see a continent of sweat asserting its independence in the light. She lifts two completed plates from the edge of a work station and exits. Ercole cuts his laughter off as if with the turn of a key, taps my shoulder, and points to the stockpot. I go back to my stirring, and he empties a saucepan of chicken stock over the leeks. Soon I am stirring risotto, ladling one cascade of chicken stock, letting the Arborio rice drink it in, then ladling in another. I feel as if I have been run through at the shoulder with a samurai sword; the entire right side of my body is aching from the stir, the whip, the chop, the occasional washing of a dish.

I have whisked cream to soft peaks, chopped a melting pot of herbs (sage, rosemary, basil, marjoram, thyme, chervil), washed six different cutting boards, each boasting knife scars of various pale colors. Now, stirring this huge saucepan, the risotto creaming into cement before each subsequent ladle thins it, my hand clutching the wooden spoon screams to open, my shoulder pulls away from the bone, and I contemplate asking Ercole for a break. But no. I begin to finish the risotto. As instructed, I fold in the fresh whipped cream, reach for the dry slivers of Parmigiano-Reggiano, and gong the wooden spoon against the saucepan lip.

"Finito!" I bellow.

Ercole throws his hands in the air, slides to my side from the cutting board, where he is loosening the soufflés from their ramekins with the back of a butter knife. He dips his fingers into my saucepan and brings them, glued with risotto, to his mouth. He puts his hands on his hips, his apron bulging like a half-earth from his chest. He nods, his hair waving. He presses his teeth together.

"Sì," he says. "Sì."

I have finished a dish in I Cannubi's kitchen. I have seen a world ruled by madmen with wooden spoons. And now I go to help him with the soufflés, the diners' last course, the final taste on their lips before bed. When I run the knife-back along the ramekins, the edges of the soufflés unfold like blanket seams from the sleeping world.

Hours pass like this, locked into simple activity: cut, plate, sauce, stir, cut . . . The restaurant empties, and, due to Ercole's manic progression of production and cleanup, we have surprisingly little wiping down to do. The kitchen, for all it has endured tonight, looks refreshed, mellow, stately. Ercole and I, on the other hand, are a mess, a wonderful, olive-oiled mess.

We sit, the two of us, across from one another at one of the inside tables, Loredana anchored like a ship's wheel at the head. The restaurant is empty of all diners except those two at my old outside table — the old man in the pink button-down and his younger leather companion. Beyond them, on the other side of the courtyard fence, a hunched man, locked in shadow, is night hunting for truffles with a feather duster of a dog.

Ercole has set a four-cheese degustation in the table's center, replete with a mound of Cognac-soaked prunes: the spoils following our kitchen performance. I can almost hear the gleaming white sliver of Toma cheese call a goat's milk "Bravo!" from the upper deck. My head is swimming from the kitchen heat, still acclimating to the air of the dining room. The air is exactly, stunningly temperate.

Loredana turns from the table, reaching behind her, tickling the air back there. She retrieves from a white-clothed two-top three fat-bottomed snifters. Ercole nods his head in approval, his hair waving like a torrential good-bye. But no, not yet, one last embrace, one last smell of the neck, one last glass of thirty-year-old Amontillado Spanish sherry. Loredana, with arms as copper as the Statue of Liberty's childhood, retrieves a bottle of the sherry, so aged it glows purple.

"Ah," Ercole sighs, leaning back in his chair, arms locked behind his head.

His armpit stains are magnificent.

"Amontillado," he calls to the ceiling and raises his fists in the air.

"This," Loredana crows, "is Ercole's first love. Amontillado sherry."

"Il mio primo bacio," Ercole shoots.

"What did he say?" I ask Loredana.

She is shaking her head, hiding her smile in the black of her hair.

"Nothing. He is stupid."

"Il mio primo bacio," Ercole fires again, this time from deeper in his chest.

"He say," Loredana says, "this sherry is, a long time ago, his first kiss."

"That's one to remember," I say to Ercole.

"Crazy," Loredana whispers to herself. "The kitchen make them all crazy."

She knocks, spider side down, on the table, and Ercole pours our glasses. The sherry fills the air like a cherry coffin, sweet age, Loredana's spider web crisped to sugar. Ercole is the first to raise his glass. Loredana and I follow. In the space between the snifter-hoist and the toast the old man outside roars like a lion, Leatherman folds like a lamb, and the truffle dog lets loose a sharp, singular bark.

We chime our glasses together and drink. The sherry slides into me not like ink but like caramelized black widow, no longer poisonous. I am zigzagged with joy and old fruit, waxed, lacquered, and my head spins like a date on a sewing needle as Ercole tosses, like a curdled Frisbee, a sliver of Pecorino Romano right at the letters. I catch it into my chest and take it into my mouth. As if in Vegas, it marries the sherry right then and there, adopts a Cognac prune, and lives together, one big happy family.

I manage to hold my hands to Ercole, to Loredana, and choke a tight-throated "Mille grazie a voi."

"Ah, ha, ha," Ercole roosters and again raises his glass.

We demolish the cheeses, trample the prunes, empty the bottle of sherry. Yes, we empty a thirty-year-old Amontillado sherry. Yes. Yes. Yes we do. My head goes both heavy and light. I think I can climb Everest. I think I can fall asleep. Then Ercole, spewing Italian all over the place, Loredana scolding him with her eyes, reaches to a liquor cabinet and nearly falls from his chair.

"Ercole!" Loredana yells, surely wishing she could send him to the corner.

He pops forward, torso collapsing on the table, laughing to himself. Loredana stands and palms the bottle that Ercole just barely missed. It is a Perdaudin Passito, that botanic garden of Italian dessert wine, and soon a glassful of the stuff is washing the sherry down with its ivy, lavender, orange, honey. The room pitches to the right, and Loredana sprouts a double. They overlap each other, and I'm amazed they can both fit on the one chair. Someone has put on some music: a slow flute driven by heartbeat bass and a cymbal as thin as a parakeet. Ercole, squinting, is telling us how, before he became a chef, he made fifty million lire in ten months selling children's books door-to-door.

"He is a wonderful salesman," Loredana says, her voice commingling with the music. "He say if he start to not like the restaurant, he quit tomorrow and do something different."

Ercole nods, whistles, and throws his hand upward as if tossing a fallen apple back into its tree. I exhale, holding my brain in place with my left hand.

Loredana stands, and I say, if only to myself, "Wow, you guys. I'm really feeling it."

Loredana sits again, and I open my eyes. Three shot glasses rest on the table like downed bells. I pick one up and try to ring it. Both Ercole and Loredana laugh and mistake my attempt as a call for booze. Loredana fills all three with clear mystery liquid.

"Di Giamaica," Ercole says, pointing to my tiny glass.

"The rum is from Jamaica," Loredana translates.

"That," I smile to her, "I understood."

She laughs, I laugh, and Ercole pleads, "Che? Che?"

She translates.

"Jamaicaaa!" Ercole yodels loud enough for the old man and his leather companion to peer inside at us.

"Americaaa!" Ercole screams over his raised glass and points at me.

"Whhoo," I exhale with too much air, raising my own glass, "to America."

The rum shoots through everything else I've ingested like an arrow and sticks out diagonally from my stomach, dyed tail feathers fluttering as I breathe. Is it any wonder that, after slamming his drained shot glass onto the tabletop, Ercole pulls two cigars from his apron's pouch — some demented kangaroo about to light her offspring on fire? Loredana rolls her glassy eyes and grunts in disgust.

"No, no," Ercole explains to her, "di Cuba."

"Cuban cigars, huh?" I mutter to Loredana in a voice that seems doomed to spend eternity inside my head.

"It is too much. He is crazy," Loredana says and gets up to pour herself a Coke.

The cigar rubs down the inside of my lower lip with its smoke, and I imagine I've been playing the saxophone all evening. I think I even get out a few notes on the cigar because Ercole starts snapping his fingers. The flute music has given way to raucous soul, some guy singing Wilson Pickett in Italian. The temptation to stand up and dance on the table is fierce, but I fear I would fall through its surface into a Hades I can't escape from. *Better stay sitting. Keep it down.* Ercole blows a wave of smoke to the ceiling. He is three-quarters finished, and I have barely smoked two inches. I watch as Ercole's cigarless hand opens and closes like a sock puppet.

"Moroccan tobacco?" he enunciates slowly, ensuring that I understand.

A chill grips my shoulders.

"Did you just speak English?" I ask him.

He remains stone-faced and brings the cigar back to his lips. His hand is still opening and closing. My heart quickens, and Loredana, sipping her Coke in the corner, scolds, "Ercole! No!"

I look at him. He looks at me. I search for the evil green in his eyes.

Taking the cigar from my mouth, I look at it and say, "Sì?"

I thought it was from Cuba.

"Aha!" Ercole stands and shuffles into the kitchen.

I picture its insides: the cutting boards, the range, the pans that were once so busy. Loredana stands, and her afterimage follows. She rejoins the table and takes my wrist. Her hands are ice cold.

"You must tell him no sometime," she hisses, "or this do not end. I tell you: he is crazy."

I'm scared but exhilarated-scared, as if Italy and its ways of living have fortified me for death.

"What is this Moroccan tobacco?" I ask her.

She grunts and rolls her eyes just as Ercole pops from the kitchen carrying a plastic sandwich bag. He sits and raises his eyebrows twice. Loredana whips him in Italian, and he grits his teeth, takes it, and whips back. She shakes her head as he, between his thumb and forefinger, coaxes a silver dollar of hashish from the bag.

"Oh, hell," I say as Loredana shrugs.

"He is a very bad influence," she says.

Ercole melts the hash with a pink convenience store lighter. He tosses in a pinch of Cuban cigar tobacco and rolls it into a cigarette.

He hands it to me, and I feel like a novice diver about to leap from an Acapulco cliff. I hope I land okay. I hope I make the water. I put it between my lips, taste tar and doughnut, and Ercole leans across the table with the lighter already ablaze. The smoke runs into me easy, a nurse smoothing a bedsheet. I feel a pair of hands sprout in my belly and begin stroking its walls. I jump, hit water, and swim along the reef. Three orange fish wink at me as they pass, and I rise to the surface, exhale the smoky saltwater, and breathe.

"Good junk," I say, and even Loredana laughs, her spider detaching itself from her hand to waltz along the ceiling with the rest of the insects.

I'm over the first high-bar, but I feel this is going to be a long dive, a dive that already has its fingers dipping into tomorrow's cake. I pass it to Ercole, and he takes it nearly to the end in one drag. He passes it across to me. The smoke takes hold of my collar, shakes me like Lodovico.

"This is great," I exhale.

Ercole takes it from my fingers and finishes it.

We talk together — the three of us — about living by the seats of our pants, about our families (it was Ercole's father who was hunting for the truffles), about food and wine. Ercole's rabid Italian never made more sense. His hand gestures spell everything out. The rest of the place, beyond the confines of the table, begins to swim in spirals, pinwheels detached from their stems.

I begin to feel a dull tapping at my back, and I think it's just the massage of the smoke and liquor until I turn to see Leatherman towering over me like an executioner. I want to jump up but seem strapped into the chair, an electric cap surely about to lock into my scalp. Next to him, standing less than four feet tall, is the old man in the pink button-down. His gray hair brushes Leatherman's waist.

"Carabiniere," Leatherman says in a henchman's voice.

"Che?" I ask.

The old man nods, tiny arms folded over his tiny chest.

"Carabiniere," Leatherman growls again, and I look to Loredana for help.

"Italian military police," she says.

My heart explodes over my chest like a water balloon.

"Oh, shit!" I cry, about to stand.

Ercole coughs into laughter. Indeed, everyone around me is laughing, and it seems I haven't yet risen to the surface. Leatherman laughs in dull throbs like an upstairs neighbor hammering a picture of a lion into the wall; the old man lets out the laugh of a cockroach; Ercole fires a rocket launcher into the air; Loredana tucks us all into bed. My own laugh sounds way too deep.

I sputter, "You all are terrible."

The old man breaks from his laughter into near-perfect English.

"You're lucky we're so nice here. In the south of Italy, very different culture. You never know what can happen down there."

I nod and he looks up to Leatherman, stretched to six-foot-five, and shoots his translation to him like a basketball through a hoop.

"Sì," Leatherman says.

This duo is perfect: the brains and the brawn. The old man proceeds to culturally dissect Italy via region. Leatherman laments that he missed our cheese course.

"Oh, formaggio!" he cries, an ape for a baby bottle.

"We're going to a disco in Alba," the old man interrupts. "Tough to get in, but they know me there — it helps to be old and a dwarf. I was going to invite all of you, but it seems you're doing alright on your own."

Ercole and Loredana stand to hug the duo and wave them out the door. The old man pokes his head inside and offers me a ride back to Il Gioco.

"I'd better walk," I say. "I definitely need the long . . . uh . . . the long . . ." I sigh and shrug; my English seems to be going. "Uh . . . air," I muster.

"Very good," the old man laughs and calls "Viene!" to Leatherman.

Ercole and Loredana walk out into the courtyard, and I, on rubber band legs, follow. Leatherman swings a helmet two sizes too small over his head and struggles with the chinstrap. The old man, geared only in his pink button-down and khaki slacks, summits the motorcycle leapfrog-style and takes Leatherman by the waist. Their attached powder blue sidecar shimmies as the engine starts. They roar from the parking lot with a honk and a wave.

After hugging and kissing Ercole and Loredana, the two of them imploring me to return tomorrow for some Barolo Chinato ("Best dessert wine," Loredana says), I stumble along the empty courtyard and up the white-pebbled archway, the cool, very-late-night wind and persimmons that flutter like fish gills.

Via Crosia and its narrow strip of grass stretch in the dark, a memory of sobriety. I must follow it, the vineyards rustling on either side of the road in whisper or warning or both. Legs teetering, I decide to lie on the grass strip and stare at the stars awhile. The earth holds me, its cold hands shivering me with the grass. It's too late for cars.

My breath compounds itself like a sentence in the air. It hangs there under the stars, a brain-shaped mist, the preborn headache that I know will join me tomorrow. And beyond it all the America I left behind and tomorrow itself, resting behind Cassiopeia like a motorcycle up the road, a motorcycle that sits just, and always, out of reach.

When I finally make it back to my tent, I'm somehow not surprised to find my perfect stack of laundry, clean and folded next to my pillow.

27

Laundry

I wake, just presunset, to find the tent door and screen unzipped, my split feet lying in a mud-puddle doormat. It must have rained overnight. Head pulsing to its own obnoxious beat, eyes shellacked like a 1930s baseball, I take a breath of air and think I'm going to swallow my tongue whole. My mouth's dryness is not to be believed, a sponge rung out and left for dead in the desert. When I smack my lips, I'm amazed they don't slough into powder. In the oak in front of Il Gioco six crows adjust their necks. In their eyes lie the motives of the vulture.

I squat at the open tent door, cup my hands into a bowl, and bring them to the mud puddle. Rinsing my mouth, then spitting thoroughly, the residual flavor is gourmet compared to Franco's tripe. My mouth, riding a wild taste roller coaster from truffle to filth, yearns for a lithium lozenge. I spit one more time, the sky folding its pink lapels over its eyes (even *it* can't bear to look), and retreat into my cave. This time I zip up.

I close my eyes and wake refreshed two weeks later. I unzip my tent door, and the sky is blued to purple, full of promise and train rides to Torino. It is two days before the Salone del Gusto, nearly the eve.

In the interim since I Cannubi, which may well have taken place in my tent with my eyes closed, I spent a lot of time in Alba and in Sandrone's vineyards. Much of his crew dismissed for the season, I picked alongside Ivo, Beppe, and Indiano. At this point in the harvest Ivo and Indiano have formed some kind of bond, Beppe now, with his tortoise tattoo and jacks, the third wheel. I never saw the sweaty woman again. Or the nieces. Maybe she was their mother. Occasionally, a clubhopper would show up, pick for a few hours, and leave. Occasionally, Sandrone would charge me with the mopping, much of his juice having been transferred to the aging barrels.

The Willy Wonka cantina was at times so quiet you could hear Luca tapping his pencil eraser against his clipboard from the other side of the building, hear him hatching his next dance. The vineyards outside held to the cooling soil, the Nebbiolo grapes, once so plump, now showing signs of death. When I wasn't working the fields, I adapted my schedule to that of the Satti bus system (which is to say, no schedule at all). Most of my days off were spent at Caffé Calissano, the brown curly-haired waitress anticipating my order of croissant and espresso by day three. I would while away the afternoons reading *Henderson the Rain King* and writing letters to friends. Eventually, the waitress, always at the right time, brought me a chilled glass of Passito.

One morning Raffaella and I took our breakfast together standing up at Calissano's indoor bar. She ordered for us: Nutella crêpes, due espressi. I watched the two of us eat in the etched mirror behind the bar, this beautiful canary feather of a woman and me with a six-day beard.

Raffaella set the demitasse mug down after only one sip, drew the lemon twist over her lips, and said, "You know, for the Salone del Gusto, Francesco has an apartment right in Torino's centro—Piazza Castello. Beautiful. You can walk to the Salone from there. Maybe three kilometers."

Francesco—Raffaella's "boy." I hadn't seen him for a while: his graveyard legs, his banker's eyes, his stoic, gray-headed, interminable niceness.

I swallowed my espresso and said, "You think I can stay there? I mean, I was planning on going for at least a couple of days."

"Oh," Raffaella dismissed my concerns, waving her hand over her crêpe as if commanding it to levitate. "He must go to work anyway. I will tell him. It will be no problem."

A leech of Nutella—that chocolate-hazelnut spread—rested at

the corner of her mouth, and it took all I had not to kiss it away or at least wipe it with my fingers.

"You, uh," I muttered to Raffaella, laughing, about to point to the crook of her mouth.

"Yes?" she asked, the Nutella holding at her lips.

"You," I exhaled and dropped my hand to my fork. "Nothing. Thanks for talking to Francesco about that."

She narrowed her eyes, a tight smile rinsing over her face. My heart dug in its nails. I hoped she wouldn't glance up into the Cinzano mirror.

That morning bled into others, some spent in the garden of Il Gioco playing baseball with Niccolo. We used broomsticks for bats, the white driveway stones for balls. We played always without talking. I spent many afternoons in Barolo's rec center, shaking down some pickup games of ping-pong with the local kids. I lost most of the time, the little rats ridiculing me in Italian. I went to the rec center's basement café to drown my sorrows. The café, unnamed, always exuded the same din of demitasse spoons tapping espresso cups. Barolo's elder locals, mostly weathered men in hats (retired winegrowers, I guessed), grew accustomed to me very slowly, looking up from their card games with suspicious and bloodshot eyes. They would soon look away, spitting their cigar smoke with an added force. I watched their faces settle again, convinced that they were all holding flushes.

The woman behind the counter, a beautiful five-foot-tall meatball with extremities, began to tell whether I won or lost in ping-pong by the way I shuffled down the stairs or by the way I held my paddle. If I won, she made me a salami panino. If I lost, a salami panino and one scoop of melon gelato.

I ran into Loredana in Alba one afternoon in a wineshop. Everyone in there — customers and employees alike — knew who she was. She chastised me, of course, for not returning after my apprenticeship for the Barolo Chinato.

"Two words, Loredana," I said. "Moroccan tobacco. And I have not yet learned to say no to Ercole."

"It is difficult," she said, "I know. I drive you back to Il Gioco dell'Oca."

We spoke on the drive about the days after the orgy at I Cannubi. A few days before Ercole had been commissioned to cook at a culinary exhibition in Hong Kong.

"Wow," I said. "Always doing it by the seat of your pants."

"Yes," she smiled, her eyes not on the road but on the sky.

By the way the car remained centered in the lane I was convinced her spider did the driving.

The days washed together in a fog, not unlike a dream, the darks of one night trickling into the whites of the next morning. I imagined that, above it all, on the other side of the Piedmont haze, Adriana sat laundering my life in mixed, oversized loads, her breath smelling of detergent and chickpea soup.

And when I wake today, it is morning or it is dusk. I could have been sleeping an hour or an eternity. In the tent's air, a seventy-degree sea, Italy asserts itself, neatly folded. I unzip my tent door, and the sky is blued to purple . . .

The Other Side of Tonight

Il passo non deve essere più lungo della gamba.
(Your step must not be longer than your leg.)

MOTTO OF TORINO

With the Salone del Gusto guide rolled into my back pocket I watch the orange lights of Torino grow big, then bigger, in the train windows. Raffaella's directions to Francesco's apartment ("only fifteen minutes from the train station") are stuck into the guide between an article on flour and an article on honey. Unlike my Monforte directions, I can't let these smudge. I step from the platform into the station — bouncing loudspeaker Italian — and into the street.

What a fashionable industrial wasteland! The slow beat of Barolo's pulse gives way to a carefully chosen ritzy chaos. They are everywhere: beautiful girls in tight black pants, horn-rimmed glasses, and platform shoes walking arm in arm with suited, tied, tortoise-shell-spectacled aficionados of modeldom. And above them all, like caffeinated woodpeckers, the smokestacks of industry are busy beating away at the sky with murky beaks. Too many things are being accomplished here by too many unseen hands. I have gone from salami to Armani, the vineyard quilt beyond these buildings only a dream, a very good dream. Perhaps the clubhoppers could exist here, but Ivo? Sandrone? Lodovico? Franco the Butcher?

The origins of this mad city lie in the founding of Taurasia by the Taurini, a Celtic Ligurian settlement, prior to 218 BC. During that year the settlement was only partially destroyed by Hannibal. Later, the Romans, led by Julius Caesar, would use Taurasia as a military stronghold. Eventually, the colony was subject to occupation by the Goths and the Lombards until the eleventh century, when it was annexed to the Savoy family. From these moments of infancy Torino has been through many rises and falls (it was the Italian headquarters for anti-Fascism during World War II), eventually sprouting into its modern-day incarnation as a decadent metropolis.

From this decadence I have to look away, if only for a second, and, wrestling free of my backpack, my shoulders find a shuttered newsstand, the Salone guide opening like a portal. And there, on the other side of tonight, I see it: a bird's-eye view of an espresso cup, steam swirling into a W; a pyramid of Parmigiano-Reggiano cheeses; a page-size tomato; a watermelon radish resting atop a bay leaf; fresh bread cracking with grain and heat; a half-pig with — yes — an apple in its mouth; blood oranges on a platter; sardines in a burlap bag; coffee beans morphing into chocolate; disembodied hands slicing prosciutto with a two-foot-long knife; a line of quarter-filled Barolo glasses; a bald old man eating a peach; a young blonde woman smelling an artichoke; yellow cherries; purple mustard; bufagella di Matese.

Cooled, calmed, but hardly collected, I hoist my backpack, step from the defunct newsstand, and hang a left at the first intersection. My eyes begin to water in the city's pollution, its orange lights, swimming diamonds. Soon I come to it: Francesco's neighborhood, Piazza Castello, a high-tech and centrally located plaza of ice cream shops, palaces, coffeehouses, museums, panini cafés, a bar, three suit shops, two dress shops, and a stand where eyeglasses run upward of £300,000 (about $150).

At the tail end of the sixteenth century, Carlo Emanuele I called on architect Ascanio Vitozzi to construct this cosmopolitan piazza where Torino's fashionistas would have an opportunity to blow off some aristocratic steam. They do so now in the piazza's famed cafés — Baratti & Milano (open since 1873) and Mulassano (open since 1900 and the favorite hangout of the Savoy family and the Teatro Regio opera stars of olde). Swathed in bronze, mahogany, and marble, both cafés serve Torino's rich homegrown beverage, Bicerin (pronounced "beach-air-een"). The drink is a mysteriously pro-portioned concoction of chocolate, coffee, milk, and fresh whipped cream, often spiced up with a dose of Vecchia Romagna.

A few doors down from Mulassano, nestled between mint choco-late chip and silk sport coat, the thinnest book on the reference shelf, is Francesco's apartment building. I press the black button on the intercom, two adolescent boys nearly run me down with matching blue motor scooters, and Francesco's voice wafts from the great beyond in a crackle of geniality and static.

"Pronto?"

"Francesco!" I yell over the din, surely spattering his eardrum over his brain. "I'm outside!"

"Ahhh."

Then: intercom silence. Horns blare; the single hum of many voices. A man, needlessly in near-midnight sunglasses, spits a straw-berry top at my feet. The wooden apartment door vibrates in an accepting buzz. I step through it into the guts of the concrete and slam it behind me. The street noise is cut off like a drunk at last call. The courtyard is draped in ivy, with walls so gray they shine.

Francesco steps like a gazelle from the second door in the far wall. He is elegant, gray as the building. He is wearing a red rayon bathrobe. His gnarled feet poke from cellulose slippers, and his toes strike me as the anti-Salone. They are the most unappetizing things I've ever seen: AAA batteries run down by an 18-wheeler. I look up quickly to his face, my own lips stretched in an involuntary sneer.

"Ciao, Francesco," I call across the courtyard.

"Ahh, ciao-ciao," he lilts, his voice as light as light.

He is all spilt glitter. Though gray, he is a cloud that will never hold rain.

"Tutto bene?" he asks.

"Sì," I say, "molto bene. Everything's fine. I'm a little tired, but . . ."

"Oh, oh, sì, sì. It is late for Barolo, early for Torino."

"Sì, capito, I'm sure," I smile.

There is an awkward pause, Francesco nodding, feigning interest in the courtyard walls he sees every single day. I walk to him.

"Ah, it is good you are here," he says in that Francesco voice, perpetually locked in vacation sigh.

Francesco the Golden Boy. What is his relationship with Raffaella?

"Raffaella," he says, "say you go to Salone del Gusto tomorrow."

"Sì," I say. "Grazie per, uh, letting me stay here."

"Ahh," he says in the middle of his vocal massage. "I put map to Lingotto on the table, very near the couch for your sleep. It is not far."

He holds his apartment door open for me.

"Lingotto," Francesco says again, filling the silence.

"Sì," I say. "It's hard to believe the Salone del Gusto is being held in the old Fiat factory."

"Ahh, yes," Francesco says. "The Fiat."

Soon I am inside and he's in bed. He has to open his bank tomorrow. His door is mercifully closed. His place is scrubbed so clean it's almost red-faced. (Raffaella told me he has a maid come in every day.) His expensive stereo, his giant TV, his silver hanging kitchen utensils. His place is black, white, and shiny. His CDs: some Miles Davis, some Italian bands, some Bruce Springsteen. Torino plays its yellowed silent movie in his living room window. Most everyone is walking arm in arm, unaware that Buster Keaton is about to drop something on their heads. Fourteen feet above me Francesco's ceiling fan spins squeakless.

Tomorrow the Salone del Gusto. My heart beats with this, rolls end over end in my chest like an old accidental Fiat — the one they forgot to recall. A lump grows like an heirloom tomato in my throat. I unhook my sleeping bag from my backpack and spread it over the white couch. It is dirty and out of place here, as if crashing a party, as if it misses the tent.

29

Billboards, Booths, and Cameras

Francesco was up early this morning, fumbling about in the kitchen with what smelled like oatmeal. I pretended to sleep on the couch, only occasionally daring to crack one eye and peer at the showhorse's breakfast routine. With the oatmeal he had a glass of milk and read the newspaper. Only once, with his mouth full, did he begin humming, then catch himself, and stop. I could hear his spoon striking his teeth with each bite.

I made sure to get out of the place before the maid came in, rolling my sleeping bag to the foot of the couch, tucking my backpack in a corner underneath a stereo speaker built into the wall. Raffaella and Francesco: rusticity meets the modern age.

On Torino's streets and sidewalks cars careen, silk people tuck in their elbows. The sky goes green. I look up to see if we're under attack. If anything sharp falls from above, I'll have to take refuge beneath one of the many hair-sprayed heads. Maybe these people are creating fashionable bunkers for themselves, setting up Fendi bomb shelters and stocking them with Armani ramen. But no: the green sky isn't the sign of alien invasion or aerial poison; it's the green translucence of a block-long tent ceiling, sheltering an outdoor market from the sun.

To the right, rows of pastries; to the left, rows of fish. This may not be Barolo, this may be a city, but it's still Italy, it's still panini and cappuccino, and there at the end of the tent it's still truffle. *God! All of these roadblocks!* All of these temptations beg to interrupt my beeline for the Salone. I guess it can't hurt to line my stomach a bit. I don't want to overwhelm myself at the Lingotto. But *moderation,*

moderation . . . This market can seduce me for at least half a day, so, biting my tongue, exercising some tranquilizer-dart restraint, I turn from the low-skied green of the market tent and cross to the other side of the street. I find myself face-to-face with a sign, black with gold lettering: Caffè San Carlo. According to a plaque on the wall and my Italian-English dictionary translation, the first restaurant in Italy to embrace gas lighting in 1832.

I obviously am meant to eat something. The café is doorless — in fact, front wall–less. I merely have to take one step up from the sidewalk, and I'm beyond the colonnade, I'm inside the place, sitting at a tiny round table, iron base, mother-of-pearl surface, big enough for one.

The waitress, like all of Torino, seems to have stepped straight from an advertisement for expensive perfume. Living in Barolo has somehow imbued me with a strange confidence in Torino. Before she can even say "Come va," her long hair running all over her shoulders and chest in a downpour of crow feathers, I smile at her and say, clumsily accented, "Ciao bella."

Her face beams like a flashlight, her eyes narrowing.

"Ciao," she manages. "Resta in Torino?"

"No," I say. "Resto in Barolo."

"Barolo?" she slithers, throwing the town's first *o* to the ceiling and catching it in her teeth before the *l* even has a chance to assert itself.

"Sì," I say.

"Americano, no?" she asks.

I guess I've just stepped from an inelegant billboard of my own.

"Sì," I say.

Soon, of course, we're talking about the Salone del Gusto, and Elena (her name) tells me that her friend Valentina is working the ticket booth at the Lingotto today.

"È possible che compro il mio biglietto per . . . uh . . . uh . . . il laboratorio di foie gras da tua amica."

I may very well buy my foie gras workshop ticket from her friend. We laugh and, soon, I'm eating a peach croissant and sending it home with a mug of cappuccino. Then, braving the narrow staircase to the café's upstairs bathroom and closing the unlockable door behind me, my stomach begins to settle, and so does Torino itself. I pull the bathroom window inward and take in the breeze, watch the people strolling one story below. I wonder which ones are going to the Salone del Gusto. The outside plays in my hair, wind swinging from the strands as if from a tire. No vineyard smell. No roasty green. Back downstairs I pay and wave good-bye to Elena. She waves back with both hands.

Again in the street I inhale and walk fast, ducking my head beneath the warmth like a swimmer. I don't come up for a breath until I see a crowd thicken around a box-shaped building, cross-hatched with vertical and horizontal columns, an inhabitable checkerboard. It is the Lingotto, and the people, wonderful specks of color and sound, are scattered all over its concrete courtyard like a spilt bag of marbles. I buy my entry ticket from the outdoor booth.

The ticket is as large as a brick, emblazoned with the same red, yellow, and green logo that fronts the guide. The woman in the booth, gray-haired with a sweet puff-pastry face, tells me that I'm going to be the twelfth person inside. My heart begins to blush. I take a step from the outdoor booth to the massive steel doors that lead to the Salone. I reach for the door handle, and, before my fingers can wrap over it, I am blinded by a white light from above.

"Good Lord!" I shout and think I may actually be calling the light by name.

Is this a leak from Heaven? And if so, am I ready? I think I may be. I think I'm ready to be taken. To kneel.

Just as I'm about to fall inside the Lingotto, guided by this light, I'm blocked by a cascading woman on roller blades. She has long blonde hair, zigzagging from her head to her waist, a swath of blue glitter eyeshadow over both eyes, and the whitest teeth I've ever seen. She's holding a microphone that has the number 4 on its handle. She gestures to the white light with a long, blue-painted fingernail, and it's only now that I can make out the cameraman behind it. She thrusts the microphone right between my eyes and shouts, above the din of the ticket-buyers, a knotted rope of Italian. It's too loud and fast for me to understand. I blink to the camera lights and force a confused and shrugging smile.

"You speak English?" she croons, her newscaster voice tapering the word *English* into a ribbon.

"Yes," I say, shaking my head and smiling.

I'm giddy. I'm going to be on the news.

"We are the Food Network," she sings, her teeth glowing in the camera lights. "What do you expect to find in there?"

She taps the door with a blue nail. I can see it but can't hear the sound it makes. Adrenaline fills my chest like neon. I start nodding, head butting the air around me. I feel like a beer sign.

"What's inside," I tell her, "is what I've been waiting my whole life to taste."

I think of Charlie Trotter and Thomas Keller and Ferran Adrià. My first catering gig rife with first fuck-ups.

She laughs like a flock of birds. I squint and see the cameraman's giant cheeks bouncing up and down. She turns to the camera, this blonde Medusa, and translates. I wonder if this is live. She stares right into my eyes, but I'm nowhere near stone. Actually, I feel softer than ever.

"What things do you most want to taste in there?" she asks.

I throw my head back. I feel like dancing, bouncing like a prize-fighter in his warm-up cloak. I shout to be heard. I spit all over the microphone.

"I'm gonna try to kick into the foie gras laboratory, and if that doesn't work, I'm gonna punch my way through to the Barolo tasting."

Again she laughs like the jet engine that shreds the birds, translates into the camera.

Then the light fades out, I blink like a madman, and she says, "That was great. It is on tonight. Channel 4 at ten o'clock."

"Excellent," I say. "That was fun."

"Go in," she says. "Go taste."

My heart beating over the speed limit, I grab the door handle like a scepter and pull.

30

Valentina and the First Taste

I could be underwater: these foreign schools, the pressure in my lungs, these people mazing themselves like star coral. The saleswoman at the taste workshop ticket booth smiles from her square of light, red Salone beret tilted toward her left eye. Her hair hangs like woven hay, rests on her shoulders, and before I can step to her I smell her perfume. It smells like the farm: the dirt, the straw, the fresh cream, maybe even a little animal tossed in. This is how this woman smells locked into her booth, her body bathed in the escaping scents of the Salone, battering her only in drips and wafts.

She must be in her midtwenties, and when my eyes stray to the gold of her name tag, her name and my choice of ticket line seem more perfect than prosciutto and melon. She is Valentina. She is Elena's friend. I envision Elena back at Caffé San Carlo, dropping her dark hair over the coffee-stained table of another. I hesitate a second too long, and Valentina cocks her head like a dog at a teapot's whistle.

"Valentina," I say as if I'm here at a high school reunion.

From around a corner the smell of port wine slithers between our faces.

"Yes?" she smiles, confused, head tilting even farther.

"How did you know I speak English?" I ask.

She says, "It was between American and German, and I guess right."

Her answer raises even more questions, but I just laugh from far back in my throat.

"I see," I nod and, for a moment, hold my gaze on my feet.

"For what would you like the tickets?" she dribbles in a water-voice over too many rocks.

Her voice is light and liquid, as sweet and basic as pabulum — she has the voice of mashed carrots, which, amid the Salone's offerings, is far more pleasant than it should be.

"Oh," I say, looking up to her face, "I'll definitely take one for the foie . . ." She starts shaking her head. ". . . gras?" I finish, a sad beggar clown rattling a handful of change.

She opens her mouth. Dark barn hay rushes all around me. I know what she's going to say.

"Oh, no. People call months ahead for these tickets. Everybody want to go to this one."

"There's none left? Nothing on hold?" I ask.

"Nothing," she gavels.

I sigh and think to name-drop.

"Oh, man," I say. "By the way, Elena from Caffé San Carlo says hello."

"You know Elena?"

"Yeah. She makes a hell of a cappuccino."

Valentina laughs, her teeth catching the light like thirty-two fish. I can see the roof of her mouth. It shines like pink aluminum.

"Yes," she says, dipping her carrot voice in sugarwater all the way up to the stalk, "she is very good."

I hear multilingual throats clearing behind me and turn to see that the lines have descended into a stock market floor–trading chaos.

"Yeah, um. I guess I'll try the Barolo workshop."

"You like the Barolo?" she asks, eyes narrowing, oblivious to the angry mob clotting behind me.

"Yeah. I'm staying over there now. Picking some grapes for Luciano Sandrone."

Her voice goes from carrot to carrot cake — thicker, denser, topped with icing.

"Oohh," she groans.

Her next three words come with the pause button hit between them.

"Very," she says, fingering the air between us, "good," she continues, my shirt collar flapping, "wine."

I smile hypnotized as she slides my Barolo ticket across the yellow countertop. Her hand is thin as a minnow, fingernails unpainted and short, a silver ring resting at the base of her pinky.

"Only two left," she says, and for a second I think she's talking about the two of us.

I'm about to give her my sly look — the one where I raise the one eyebrow — when I realize she's tapping the ticket with the moon face of her finger.

"Yeah," I say, "I guess I'm lucky to get in."

"Enjoy," she continues. "Come see me for more tickets. There are many more laboratories."

She pronounces the last word like a classic film villain, accentuating the *bor* and *tor*. I take my ticket and hope it keeps its promise. I step from the line and look back to Valentina. She is busy, so I don't wave.

There's another set of doors to go through, a long set of glass doors. I have an hour before the Barolo tasting, six of them spanning 1990 to 1997 — in the opinion of the Slow Food movement, the six best of the nineties. I step forward, and a glass door slides automatically left. A cyclone of smell releases itself like rain, and I'm in it: the storm's eye, colors streaking all over the room, a collective downpour of chewing and swallowing. I walk forward, my legs working without my brain. The Salone del Gusto, and the question hits me, an ancient riddle: in a Salon of Taste, what does one taste first? A meat? A cheese? A fruit, vegetable, grain? Do I start with something Italian? Do I begin with the comfort of something American? Do I go completely exotic? This is important. I need a sign.

I close my eyes and look up. The white lights of the ceiling turn my shut-eyed vision from black to purple. The purple spreads into circular dots like bulbs or checkers or figs. *Figs.* I open my eyes, go back to that Alba morning, the market, the smiling round frump of a man who busted that fig in half and held it to me with his bare hands. Fig: as comfortable as my crib, as Italian as Alba. Past, present, and future merge into a single fruit.

31

Six Barolos, Four Figs

Glasses poured. Wine that evokes images of ancient Greek pillars, columns, buttresses both flying and grounded. I have headphones over my ears, pumping belated and broken English past the white-cheeked cherubim, the floral wreaths, the gargoyle with only one eye.

This is the Barolo workshop, the great masters painting our bodies with wine: Gromis, Sandrone, Scavino, Conterno, Cogno, Pira. These men, just beyond Torino's confines, buy their meats from Franco's butcher shop and their grissini from the panetteria, witness their labor for sale in Il Bacco.

The headphones stress: "Gromis" Barolo is not made by Gromis at all. Famed Vintner Angelo Gaja rented the Gromis estate in La Morra to produce this silk curtain of a wine. Gaja, a man both revered and resented in the business for bringing the Piedmontese wines to the attention of the tourists and the commercially minded international public (he regularly imports and distributes French and Californian wines throughout Italy), has had winemaking in his family since the 1850s. When Gaja took over the business, he sold his family's property in Barolo in order to focus his efforts on his Barbaresco wines. The Barbaresco zone (often called "Barolo's Backyard") offers Nebbiolo-based wines made in a similar process to Barolo with shorter barrel-aging requirements. To publicize Barbaresco, Gaja, much to his father's dismay, began to untraditionally cultivate Chardonnay and Cabernet grapes. Hence, his Cabernet vineyard is dubbed Darmagi, or "pity."

The Paolo Scavino estate, now run in Castiglione Falletto by

Enrico Scavino, Jr., and his daughter Enrica, has been at the fore-front, with Sandrone, of Barolo's modernist processes since the early 1980s. The winery was among the first in the Langhe to employ temperature-controlled tanks and storage units.

The Conterno label involves a bit more familial drama. Brothers Aldo and Giovanni Conterno, sons of Giacomo Conterno, disputed bitterly over the nuances of winemaking. Aldo was more willing to adopt modernist methods, while Giovanni remained a passionate traditionalist. Their differences irreconcilable, the brothers split their father's winery, Aldo producing under his own name, Giovanni pos-sessing the Giacomo Conterno label. Both brothers produce excel-lent though markedly different wines a mere mile from one another in Monforte.

Elvio Cogno, choosing the more modernist side of the coin, began to make wine for a living in 1964. His current estate is situated in Novello's Ravera district, the area in which he was born. At age sixteen Cogno received a scholarship to the prestigious hotel man-agement school in Stresa. Soon afterward, with his brother Giovanni he became a struggling restaurateur, then a winemaker for his father, Luigi.

Another Luigi—Luigi Pira—produces wines out of the hamlet of Serralunga and is famous for his single-vineyard Barolos: Marenca, Margheria, and the ultrarare Vigna Rionda. The headphones convey: it is the latter that now fills the glass before me.

I drink their wares; even the modernist wines taste ancient, frayed, sepia. But then the swallow, the wine holding in the microscopic grooves of the mouth, dissipating like kettle steam in a white kitchen light. The barely English headphone instruction drones on, becomes background music.

Before the Barolo workshop I strolled the grand market where I bought my four-fig snack this morning. The man who sold them—bald, copper, aproned—did not bust them in half with his thumbs. Instead, he placed them delicately into a paper bag as if they were glass. I ate them all as I strolled the market rows, delicacies from all seven continents, from both above and below ground, land and water, stretching for miles.

A group of locals ooohed and aaahed at a booth selling American southwestern cuisine. To those raised on truffles and Barolo, tamales, I guess, are the peak of exoticism. I ate one fig while I passed them, watched them struggle with the inedible outer corn husks. I ate my second fig watching a seven-piece German family take prenoon shots of ouzo and chase them with bites of dripping, small-batch feta. My third fig (and the best of the bunch) was taken down in front of a booth perpetuating the best flavors from "The North": crab from the Baltic and North seas, wild herb soup, carp, lamb, all accompanied by traditional beers.

Having passed booths of truffle, wine, fresh pasta, and prosciutto (the old hat . . .), I bite into my final morning fig at a booth immortalizing Venezuelan chocolate and rum: some chocolate "complete," some chocolate "raw," some rum young, some rum aged sixty years. I look to my fig for an answer, eat it, and am transported south — not, though, to South America but to South Lingotto and the hall of open-doored classrooms, each large enough for a crowd of seventy-five.

I am sitting four rows from the back, watching the wine experts lecture from the front of the room. The headphones pump the lecture into English on a two-second delay, the translators locked into a glass-walled closet at the back of the room. I have finished all my Barolo save the Sandrone, and so I pull the headphones from my ears and listen to the music of the original Italian. I think I get the gist; at least fifty percent of the lecturers' words end in *isimo,* a variation of *very.* Yes. Of course. This wine is very. *Very* very.

I sip the Sandrone, a 1990 Le Vigne, the same wine he gave me as payment for my grape picking, and it tastes like home. It tastes like the raisin smells of my grandmother's makeup, my old front lawn in late summer, my first kiss with Dawn Seckler in the junior high parking lot after graduation (she forgave me my Led Zeppelin trespasses), my mother's chocolate-chip mondelbrot, my father's sneezes, my sister's laughter, my tent at Il Gioco dell'Oca, my own bottle of Sandrone 1990, Italy itself. I swallow and age noticeably. I feel it thick, like motor oil. I can feel it in my kneecaps.

After about an hour of tasting and learning and tasting again the workshop is dismissed. Woozy and somehow sore, as if I've just snowshoed across the Arctic, I step from the hall blinking fluorescence. I will eventually return to the market, but I feel the need to talk to someone about the Barolo tasting. Does the Salone del Gusto have therapists on staff? I hope Valentina's not on her lunch break. I step toward the sales booths, my stomach growling like an old stray dog.

32

From Barolo to Vinegar

9:00 Mystery of salamina da sugo. A gentle myth:
the salamina da sugo. . . . A myth straight out of the
Renaissance, a great dish to share with friends. Here we
taste three types of this outstanding, inimitable sausage:
the Slow Food Presidium anarchic version, a farmhouse
version, and an industrial version. Accompanied
by the wines of the Umberto Cerari cellar.

SALONE DEL GUSTO GUIDE

Anarchic sausage? Count me in. Valentina is not on her lunch break but has little time to talk. It's limited to:

"You like to taste many different things," she says.

"Yeah," I say, "it's all wonderful. Completely overwhelming."

I stroll the market rows awhile, gawking at the wares. I stop at a vinegar booth, the skinny old man behind the counter dripping a thick, century-old balsamic over pear slices. The man concentrates with marble eyes pressed, as if with ghostly hands, a half-inch too deep into his head. I imagine what his skull must look like. He unravels his pipe-cleaner arms from his hip and holds his hand out to me, fingers long as unsharpened pencils.

"Prego," he says.

His voice is as resinous as the vinegar. This balsamic has regressed to sap, more solid than liquid, settling like taffy scars on the pear faces. This is a vinegar to reforest the land, carrying in its tang the blueprints for oak, ash, mulberry, chestnut, cherry, juniper, acacia . . .

This vinegar, once sealed with red wax and cork, has been exhumed before my eyes by the man with the world's longest fingers.

When he repeats "Prego," I wonder if he should have disturbed the vinegar's bottled slumber, if he's committed some kind of cursable sin. We have stepped between the mother vinegar and her cubs. He smiles and, toward the back of his mouth, I spot a single fang. I reach for a pear, slow, hesitant. I envision myself at fourteen years old, reading some Stephen King novel at night, alone in bed, the first tendrils of a supernatural fear growing inside me like a sapling. My hand pauses over the pear, careful not to touch the vinegar man's hand, his fingers surely perfect for curving around a shovel's handle, swinging it above his head, and smashing my brains all the way back to Valentina.

I blame Stephen King for this. Such irrational hesitancy! Long fingers? Fangs? I blame Stephen King. Shaking my head, swallowing, I scoop a balsamed pear slice into my hand. It rests weightless in my palm, and I fold it, vinegar side down, onto my tongue. I expect Fingerman to cross himself and give me Communion, once again sending my dead grandmother into coffin-bound hysterics, but he only smiles and nods, blinking his eyes another quarter-inch into his head.

The balsamic breaks in half in my mouth, cracks itself from its urn, releases candy-sweet evergreen, acid as mellow as Cognac, the fruit of the tree trunk, falling like water over the forest floor, and all cut by the pear's fresh blur, the tickle of its rind, the mist-run of its weedy juice. This is a marriage that will last. I swallow and my mouth is actualized. It has traveled through time and guillotine; it has returned to thank this man.

"Grazie," I say. "È bellisima."

"Prego," he says, voice full of mucilage.

He turns behind him and retrieves an orange box about a half-foot tall. I see the picture on the front. It is a hibernating bear. It is an entire bottle of century-old balsamic vinegar, still at peace behind box, cork, and wax. Each drop of this stuff is so intense that to finish the bottle would take a lifetime and a half. I decide that I should be satisfied with my taste. That, and the fact that the bottle costs the equivalent of seventy dollars. That such a bottle would probably run over five hundred dollars in the United States still doesn't increase the thickness of my wallet. I have to say the words that sound so out of place in Italy.

"No grazie, ma . . ." and I kiss my fingertips.

He laughs like a kick-start motorcycle and wraps his fingers over my hand. They stretch up to my forearm.

Soon I am surrounded by six wine barrels: two Dolcetto, two Barbera, two Nebbiolo. I pay for a wineglass — an actual glass glass — and find that, for my four dollars, I can taste from these barrels unlimitedly for the rest of the day. Starting now . . .

I sway along the rows, almost drunk, coming to rest at a pasta booth. A tiny elbow-bodied old woman is dressed in a red and white checked shirt with a matching chef's hat. Black-gray hair pushes from underneath. Her glasses sit low on her nose, and her apron is spattered with flour. She grasps a handleless rolling pin in both hands. The massive tube of wood must be heavy, but she maneuvers it with ballerina grace over a yellowed ball of fresh pasta dough. It's all she uses. No pasta press. She looks up at me once and smiles. She is missing one front tooth. She could be the sweaty woman's mother.

In no time at all she has the dough down to a curtain. She lifts it, and I can nearly see through it. I stare, empty wineglass dangling from my fingers, as she cuts the dough into fettuccine, drapes it like blonde dreadlocks over a drying rack. Her eyes stretch to meet mine, and there is a wink in them, though she doesn't wink. I smile and have to look away. My eyes find my watch. The hands and numbers make little sense. I look up, and she has started on another ball of dough.

33

The Truffle of the Barn

The fluorescence of one room bleeds into another with only minor differences: a blinking flicker here, a snoring hum there. I sit again beneath these flickers and hums, just past 9:00 PM, in the salamina da sugo workshop, ready for the gentle myth, ready for some anarchy.

A hush falls over Ferrara, a small city in Italy's Emilia-Romagna region. Talk of its indigenous salamina da sugo rarely breaches its borders. Perennially crowning the Christmas tables of the Ferrarese, the mysterious and controversial dish remains out of reach for the rest of the world.

The salamina was first documented in a fifteenth-century letter from Lorenzo il Magnifico to Duke Ercole II d'Este. Apparently, the first to produce salamina were the *porcaioli* of the Trentio and Bormio mountains. Eventually, they migrated into the Po valley and then into the area that was to become Ferrara. Not a single discovered document mentioned salamina da sugo again until 1722. Capturing the artistic heart and palate of writer Antonio Frizzi, salamina da sugo became the object of his poem "Salamoide." Frizzi writes, "I mix the pig's liver with its meat, put an iron on top, and step on the iron." Frizzi went on further to speculate that the pigs destined to become salamina are born carrying the spirits of all dead women. In tasting it, the headphones proclaim, one has difficulty separating flavor from verse. Often invoked as an incurable aphrodisiac, the salamina (or salama, as it is often called) was a popular meal at wedding banquets and brothels. The dish was reputed to soften the skin and add life to the blood of newlyweds as well as prepare the ladies of the night for their customers.

The night outside the Lingotto stretches its legs, brothelless, and blows its yawn over the old factory, and the building itself seems to settle in a posttasting bliss. This is the last workshop of the day, and it is run by representatives of the Slow Food movement, their Italian taking the form of culinary protest. The translation whistles flutelike into my ears, discussing this nearly extinct breed of sausage, stirring the Slow Food movement to educate the masses in an attempt to lift it from certain death.

This salamina is commercially illegal. The Slow Food movement had to hew through bureaucratic barbed wire just to get this workshop off the ground. It is virtually number one on Slow Food's endangered foods list, holds a top-shelf position in their Ark of Taste. The dish begins with the grinding of the "less noble" but more flavorful parts of the pig: liver, tongue, belly, shoulder, chin, top neck, throat lard, cheek, thigh. The ground meat is then coupled with an array of spices — types and amounts differ with each producer. Typical spices include salt, pepper, nutmeg, cinnamon, clove, and garlic. Red wine (approximately two liters per ten kilograms of meat) is added to the mixture — usually a Sangiovese, Barbera, or Semisecco del Bosco Eliceo. Certain producers also add rum, grappa, or brandy.

The mixture is then packed into a pork bladder, tied with twine, and traditionally divided into eight segments. In a well-ventilated dark chamber, at about fifty degrees Fahrenheit, the salamina is hung to ripen for at least one year. During this time the salamina is periodically brushed with olive oil and vinegar. Once sufficiently aged, the salamina will bear a protective coating of white mold. Prior to preparation, the mold is rinsed away, and the cased meat is soaked in lukewarm water for at least twelve hours. After the soaking session the salamina is placed inside a cloth bag that is then tied to the center of a long wooden stick. The stick is draped across the top of a large stockpot so that the salamina bag is hanging in the middle, away from the pot's bottom and sides. The pot is filled with water, and the salamina cooks for about four hours at a low simmer. Once ready, the salamina is cut from the bag and gently removed from its casing with a spoon. The salamina's wine is released during the cooking process, yielding a viscous and spicy sauce.

Three types of salamina line the plate in front of me, each cresting a small mound of mashed potato. The first is anarchic; Slow Food's own farmers producing their ideal version sans governmental regulation. It is pink and brown and dripping with its internal, natural "sauce." The next is a small farmhouse version produced, as it has been for Italian centuries, against the rigid health department standards, left to hang for months from a pigsty rafter. The truffle of the barn. The final slice is an industrially produced, commercially regulated sausage that does its best to mimic salamina da sugo. The Slow Food movement wants us to know the difference.

We lift our forks in choral unison and, slowly, like the simultaneous bowing of fifty veiled heads, bring them to our plates as we are instructed to taste the first sample. Upon biting, the salamina oozes smoky gravy into our mouths, collecting a texture somewhere between ground meat and rose oil. If this sausage were a cheese, it would be baked Brie. Just by chewing together, with our arsenal of taste buds, we march on Roma with torches ablaze.

The farmhouse salamina is a little less sweet but just as runny, scampering over the tongue like a mouse, feet soaked in licorice. Together we burp terrestrial elegies. The industrial version is tasty but common, a mere smoked sausage injected with hormones and cardboard crumbs. We sneer. We save the whales.

We have tasted, the thin, black-haired representative declares with a snap of his fingers, what may be the last barely legal taste of salamina da sugo ever. After this Salone del Gusto the book may very well be closed. I imagine an underground, gathering in windowless attics, reading by candlelight ancient farmland recipes, and passing samples of this banned foodstuff. They will weep over the crushing of pleasure in favor of the illusion of health. They will smoke banned cigars, drink banned liquor, and toast to anarchic sausage. We, and the salamina, will survive in the basements of the world.

This black-haired representative of Slow Food widens his eyes and stares, cultishly, into the ceiling's holy but fleeting fluorescence . . .

34

Sleeptasting

It is a sparse midnight walk back to Francesco's, the bastions of Torino's treasured fashion sense surely laying their gelled heads onto silk pillowcases. Francesco is sleeping when I sneak in, my mouth glowing, my stomach in full chaise-longue recline. I am a birdwatcher having just checked off three-quarters of his "must-see" list. My sleeping bag waits to be unrolled, eyes me as I scan Francesco's mantelpieces for more pictures of Raffaella. There are four of them, one with her, him, and Niccolo. I imagine all of the Piedmont's farmers sacrificing their hours, fingers, backs so Francesco can have this apartment, modern kitchen, shelves of music, pictures.

Stomach snoring, dreaming of digestion, I strip down to my red boxer shorts and my green "Frank and Dino's Deli is the Place to Fill Your Belly" undershirt. The ceiling fan spins its chill. On Francesco's wall a beautiful angular black woman squints at me in profile. The poster, in Italian, advertises a West African Film Festival at Torino's Mole Antonelliana cinema museum. The woman's hair is strung upward into a cone, horizontal braids freezing it into shape. Her earlobes hang to her shadowed jaw, chin reaching downward toward the text. I step closer and see that she is not squinting at all. Her eye is closed, upper lid deflated over her lashes. She can't bear to look.

I unleash my sleeping bag onto the couch and climb in. My stomach spreads over my ribs like a sandbag leaking its sand. The white ridges of the ceiling offer themselves like a foreign and faraway landscape, a landscape where the sky is sleeping and the Earth is the abyss. I can't wait to leave this apartment tomorrow. And tomorrow — day two at the Salone — is a bird building a new wing in sleep.

Countless Italian hands are passing me through the Salone del Gusto's market corridors, gold rings shifting on their fingers. A man with a handlebar mustache so thick he could be ridden like a bicycle plates a tower of herb-roasted pork. It disintegrates on my tongue like a lozenge. As soon as I swallow the hands return, warm as a blanket, to advance me.

An old Italian woman with dyed red hair and a hockey-puck bald spot spins a slice of Pata Negra prosciutto into a rose. I eat it, this rare pig near extinction, and I feel as if I can perpetuate a new species in my guts. I start to work on it when the hands lift me nearly to the ceiling, deposit me in front of a young woman, hair fresh and yellow as corn, as she hoists a slice of buffalo mozzarella from its milk. I think of rabbits, doves, magicians' hats as I finish the musky cheese, follow it with a goat's milk gelato flavored with lemon and sage. The ice cream is from Italy's Valle d'Aosta region, the northwestern corner of the country, and it tastes of mountain and border, the stones of the earth that could not be contained, a natural cathedral reaching for something holy, Italy garnished with France. It tastes of animal, and of ambition.

Soon the ceiling of the Salone breaks like glass and begins raining twelve different olive oils — some smooth, some grainy, some full of fruit, some drenched in ocean. In this deluge Athena appears, tongue kissing Poseidon, the Etruscans cheering them on. This cloud passes and a new one drifts in, thicker at the middle, thinner at the edges. It lets loose with white anchovies and marinated Sicilian yellow peppers, then Parmigiano-Reggiano soaked in truffle honey. The rain goes brown with Italian coffee, then pink with rosolio drops. The drops, or gocce di rosolio, indeed the size of coffee beans, consist of a thin, fragile sugar crust filled with liquid rosolio — that elusive liqueur made from rose petal and oil. The sugar casing is hard enough to prevent leakage but fragile enough to be crushed against the roof of the mouth with the tongue.

I buy a package of the drops for Francesco and a box of balsamic chocolates for Raffaella. I say good-bye to Valentina, and she dips behind her ticket booth, rises with sesame biscotti.

"They give us these to eat while we work," she lilts. "They are good, but I am tired of them."

I eat one while I shake her hand, fluttering in mine like that new wing, and I tell her it was nice to meet her. She passes me a card with her phone number and slurs, "If you return to Torino . . ."

Maybe I'll call her sometime. Maybe the Barolo pay phones will work for once. I smile at her, sesame seeds all over my teeth.

The hands return, stitch the ceiling of the Salone back together, and walk me through the orange night lights of Torino back to Francesco's. I unleash my sleeping bag onto the couch and climb in.

I wake to the slamming of the front door and the ceiling fan. Francesco has left for work, the black woman on the wall still on the brink of weeping. I have slept well. My arms are strong, renewed. On the kitchen table a note. The handwriting is abysmal and Francesco's. I struggle to piece it together. He is leaving work early today to go see Raffaella. I am to wait. No need for the train. He is going to give me a ride. I think to pass the time in Caffè San Carlo. I hope Elena is working. I'll send Valentina's regards. I am the *hello* emissary between two beautiful Italian women. It could be worse.

On my way to the bathroom I glance at Raffaella's pictures in profile with only one eye. The sink water is cold on my face. The haze of sleep, salamina, rosolio . . . I open the bathroom door and see the maid at the couch, folding my sleeping bag. Her hair tangles itself black on her head. It is a mess of night-weeds. She wears a thin pink blouse, untucked. It catches the light at the window, the voices of Piazza Castello. She is lit like the child of the sun and the moon. When she turns, raising my pillow over her head, I can see that she is pregnant.

35

One More Song

It's really strange, this riding next to Francesco, seat-belted into the
passenger side, as he drives his fancy Fiat from Torino to Barolo, our
two bobbing right fists raised to the car's navy ceiling, calling out
the lyrics to song after song on Bruce Springsteen's *Greatest Hits*.
Francesco does a mean "Born to Run," his banker's Italian flipping
the horn-rims from its face and loosing a mess of hair from its pins.
He's got a great rasp on him; he really does. Puffing my ribs like a
rooster, I try to outdo him with a "Thunder Road" straight from a
rosolio-painted diaphragm. My rasp, though, gets lost in a bout of
coughing. Francesco was nice enough to let me taste a few of the
gocce di rosolio I bought him, and now this is how I repay him,
by coughing in his face while Springsteen testifies to the waving of
Mary's dress. Francesco is undeterred. On "Badlands" he covers
three instruments, voice, guitar, sax, all crescendoing in an Italian-
accented *Ba-ba-ba-baaahhh!*

Corny as it may be, we sing "Born in the U.S.A." together, his
black-tie Fiat swerving all four lanes of the Autostrada. Pounding on
lap or steering wheel in countless drum solos, Francesco sheds his
embalmer qualities, becomes a middle-aged Paul Newman of sorts,
becomes worthy of Raffaella's affections. This is a man who's willing
to spit all over his own windshield while trying to out-Springsteen
me.

Barolo's castle shows itself, still miles away, the skinny orange
flame of a single swaying lighter. I look to Francesco and wonder if
we should do an encore. I wonder if we have the time. He presses
the gas pedal in one smooth stroke, and the castle begins to define

itself as stone, inanimate, indifferent to one more song. We swing left onto Via Crosia. The sky struggles to hold its dim blue, the sun long down, the light dying like a bulb beneath a sheepskin lampshade. We stop the car at the black iron gate, and Francesco presses the red call-button. Raffaella's voice sparks from the speaker-box as if expecting a tourist. It is that beautiful, petal-in-the-wind "Pronto."

When she hears Francesco's voice singing, "Ciao, ciao, Raffaella," still with residual rock-and-roll rasp, the hostess leaves her voice.

"Sì, sì," she says impatiently through intercom static.

The iron gate folds inward. Francesco pumps his fist to me and gets back into the car, his gape-mouthed smile large enough to hold a hive of bees.

"It is okay," he yodels to the Fiat ceiling, the ceiling where our two right fists once held such close communion. "She let us in." His voice is thick with honey-in-progress.

I clear my throat, whisper, "Eccellente."

Raffaella's box of balsamic chocolates shifts at my feet. Of course, she charges from the two front carved double doors in that typical Raffaella way: heavy but light, the cirrus cloud that defies science and impossibly carries rain.

"And yes?" she sings, not like a parakeet, not like any bird at all. "How was it? How was the Salone del Gusto?"

I exhale. I consciously try to seal my heart like an envelope, but the glue is old and comes undone.

"Oh, Raffaella," I say, "it was ridiculous. It was amazing. I don't know what to say. I don't know where to begin. Or end."

I wish her courtyard was full of harps. The background music necessary to talk about a vertical tasting of Barolo. As I speak to her, her eyes flit to Francesco. I hold the balsamic chocolates to her like a tray of hors d'oeuvres.

"I picked these up for you there," I say.

Her hands close in on the box from both sides, tighten around it, and I think of Sunday mornings with my father, watching the Three Stooges over bowls of bad, sweet cereal, Moe inevitably crushing Curly's skull in a vise. Some Sundays, when he was feeling especially philanthropic, my father would microwave omelets for my sister and me, these yellow rubber wheels of egg that neither my sister nor I had the heart to badmouth in front of him.

"Cioccolatini," Raffaella cries. "You are wonderful," and she leans in to kiss my cheek.

Her lips melt into me like candle wax, and Moe turns the vise lever one notch tighter.

"There's, um," I muster, coughing the dust from my throat, "some aged balsamic in those."

"Oh, yes," she beams, reading the side of the box, and I envision the Vinegar Man, his javelin fingers, the resin on his breath.

"You must come inside," she says. "My parents are here. They want to hear about it."

"Ah," Francesco sings and spews something about Raffaella's parents and Niccolo.

She rolls her eyes, laughs, and, finesse dripping from her voice, slurs, "My mother make her famous ceci soup."

Chickpea soup is exactly what I need right now. Something warm and heavy.

"Come, come," Raffaella preens, holding her balsamic chocolates above her head like a weightlifter or a cocktail waitress. "We go in."

She leads us to the double doors. I slow my pace so Francesco can walk behind her. The two of them disappear into the sliver of inside yellow light. I touch the knob. It is copper and cold. Adriana's voice vaults across the ceiling, crows through the open doors like an escapist hen. I'm looking forward to this dinner. To being with the whole family. Before I go in I turn to the courtyard. It amazes me that I can see the moon, flashing like a dime, and the stars surrounding it, but, even squinting, even stretching my neck as far as it can stretch, I can't even see my tent out there.

36

Heroes and Villains Commune over Ceci

Adriana is caped in arm fat, Michele in the gray straw of a long-forgotten scarecrow costume. Raffaella shines her blonde heat, and Francesco gallops like the old horse who hides his strength in his haunches. And Niccolo sits at the head of the table, this tiny copper soldier holding his seven-year-old evil beneath his tongue like a butterscotch. He wears a plain red sports cap that covers too much of his head.

I feel I have crashed a superhero party or, rather, a party where the heroes and villains smear together like crème anglaise and raspberry coulis on a carved and wooden dessert plate — a dessert plate that now holds, beneath four white folded bath towels, a sinister black cauldron of Adriana's steaming ceci soup. The six of us blur into its mist. Raffaella, just a few minutes earlier, called it *famous,* and I wonder, if only a month ago, she would have slipped her descriptor into an Italian envelope, and opened it, perfumed, reciting *famoso.* I feel a bit guilty for forcing English upon her. This intercourse of language stirs my belly, and as I sit to Raffaella's left (Francesco to her right), Adriana clucks "Zuppa di ceci" upward into the yellow chandelier.

"Bravo, bravo," Michele calls, fingers waving expectantly in the air, playing an invisible piano.

Adriana ladles the beige nectar, stuffed with carrots, smooth as earthenware, into my bowl first. I am the guest, and here I have forgotten not only my costume but my superpower. I wonder if I should deconstruct "I Am a Rock" for the table.

Niccolo pounds his chair's arms and squeaks a gravelly "Nonna!"

His red hat holds its place.

Adriana turns to him. "Ay, Niccolo, quando . . ."

"Nonna! No!" Niccolo screams, complaint thick as glue in his mouth.

The evil can't be contained. He is menace at the dining room table. Raffaella glares at him and mumbles through clenched teeth. The kid wants to be served first. I go to slide my bowl toward him, but his eyes narrow like an oiled mustache, and I can see that he wants to spit his venom in my face.

Adriana serves him next and musses his hair, clucking "Niccolo" in duplicate, her arms waving. Michele, Adriana's understudy, laughs and attempts a cluck of his own.

"He is terrible," Raffaella whispers to me of Niccolo, her breath a blessing, the whipped-cream wind of Zion, and I trace my eyes around the bend of her lips to see that the kid also regards Francesco with tightly folded arms.

Michele fills our wineglasses with Ettore Germano Barolo 1993, and Francesco vacation-whinnies "Aah," Niccolo raises his glass of milk to our toast, and everyone at the table, save Raffaella and myself, fusses over him as if he has just reinvented the lightbulb. He swills his milk like the anti-Machiavelli, *The greatest good for me alone,* bubbling white and silent over his lips. I swallow my wine. As it unrolls its cherry and chestnut over my tongue I again wonder if my superpower has something to do with tasting. *Can't cook for shit, can't make his own wine, but boy, can he ingest!*

Michele and Francesco tuck their napkins into their shirt collars, and I follow suit. Raffaella drapes hers over her lap. Niccolo and Adriana leave theirs on the table. We all dredge the bottoms of our soup bowls with silver, unearth potato, carrot, sage, and chickpea, culinary archaeologists. With each subsequent spoonful, bursting with root and bean, herb and balm, each inevitable swallow of wine, I begin to feel more and more like part of the family. I tell them, into our second bowls now, of the Salone.

"Aah!" Adriana screams as if laying a platinum egg, stealing Francesco's line and making it her violin string–breaking own.

The chandelier burns into our scalps, this blue-blooded inter-rogation lamp.

"Salaminaaa," Adriana lets loose in an extended tweet.

Michele reaches across the table, nabs my shoulder in his talon.

Niccolo hisses like a snake forced from its nest, Francesco sighs and tells them something about Springsteen, and Raffaella, trying her best to ignore her demon seed, bats her lashes.

"It sound so wonderful," she says and fans her fingers. "Perfect."

"It really was," I tell her, and Adriana, waving her hands from the other side of the table, calls, "Che? Che?"

Raffaella translates.

Michele yells, right hand on his heart, left arm extended outward, "Chicago! Chicago! Al Capone!" and points his finger, again like a gun, dead at my chest.

Francesco mutters something to Raffaella, and they kiss like a thimble while Niccolo kicks, with both feet, the underside of the table. I want to do the same.

The cauldron nearly drained, and eight bottles of Barolo later, we all hit that point in the meal where we lean back in our chairs. The table cluckings descend into putters, Niccolo's head reaching for sleep on his shoulder.

I kiss them all except the kid, Michele's skin like bone, Francesco's surprisingly warm, Adriana's even warmer, and Raffaella's even warmer than that. I watch them all, except Adriana, start for the stone stairs and their bedrooms. Raffaella's hand is in Francesco's. It could be the wine, but I think I may be happy for them.

Adriana and I clear the table, and I help her do the dishes — she washes, I dry. As I wipe down the range she tells me in deliberate Italian about the government, how it favors the southern portion of the country because of the Mafioso concentration. She shakes her head, chin pressing to me like a halved biscuit, as she explains that above a certain Italian latitude, at retirement one receives the equivalent to Social Security at age sixty-five; below this latitude, age forty-five. Now that she is alone, Adriana's demeanor is more serious, her voice deeper, more human. She is beautiful.

We finish our cleanup and she hugs me, soaks me up like a sponge. Outside the temperature flits around freezing, and, touching my tent, its cold vinyl pushing frost to my fingers, I turn to look at the house. All is dark, save the muddy yellow of Raffaella's balconied window. At night the farmhouse reveals its full size. Il Gioco dell'Oca: it is huge and frightening but comforting and yet somehow out of reach. It is an elk asleep, standing up in the moon. It is something I will always remember. I don't know whether it is a shadow across Raffaella's bedroom ceiling or a star, but something about the house shoots like a comet.

37

Nightpicking

The vineyard green is going to yellow, some, even, to red. Sandrone has summoned us to an evening pick, a small group. Last night in his bedside notebook he must have written his plan while I ate ceci soup with the family. *Send Mariuccia to Il Gioco at 4 PM. Get the last of the grapes before first frost.*

We pick, the tractor crew working in the rows above me, and above them, two remaining clubhopper boys. That's it. For the first hour Sandrone worked alongside us, a tie-dyed fleece pullover hiding his suspenders. The air cold. The ground hardening. The sky losing its light quickly, getting dark earlier. Its blue is a blue that promises snow. Winter is coming.

As Sandrone cut the grapes he muttered to himself, *Allora, allora . . .* A lullaby to his fruit. A swan song. Simply *Well then, well then . . .*

After the first hour he drove himself back to his cantina in one of the tractors. Ivo tells me he is busy transferring young wine from the steel tanks to the aging barrels.

"Hoses all over the place," he says.

The juice is pumped from the steel tanks via an airtight vacuum device, calibrated to specific pressure, where it journeys along a tangle of sterile hoses and into the barrels. The hoses are designed to be flexible, to bounce back after being run over by tractor or forklift, not to impart any adverse flavor to the juice. Each hose houses an inner hose that traps most impurities and bacteria.

Luca hangs a small chalkboard over each barrel, recording the date of the transfer and the vineyard from which the grapes were picked. His hands surely shake as he writes, his brother watching over him, his European-style 1s rendered in chalk like windsocks. This while we pick, the arteries of wine beating in Sandrone's House of Transfusion.

We pick until dark, Ivo, Beppe, and Indiano eliciting soft groans, the clubhoppers lost in shadow. Still in the air the smells of fertility, or fertility dying, wet green going crispy, the orange lights of the hilltop towns winking on around us. From this angle I can't tell which is La Morra, which is Castiglione Falletto. Only this dark hallway of night, feeling our way along the grapevine walls, the wind tunneling the rows, Ivo pulling on a fleece top of his own, cursing the wind in Italian. Soon his coveralls will be tucked away in a drawer until spring, his hairless bare chest finally covered.

We clip cold grapes, fill our crates, ditch them in Tractor Alley. Our hands cramp in this weather, the blood closer to the skin, the metal clippers freezing. As the sky shuts off, the sound of an engine approaches. A flatbed pulls up and Sandrone dismounts, cheroot blazing. When he exhales, it's half smoke, half condensed breath. He shivers. I palm a bunch of grapes. Smooth as fish skin. Even in this dark I can tell the crate at my feet is full. The clubhoppers leave their rows uncommanded, their hair bouncing as they walk toward the flatbed, carrying their crates. When Sandrone calls *Basta!* I know it's probably not for the day but for the season.

He unloads from his flatbed not a new team of empty crates but a thermos of chamomile tea, a couple bottles of Dolcetto, a loaf of bread, a dish of butter, and a curtain of speck, a smoked prosciutto. The wrought iron table and chairs are cold, and I zip up my windbreaker, press my elbows to my ribs. We sit and, with red hands, eat, drink by the headlights of the tractor.

Ivo tears into his speck, raises his glass of Dolcetto. He says something in Italian, and the clubhoppers grunt dismissively but raise their glasses. To them Ivo is a corny old man. With Beppe and Indiano I raise mine as well. Not enough chairs, so Sandrone stands, circles the table with his mug of tea steaming. He chimes his mug against the lips of our glasses. Beppe scratches his cheek, the shell of his tortoise tattoo bouncing up and down.

Ivo turns to me. "I say, basically, 'To the wine,'" he clarifies.

"Here, here."

Indiano finishes his glass first, and for this Ivo playfully gives him shit. The two of them become all elbows in the night, their mock fight intermittently captured in the spears of tractor light. Sandrone laughs deep. The clubhoppers wave their hands, clearly too cool for this. Ivo forces Indiano into his chair again, and Beppe stands, whispers something to Sandrone.

"Motherfucker is the quietest drunk in Barolo," Ivo tells me about Indiano.

Behind me Sandrone laughs again, bear-hugs Beppe.

"You know what he does when he's not out here?" Ivo asks me.

"Who? Sandrone?"

"No. Sandrone's always with the wine. Indiano: you know what he does?"

The wind shoots between us. Above us tonight's first star.

"What?" I ask.

"Opera," Ivo tells me. "He's an opera singer."

I turn to Indiano. His pale, veiny skin encased in long sleeves, long pants. His thinning black hair. He's working on his second glass of wine. Somewhere in his chest, his throat, comedy, tragedy, overture, and aria. I can't believe it. I've barely heard him speak. Ivo nods.

"It's amazing," he says.

The clubhoppers are the first to ride the flatbed back to the cantina, curling their bodies among the last crates of grapes. Mentally I prepare for my walk back to Il Gioco — the silence, the strip of grass, Lodovico's barrel, Pongo trying to keep warm in his doghouse. With the tractor crew I finish the bread, the wine, the speck in darkness. In spite of the cold, none of us drink the tea.

Around me, probably for the last time, the crew. Barrel-chested, tattooed, skinny with their secrets, their Rottweiler scars. Bodies filling, or trying to fill, their coveralls. Bloodshot eyes. Knucklebones in their pockets. Songs in their heads.

"You wouldn't be up for a rematch?" I ask Ivo.

Beppe and Indiano wrinkle their foreheads as Sandrone returns with the flatbed, allowing us once again a little light.

"What, the arm wrestling?" he asks. "You can't be serious."

But even as he says it he places his elbow on the tabletop, opens his big hand. Sandrone leaps from the driver's seat to watch. I grasp Ivo's palm with two hands, one on top of the other, and tighten my body. Ivo's fingers are warmer than they should be. Beppe begins the countdown. Indiano, holding his aria at least until winter, pours himself a third glass of wine. Sandrone lights another cheroot, smiling, the red flame winking like a radio tower. A warning to airplanes. This is his party. His quiet, end-of-the-season bash without a bash. In this temperature our heartbeats are nearly audible. In the beams of tractor light so many things that we can't see are living.

38

La Partenza della Filovia

That night in the tent my pillow retains its cold, holds it like a bouquet of roses to its chest. Whether I am lying on my right or left side my ears can't shake this floral chill. The moon is shameless, obscene. When I fetch *Henderson the Rain King* from the corner of my tent, my flashlight is hardly necessary to finish the book. My camping clock flashes its time, and I watch it until 2:35 AM becomes meaningless. Henderson at the end of the novel whoops around the Arctic, and I feel I may be catching his breath in my lungs, engaged in some frigid and literary mouth-to-mouth.

I have nothing to read. The stars, skipping their light like shale through the tent screen, maintain their distance. In an effort to be closer to them, to hear their whirring electricity, I unzip the tent door. The sound, a moan, is deafening. The night is so quiet. I don't hear a single cricket. I step sockless into my shoes. The grass crunches, brittle, elongated grains of half-cooked rice. The tractor crew dreams in rooms I will never see.

The mud is hard. Tonight the earth does not want to move. I scan Il Gioco's face, Raffaella's caged windows now dark, as they must have been for hours. Pongo is silent in his doghouse. The chickens don't shuffle a feather. The cats are nowhere to be seen. I don't think anything or say anything.

In this weather the Nebbiolos become that much more fragile, their skins so thin. I wonder if Ercole and Loredana are still awake, drinking from some exotic bottle, if Lodovico is snoring, if Square-Head's pillow is square. I wonder how Michele and Adriana hold each other in sleep, if, inside the farmhouse, Raffaella and Francesco are twined together like Ss? I wonder if Beppe Fenoglio realizes from the great beyond that I am now touching what was once a piece of his home?

The handle bucks. The door settles inward like a sow shifting in sleep, shivers its belly across the stone floor. As quiet as the night is, the house is quieter. I curve into the living room, stare at the piano on the far wall. At this hour it is unplayable and finished, laminated and castaway.

Above the piano a plate holds to the wall. It has a white background and a blue painted picture of a slumped horse pulling a man sitting on a plow. Its eye is smudged and unknowable. Next to this plate is a sepia photograph of an old trolley car. Its nails are visible, and it seems ready to collapse like a toothpick blueprint. The picture must have been taken at least a century ago in Barolo. A crowd of men surround the car, staring at the camera from beneath black-brimmed hats. The driver rests hidden in shadow and square engineer's cap. At the photo's bottom left corner a boy wears a beret. His short pants are tucked into tall socks, and his hands are pushed into his pockets. He has huge cheeks and eyes that teeter between sadness and confidence. His left foot is resting at the base of the building that years later would hold Franco's macelleria. I wonder if the boy, all those years ago, could smell the burgeoning meats. The raw tripe. A pocket-watch chain dangles from his blurred belt loop. I wonder if it is real gold. It gleams white as if catching the sun. It is the brightest thing in the picture. There is a caption, handwritten in white. The letters waver as if penned by a dying hand. It reads: *La partenza della filovia.*

Even before I walk to the bookshelves, before I look this phrase up in Raffaella's Italian-English dictionary, I feel something unnamable growing in me. It stretches from belly to heart, and it is not cold. It is temperate and moving. Somehow I feel not in this house, not on this stone floor at all, but elevated, weightless, on horseback. Tasting things in the wind. I find the words, the dictionary pages shuffling like a mane. The caption means: *The departure of the trolleybus.*

I touch the walls, the stones' grains, sidestep into the dining room.

The fireplace holds its ashes, scraps of burnt newspaper that once held the news. Stacks of board games line the mantle. Everything unplayed adding up to *home*. The obviousness of comfort: on the bookshelves, books; on the wine rack, wine. In the dining room the table is empty and clean. The table once held a cauldron of ceci soup, once presented plates of pasta draped in truffles. There's Francesco's dinner chair. There's Adriana's.

I walk to the wine rack and stare at the names on the labels, the families who make some of the greatest wines in the world: Gigi Bianco, Pio Cesare, Giacomo Conterno, Pira, Paolo Scavino, Luciano Sandrone, Elio Altare, Aldo Conterno, Elio Grasso, Ettore Germano, Angelo Gaja, Bartolo Mascarello, Ivo Mascarello, Fratelli Alessandria, Lodovico Borgogno, Elvio Cogno, Ceretto, Mauro Veglio, Luigi Pira, Francesco Borgogno, Francesco Boschis. One day they too will be pictures on a wall.

I breathe in and hold it for a few seconds. I hear the blood ticking in my ears and turn to look at the stairwell. Only the first four steps are visible. Up there, a sleeping family. I let out my breath in a stutter, and weight runs back into my legs. Winter's coming, but I close my eyes and imagine it's spring. I open them and think I see roses flashing through the room like traffic. When the flowers descend into afterimage, I touch the coiled radiator with both palms. The heating oil trickles like a metronome. I look at my shoes. They are set in sludge. As my hands warm I decide to go back to America.

39

The Dateless Label

When I wake, Italy seems to have descended into January overnight.
I, like the year, am new, fingernails softer, and cold. My sleeping bag
is powdered with frost, and I squeeze from it like custard. In some
sort of sleepwalking stupor I must have taken the Satti bus to Alba
and settled my open-ended plane ticket with a dark-haired travel
agent. I see the ticket poking like a false bookmark from the middle
of a long-finished *Henderson the Rain King*. The faded red and green
of its Alitalia face. My return is tomorrow. After all this time I have
almost nothing to pack except the unexpected foodstuffs. The words
Malpensa and *Milano* printed across the ticket face in distinguished
black. Airport. Airplane. All words with air in them.

After visiting the travel agent I walked into Barolo for a handful
of good-byes. All were less difficult than imagined, almost nonchalant. And the surprising gifts: from Il Bacco Franco a half-bottle of
Marcarini Barolo 1995; from the panetteria twins and Square-Head
brother a white cardboard box of baci di dama ("Grissini non per il
aeroplano," they harmonized); from Ercole and Loredana kisses on
both cheeks and a demand for a postcard from Chicago, something
with the Sears Tower on it; from Franco the Butcher — what else? — a
string of fat wild boar salami. He even held a nickel of tripe to his
eye like a villain's spyglass as I left. Through tripe: that's how we
last saw each other. From Michele and Adriana laughs, very loud
laughs. I didn't dare try to find the Alessandria cantina again, and
the Borgognos . . . Well, I let them hibernate.

I collect these foodstuffs into a small pile at the tent's left foot.
Stretching my backpack top open, I shove these gifts to the middle,

sandwich them between clothes to avoid detection by customs. This packing and burying . . .

I unzip the tent screen, then the door, and the outside air bursts in like the taxman. Pongo is huddled in his doghouse at the base of Il Gioco. Raffaella's car is gone. As I step from the tent the dog doesn't move. He looks at me, quickly looks away. I am in my blue sweatpants and burgundy fleece shirt. My black Eagle Crest winter jacket will only zip halfway. I am barely warm enough.

After a few failed attempts to catch Sandrone at his cantina I had to organize with Mariuccia to see him this morning. Soon I am again on that narrow strip of grass. The wild cars have become second nature; the ditch, now frozen, offers no sludge. My shoes are as dirty as they're going to get. Sandrone's cantina rests in the distance, and I want to run to it in slow motion, arms spread wide, string music swelling, mouth agape, tongue draping the wind like a dog's. Looped on film, the black-and-white reuniting of eager long-lost lovers. I reach for those heavy double doors — both of them — and push.

I have no idea what I am going to do when I return to America. Something with food? I envision the Piedmontese postcards I bought: the Castello di Barolo, La Morra's Belvedere, Torino's Piazza San Carlo, Alba's Duomo, the white awning of Caffè Calissano visible in the lower right-hand corner. Am I merely going to hang these on a Chicago apartment wall, magnet them to the refrigerator?

As I listen to the doors creak inward and catch my first glimpse of Sandrone in the machine room pacing the scaffolding at the lips of his holding tanks, these questions steam away as if in a Moroccan tobacco haze. Red hoses snake every which way from steel tank to wooden barrel. Today Sandrone's suspenders are purple. Perhaps he's taking wardrobe lessons from his brother. I envision Sandrone in Bermuda shorts, and my call to him is laced with a chased laugh.

"Luciano."

Even at our distance I swear I can hear his eyebrows raise. It sounds like the strained cables of a dumbwaiter.

"Allora," he calls.

The word in his mouth is a gift, echoes from the holding tanks like wrapping-paper tearing. He walks heavy down the metal stairs, his footsteps ticking like the clock that will soon bring my plane to Malpensa airport. With his thumbs he flings both loops of his suspenders outward. They snap back against him.

"Ritorna a America?" he solicits, though he knows the answer.

His glasses slip on his face. He is cigarless, and, for some reason, this makes me sad. Today I want to see him with all of his accessories. We talk awhile, I understand about one-third of what's being said, and I touch his shoulders a lot. He is soft and hard and supportive. A thrift-store recliner with impeccable taste. We talk of possibly meeting up in New Zealand in March for the wine harvest. I know this is unlikely. I know I'd have to find a quick and high-paying job in Chicago to pull this off, but every time Sandrone mentions it I say, "Sì" anyway.

I walk with him to the far end of the machine room. We flank the door from where I spied on Luca that day. Sandrone reaches to a box on the floor and pulls out a bottle. From the blue foil on the bottle neck I know it is his Cannubi Boschis, and my heart, like a catcher for a fastball, readies itself with pads. Sandrone is nodding. He is not looking at me but at the bottle. He is nodding. He is small but wide. Gray hairs poke from his neck like wheat. Even his wrinkles look strong.

The bottle is unfinished, or, rather, its label is. The blue square is there, and the tall letters that spell Sandrone, and even the shorter ones that spell Cannubi Boschis. But the label is dateless. Sandrone's hands are so dirty, but the dirt looks clean. He pulls a pen from his breast pocket—a blue one—and writes something on the label. From the way the back of his neck is stretched, I can tell that he is smiling. He spins the bottle to me, his mouth so happy.

In blue ink I see the four numbers I had braced myself for: 1, 9, 9, 7. A 1997 Cannubi Boschis. This blockbuster vintage. This bottle he has personally aged. The cantina goes cold, drafty, wearing January like a badge. Sandrone passes me the bottle; it hangs heavy as an infant. I examine his handwriting, the date asserting itself in pen like an autograph. His 1 is arced like an upside-down V, his 9s curve at the bottom like lowercase Gs, and his 7 is perfect, right-angled and casting its glance at the previous three numbers. I am holding a small piece of history and am surprised at how light it is.

Sandrone sighs. We hug one another and hold the backs of each other's necks. When I leave this cantina, I know he will go right back to work. Hoses. Tanks. Barrels. At the double doors I turn back to Sandrone, and his wave is an open palm held stationary above his head. His glasses rise and fall.

Outside the air is sharp as a pencil. I hold the bottle by its neck. At my feet the narrow strip cracks its grass. I look to the sky. It's so blue it's ridiculous. Even the birds have shunned it.

40

Something Small to Tide Me Over

My tent swoons, collapses flat into Raffaella's garden, gushing its air over the frozen mud. I roll it tight and blink at the square of dirt it leaves behind, stripped of grass. If this patch of dirt was warmer, it would be crawling with worms. I can't believe how small it is.

It's barely evening. The sky is the color of glass. Pongo steps from his doghouse, his white fur parted by the wind. At this distance his eyes, marble black, should be undefined, but they're not. They're curious in a trying way. His eyes know his brain is pondering things that it will never understand. I stare back at the dog, and his ears rise toward his scalp. We watch each other like this. We watch each other for a little while. Pongo looks away first. His body curls into a circle, and he noses the entrance to his doghouse. Like a bad movie he turns back over his shoulder. His eyes are no different. Then he goes inside.

I know that soon Raffaella will be coming out to say good-bye. My heart's high, right in my mouth, and if I smile or sigh, anyone who's looking will see it. I am hungry and thirsty. Belts of cold smoke bat from my mouth, lit by the hot lining of another empty stomach. I will have to grab a panino at the train station. Something small to tide me over. My throat is on fire, and the Piedmont roars its wind like a dragon: substantial, erratic, fictional. Tonight I will attempt to sleep on the train from Torino to Milano. I hope I will have the sleeping car to myself. I look at my feet on the mud. I am packed full.

Beppe Fenoglio's former front door is open, and I squint to see inside. Niccolo paces the top landing. When he sees that I have spotted him, he runs for the shadows, and Raffaella, like sleight of hand, replaces him. She gallops down the stairs, hair bouncing, eyes down, brow furrowed as if she's counting each grain in the granite. Her descent down the stairs appears so difficult, laced with faith, the stepping, releasing, rotation of her muscles, falling and falling forward, trusting her back leg to sneak up in time to catch her. I'm amazed she reaches the bottom unscathed.

My legs don't want to go to her, withered to catatonia by winter. Raffaella is shoeless but stands impossibly tall. Her feet, long as fish, copper as the rest of her, must be freezing, but she doesn't show it.

I am standing on the driveway stones. I have moved to her without knowing. Her mouth is closed. My chin hurts. My stomach, perhaps sensing its return to America, breaches all time change and calls for the comfort of a boring breakfast. Cereal. Oatmeal. Toast.

Raffaella stretches. She smells of hay, somber, twilit. She smells like Raffaella. We appear to be standing at the bottom of a bowl, fragile as Rice Krispies, and I hear the tires of my taxi spin the stones outside the front gate. My blood lights as if plugged in, and I feel drenched in milk, an inch from electrocution.

"This is your taxi," Raffaella says.

An affecting sentence. Full of identification and truth. I bob on the balls of my feet. My hands trace my sweatpants, stopping at the knees, braced like a shortstop. I am afraid to talk. Raffaella's eyes crumple. Her right hand holds at the base of her throat, fumbling with the skin there. She coughs once, and the sound of it, the lilt, pulls me from the bottom of our bowl, saves me from being crushed to beige dust with the convex side of a spoon.

"My cab," I say.

She laughs wet, and I realize she's crying. This science project: we're filled to the rim with water, held in place by surface tension alone. Now Raffaella makes me spill my sides. An egg, bursting with a thousand canaries, opens up in my chest.

"Thank you for everything," I say to her ear, its topography smooth as an aqueduct. "Thank you for everything," I say.

I wipe my face with the heel of my hand. It is hot, and its dampness opens the lines of my palm. My hand fissures and, in a chain reaction, every fault line in me cracks a little wider.

"You must write to me," she says.

I fall forward and she catches me. Her body presses its bones, its blood . . . I don't want to say the words. I don't want to say them. The cab driver doesn't beep his horn. We let go of each other. The warmth of her face stays. The stones begin their shifting.

The driver, a boulder of a man, tosses, like a matchstick, my backpack into the trunk. I want to draw a chalk outline around it. I sit in the passenger seat. His neck skin ripples, but he says nothing. As he puts the car in gear I look out the window. Niccolo, without his red cap, is standing with his mother at Fenoglio's door. His left hand is rising and lowering, fingers confused whether to wave or to stay down. He has her blonde hair.

41

Late

While the train wanders from Torino to Milano my eyes close as if on sawdust, then open again. The window, slack-jawed, discloses its night. So far I have the sleeping car to myself, and though I don't want to share my oncoming slumber with anyone, I crave a measure of company.

Italy becomes a foreign country again. Before my chin nods forward onto my chest I stare at the passing hillsides, darkened as ash, and signal to them with my eyes. At this hour they don't signal back.

42

He Was Right

In a train-suck and train-snap I'm at Malpensa airport, waiting in a line. Between loudspeaker blasts I realize that the word *Malpensa* may be Italian slang for "evil thought." O Glory. My backpack shifts on my shoulders, some B-movie beetle. The commotion here is worse than on the streets of Torino, people swimming in all directions, their movements dictated by the impenetrable loudspeaker, boasting more static than voice. Here in Malpensa we face the wrong higher power. And the line is long.

In front of me a mother stands with a small blonde son, the boy kicking as hard as he can at a black valise, but the case won't budge. The boy is wearing a mean face, but still, kicking first with the toe of his shoe, then with the side of his foot, nothing. His mother does a beautiful job of ignoring him.

When I come to the front of the line, I want to lean my elbows on the desktop and confess my sins. The woman's face is young and tablecloth white, her mouth gorged with purple lipstick, some of it staining her front two teeth. She suspects this or tastes this and drags her tongue over them. When she smiles again, her teeth are clean.

"Chicago," I say, handing her my itinerary.

Her nametag says *Chiara*.

"O'Hare Airport?" she asks, her English tickled with only a goose-feather of Italian.

"Yeah," I sigh, envisioning O'Hare: the white lights, the American billboards lit with ads for pizza joints.

Her fingers prance over a hidden keyboard. Chiara doesn't lift her eyes when she says, "Oh. This is going to be delayed for a little more than one hour."

Her Italian defines itself in the hard *h* of her *hour,* as if that single feather had collected its flock. I want to wipe the lipstick from her face with a Kleenex and kiss her lips. I remember Raffaella's analysis of Alitalia airlines.

Your plane will be two hours late, your luggage will be lost, but the hostess will be incredible.

With a muster of faith welling up, I check my backpack and take my boarding pass. It is heavier than cardboard should be. I have some time on my hands. A little over three hours. I step through the airport's automatic glass doors and inhale the length of the drop-off sidewalk. The air is industrial, reeking of burnt glue. Car horns preach their sermons, offering exhaust to the heavens in a billow of bass and stink.

I turn my face into the wind. The air is cool, and I want it on my skin. I unzip my Eagle Crest jacket all the way down and unbutton the top two of my fleece. The breeze lifts me from the train-car ache, and I increase my pace, walking into it. As a child — six years old, maybe — I dressed up as Count Dracula for Halloween and remember walking into a wind much like this one. My black cape flew behind me, and I extended my arms forward, leaned into the weather, and growled through white face paint, bottled blood, the drool-soaked plastic of the fangs. I remember lifting from the sidewalk and being carried by the wind and cape across Pinehurst Lane to where the older kids were busy filling their sacks with full-size Snickers bars — at the time, the epitome of fine dining.

At the end of the airport there's a six-lane highway and across that a line of cafés. One in particular, still in this cold, has a few umbrellaless outside tables set up. I step to the curb, watch the minicars snake in and out of sight for a tangle of off-shooting ramps. I step into the street, and a gray Fiat shoots from around a corner, its horn moaning like a shot duck. I step back to the curb. Look left and right and wait.

After the red car.

The red car passes, and again I step into the road. This time it's a white mini that shoots past my legs, its horn whooping like the duck hunter. My shoulders slump. Back at the curb I rebutton my fleece. A police car approaches slowly, dragging its blinking lights. There is no siren. The car stops on the shoulder in front of me, and my jacket shifts uncomfortably, readying for another takeoff.

The passenger door swings open, and a middle-aged policeman, fat as a doorknob, steps out. The driver remains hidden in shadow, eyes at me, badge catching the sun like a robot heart. The policeman's Italian is warm as oven grease, burnt-on and old, teetering between noxious and fragrant. He's wearing a hat, but I can tell he's bald underneath.

I can't make out what he says over the roar of traffic, but there's concern in his voice, a lack of desire to scrape me from the Autostrada. I nod, figuring it's the thing to do. He nods back and unbuckles a flashlight from his belt. Flashing the light violently to his left and right, he steps from the shoulder and in what seems like a dangerous and extraneous move strolls between the braking cars to the middle of the Autostrada. Soon, his light blinking in warning, traffic stops.

"Prego," he waves, his voice deglazed by wind, effort, and adrenaline.

"Grazie," I say to him and clap a hand on his shoulder as I pass.

His belt shudders in a metallic rattle, and then I'm on the other side. I zip my jacket. I walk to the café — Il Ventaglio — and sit in an iron chair at a white plastic table. The chair is cold, and my teeth press together for warmth, but I want to be outside. I use the armrests.

Somehow I think this wind allows me to stay close to the Piedmont and its meats and breads, its streets and people. It must carry traces, however small, of the vineyards, the Nebbiolo. Raffaella is surely running her fingers through her hair, cursing me for killing that tent-sized patch of grass in her garden. I look up over the airport for a while, watching the arrivals and departures.

With the passing of a yellow plane I think of Raffaella's hair. With the plane's sky-written exhaust I think of Al's beard, Al in Alaska. I wonder if he's still alive. I want to tell him: he was right.

In a breath, then another, I pluck the menu and wine list from a silver ring at the table's middle. At the words, their smudged black letters, my heart crawls back into my chest, knowing it's going to stay there awhile. I'm going to have to get used to this.

On the menu only sandwiches. On the wine list not a single Barolo.

IN THE AT TABLE SERIES

Corkscrewed
Adventures in the New French Wine Country
Robert V. Camuto

Spiced
Recipes from Le Pré Verre
Philippe Delacourcelle
Translated and with a preface by
Adele King and Bruce King

A Sacred Feast
Reflections on Sacred Harp Singing
and Dinner on the Ground
Kathryn Eastburn

Barolo
Matthew Gavin Frank

How to Cook a Tapir
A Memoir of Belize
Joan Fry

Eating in Eden
Food and American Utopias
Edited by Etta M. Madden and Martha L. Finch

Recovering Our Ancestors' Gardens
Indigenous Recipes and Guide to Diet and Fitness
Devon Abbott Mihesuah

Dueling Chefs
A Vegetarian and a Meat Lover Debate the Plate
Maggie Pleskac and Sean Carmichael

A Taste of Heritage
Crow Indian Recipes and Herbal Medicines
Alma Hogan Snell
Edited by Lisa Castle

The Banana
Empires, Trade Wars, and Globalization
James Wiley

AVAILABLE IN BISON BOOKS EDITIONS

The Food and Cooking of Eastern Europe
Lesley Chamberlain
With a new introduction by the author

The Food and Cooking of Russia
Lesley Chamberlain
With a new introduction by the author

The World on a Plate
A Tour through the History of America's Ethnic Cuisine
Joel Denker

Jewish American Food Culture
Jonathan Deutsch and Rachel D. Saks

Masters of American Cookery
M. F. K. Fisher, James Beard, Craig Claiborne, Julia Child
Betty Fussell
With a preface by the author

My Kitchen Wars
A Memoir
Betty Fussell
With a new introduction by Laura Shapiro

Good Things
Jane Grigson

Jane Grigson's Fruit Book
Jane Grigson
With a new introduction by Sara Dickerman

Jane Grigson's Vegetable Book
Jane Grigson
With a new introduction by Amy Sherman

Dining with Marcel Proust
A Practical Guide to French Cuisine of the Belle Epoque
Shirley King
Foreword by James Beard

Pampille's Table
Recipes and Writings from the French Countryside
from Marthe Daudet's Les Bons Plats de France
Translated and adapted by Shirley King

Moveable Feasts
The History, Science, and Lore of Food
Gregory McNamee

To order or obtain more information on these
or other University of Nebraska Press titles,
visit www.nebraskapress.unl.edu.